LABOUR'S PATH TO POWER

Labour's Path to Power

The New Revisionism

Giles Radice

MACMILLAN

First published 1989

Published by
THE MACMILLAN PRESS LTD
Houndmills, Basingstoke, Hampshire RG21 2XS
and London
Companies and representatives
throughout the world

Printed in Great Britain by
Billings of Worcester

Typeset by TecSet Ltd, Wallington, Surrey

British Library Cataloguing in Publication Data
Radice, Giles
Labour's path to power: the new revisionism.
1. Great Britain. Political parties: Labour Party
(Great Britain). Policies
I Title
324.24107
ISBN 0–333–48071–6 (hardcover)
ISBN 0–333–48072–4 (paperback)

To all those who want to see an end to a
long period of Conservative governments

Contents

Preface

The Labour party can win power in the 1990s, provided it changes direction. To change direction, it will need new maps. This book attempts to provide a map.

Because my work covers such a broad terrain, including analysis, philosophy, strategy and policy, I have sought the advice of over 50 politicians, journalists, academics, economists, industrialists and trade unionists. I would like to thank them for their help. I have been fortunate to have discussions with politicians and experts from France, West Germany, Spain, Sweden and Austria. In the spring of 1988 I visited the United States and also met leading Soviet foreign policy specialists at the Anglo–Soviet Round Table in London.

My gratitude to Penny Cooper, David Lipsey, Geoffrey Norris, Lisanne Radice and Peter Riddell who have all read drafts of the book. Professor Raymond Plant has commented on the philosophical section, while I have consulted with Professor Ivor Crewe, Anthony Heath and Robert Worcester over psephology. Gavyn Davies, Professor Paul Ormerod, Jonathan Radice and Michael Stewart have commented on the economic and industrial chapter(Chapter 7); Alan Cave and Lord McCarthy on the trade union chapter (Chapter 8); Gordon Best, Frank Field, MP, John Hills and Professor John Kay on the welfare state chapter (Chapter 9); Peter Hennessy, Anthony Lester, QC and Professor Michael Zander on the democratic agenda (Chapter 10); Professor Lawrence Freedman, the Rt Hon. Denis Healey, MP, and George Robertson, MP, on the foreign affairs and defence chapter (Chapter 11). My thanks to the House of Commons Library staff for their help.

I am especially grateful to two people. Penny Cooper's diligent research, informed criticism and sustained enthusiasm have been invaluable, while Gillian Jacomb-Hood's skilful work on the word processor, remarkable patience and good humour have ensured that the book was produced.

I take sole responsibility for the opinions expressed in the book.

GILES RADICE

Introduction:
the Case for Revisionism

After three successive defeats, the Labour party needs to change. The main argument of this book is that, if Labour is to have a chance of mounting a serious challenge to Conservative political supremacy, it will have to become a fully fledged revisionist party, not so much in the classic sense of breaking with a Marxist past, but in the wider sense of being prepared to reassess its values, strategies and policies in the light of rapid economic and social change. The Labour party has always been a 'variegated, ideologically confused party'.[1] Though in the past it has been able to get away without defining its position, the party is now paying a heavy price for its pragmatism. Unless it is prepared, like its sister Continental parties, to adapt in a principled way to changing circumstances, it is in danger of becoming a permanent minority party. If Labour is to gain power over the next decade, it has to set out an alternative political agenda which will be relevant to the needs of the 1990s and around which a new progressive majority can rally.

* * * * *

THE REVISIONIST HERITAGE

Revisionism has a rich intellectual heritage within the European Socialist movement. The earliest revisionist was Eduard Bernstein, the German Social Democrat. In March 1899, he wrote his major book *Evolutionary Socialism*, which set out for the first time a powerful revisionist critique of Marxism.[2] In this work, which had a profound impact not only on the German Social Democrats, but on other European Socialist parties, Bernstein decisively refuted the Marxist theory that capitalism was about to collapse.

1

He pointed out that, contrary to Marx's predictions, the working class were becoming better off, the numbers of capitalists were growing and there was no evidence of any general economic breakdown. Bernstein's explanation for the failure of Marxist predictions to materialize was that Marx had underestimated the economic and social consequences of a free political system upon its mode of production: 'In all advanced countries we see the privileges of the capitalist bourgeoisie yielding step by step to democratic organisations . . . Factory legislation, the democratisation of local government . . .the freeing of trade unions and systems of cooperative trading from legal restrictions, the consideration of standard conditions of labour in the work undertaken by public authorities – all these characterise this phase of evolution'.[3]

Bernstein also firmly rejected the Marxist concepts of revolution and 'the dictatorship of the proletariat'. 'Is there any sense', Bernstein asked, 'in holding to the phrase "dictatorship of the proletariat" at a time in which Social Democracy has in practice put itself on the basis of parliamentarism, equitable popular representation and popular legislation, all of which contradict dictatorship?'[4] He showed that increasingly Socialist and working class parties were winning votes at national elections and seats in national parliaments, that at local government level they were beginning to run things and that trade unions were making significant industrial gains. Democracy, he concluded, was both essential to the development of Socialism and a key Socialist objective.

Finally, Bernstein criticized the unscientific nature of Marxism. He accused Marx of ignoring economic and social improvements because they refuted his theories. The problem with *Das Kapital*, argued Bernstein, was that it aimed at being a scientific inquiry and also at proving a theory laid down before its drafting. 'It thus appears that this great scientific spirit was, in the end, a slave to a doctrine'.[5] It was also unscientific to believe that Socialism could have a 'final goal'. To Bernstein, Socialism was rather an ethical framework and a way of changing things: 'To me that which is generally called the ultimate aim of Socialism is nothing; but the movement is everything'.[6] The priority for Socialists in the here and now was to extend political and social rights by democratic means.

Anthony Crosland saw himself as Bernstein's successor. He

wrote: 'I am revising Marxism and will emerge as the modern Bernstein'.[7] His most important book, *The Future of Socialism*, published in 1956, certainly shaped the thinking of a whole generation of British Socialists. It was ambitious in conception, wide-ranging in scope, and written with wit, lucidity and authority. Even today the brilliance and sharpness of Crosland's mind stand out clearly from its pages.

Crosland's message was that the harsh world of the 1930s had been transformed by the war and the post-war Labour government. The Marxist theory of capitalist collapse, so firmly believed by Socialist intellectuals in the 1930s, had clearly been disproved. On the contrary, output and living standards were rising steadily. At the same time, the commanding position of the business class had been reduced by the increased powers of government and improved bargaining strength of labour. Managers, not owners, now ran industry. The combination of rising living standards, redistributive taxation and welfare benefits and services had substantially reduced primary poverty. Crosland argued that, in the new situation, ownership of the means of production was largely irrelevant. 'I conclude', he wrote, 'that the definition of capitalism in terms of owner-ship . . . has wholly lost its significance and interest now that ownership is no longer the clue to the total picture of social relationships: and that it would be more significant to define societies in terms of equality, or class relationships, or their political systems'.[8]

One of the key points about *The Future of Socialism* was the clear distinction it drew between ends and means.[9] 'Ends' were defined as the basic values or aspirations and 'means' as describing the institutional or policy changes required to pro-mote these values in practice. It was incorrect to try and define Socialism in terms of a policy like nationalization which, as Crosland pointed out, had been applied for very different purposes in Nazi Germany and the Soviet Union. The revisionist task was to subject means to searching scrutiny in the light of changing conditions. As he pointed out, 'the means most suitable in one generation may be wholly irrelevant in the next'.[10]

Modern Socialism, Crosland concluded, was about improving welfare and promoting social equality: 'The Socialist seeks a distribution of rewards, status, and privileges egalitarian enough

to minimise social resentment, to secure justice between individuals and to equalise opportunities; and he seeks to weaken the
existing deep-seated class stratification with its concomitant
feelings of envy and inferiority, and its barriers to uninhibited
mingling between the classes'.[11] Significantly Crosland gave first
priority to educational reform, including introducing comprehensive secondary education reform and opening up entry to
private schools. 'If Socialism is taken to mean a "classless
society", this is the front on which the main attack should now
be mounted'.[12]

Nearly twenty years after the publication of *The Future of
Socialism* and two years before his death, Crosland restated the
revisionist position: 'Socialism, in our view, was basically about
equality. By equality, we meant more than a meritocratic society
of equal opportunities . . . we adopted the "strong" definition of
equality . . . We also meant more than a simple . . . redistribution of income. We wanted a wider social equality embracing
also the distribution of property, the educational system, social-
class relationships, power and privilege in industry – indeed all
that was enshrined in the age-old Socialist dream of a more
"classless society" '.[13]

It is relatively easy to criticize these two great revisionist
thinkers. Both Bernstein and Crosland were over-optimistic
about economic improvements. In one celebrated passage, Crosland proclaimed 'I no longer regard questions of growth and
efficiency as being, on a long view, of primary importance to
socialism'.[14] Both were inclined to be over-complacent about
Conservative opposition to Socialist ideas and policies.
Bernstein's 'capitalist bourgeoisie yielding step by step' was
matched by Crosland ruling out 'a wholesale counter-revolution'
by the Conservatives. Both had little to say about the international context in which Democratic Socialists had to work
Though Bernstein eventually broke with the SPD over their
support for the German war effort, he had not foreseen the
coming of the 1914–18 war and on 4 August 1914 voted for war
credits.[15] Crosland became Foreign Secretary but he used frequently to say that he was not interested in foreign affairs and he
certainly did not write anything of note about them. Specific
policies or methods with which Bernstein and Crosland were
associated or admired have either failed to live up to their hope
or have come under attack. Thus Bernstein passionatel

believed in cooperatives and Crosland was a somewhat uncritical advocate of public expenditure (though he latterly added qualifications).[16]

But the shortcomings and inadequacies of the Bernstein and Crosland models do not undermine the revisionist case. Far from it. Both actively encouraged new thinking, new strategies and new policies. Indeed, the whole point of revisionism is that it cannot be a final position. By definition, it is provisional, always open to reappraisal.

The revisionist approach is made up of a number of crucial processes.[17] First, analysing what is actually happening as opposed to what a particular dogma says ought to happen or what one would like to happen; secondly, distinguishing clearly between values and methods; thirdly, subjecting values and methods to scrutiny – and, if necessary, being prepared to modify these in the light of changing conditions; fourthly, supporting open and pluralistic procedures, by which ideas and policies are not only tested against criticism but changed in the light of that criticism. In short, revisionism is a radical cast of mind, a critical way of evaluating human affairs and politics, in order to develop strategies and policies which take account of change.

* * * * *

CONTINENTAL REVISIONISM

All the most successful Continental Socialist and Social Democrat parties are revisionist – both in the narrower technical sense of having broken with Marxism and in the broader sense of being prepared to rethink, reexamine and reassess their direction and policies.

The classic revisionist statement is the 1959 Bad Godesberg programme of the German Social Democrats (SPD). In this programme, the SPD not only sent a signal to the West German electorate that it had broken with its Marxist past but also created a modern Socialist identity which was in tune with the post-war world.

The SPD, which had expected to dominate the politics of post-war Western Germany, had been beaten by the Christian

Democrats (CDU) in three successive federal elections – in 1949, 1953 and 1957. It was against the background of electoral defeat that the SPD's leading politicians and thinkers worked out a new political programme which was adopted by an overwhelming majority at a special party conference at Bad Godesberg.

A key feature of the socialism of Bad Godesberg was its commitment to values. 'Freedom, justice and solidarity which are everyone's obligations towards his neighbour and spring from our common humanity are the fundamental values of Socialism'.[18] The programme also underlined support for democracy and opposition to dictatorship, whether of right or left: 'Socialism can be realized only through democracy and democracy can only be fulfilled through Socialism'. Willi Eichler, the main author of the programme, called it 'an ethical revolution'.

Echoing Crosland in *The Future of Socialism*, Bad Godesberg gave a high priority to social welfare and stressed the responsibility of the state in social affairs. 'Established fundamental rights do not only protect the freedom of the individual in relation to the state; they should also be regarded as social rights which constitute the basis of the state. The social function of the state is to provide social security for its citizens to enable everyone to be responsible for shaping his own life freely'. It outlined an ambitious plan of social reforms, including extensions of social security and health protection, expansion of the housing programme, reduction in working hours, more codetermination, and opening up education to provide better life chances and greater redistribution of income and wealth.

But the crucial difference between the Bad Godesberg programme and previous party programmes was the abandonment of comprehensive public ownership as an objective and the acceptance of private ownership and the market over large parts of the economy. 'Free choice of consumer goods and services free choice of working place, freedom for employers to exercise their initiative as well as free competition are essential conditions of a Social Democratic economic policy . . .Private ownership of the means of production can claim protection by society as long as it does not hinder the establishment of social justice'. But the acceptance of the market was not unconditional. There was a key role for Keynesian policies. 'The state cannot shirk its responsibility for the course the economy takes. It is responsible for securing a forward-looking policy with regard to business cycles and should restrict itself to influencing the economy mainly by indirect means'. And the state had to intervene to prevent abuse of economic power: 'The most important means to this end are investment control and control over the forces dominating the market'. It added that where 'sound economic power relations cannot be guaranteed by other means, public ownership is appropriate and necessary'. The formula which best sums up the Bad Godesberg approach is 'As much competition as possible – as much planning as necessary'.

In a discussion of the significance of Bad Godesberg, a leading British journalist has acutely observed: 'If socialism is prominently about the socialisation of production, the Bad Godesberg Programme kills it off. If socialism, on the other hand, is concerned with something different – the emancipation of men and women so that all have an equal right to shape their society and to control their own lives – then Bad Godesberg can be presented as a fresh vision of socialism'.[19] For the SPD, Bad Godesberg did not lead immediately to electoral success. It was not until 1966 that it joined the 'Grand Coalition' with the CDU and not until 1969 that it was able to form an SPD-led coalition, with Willy Brandt as Federal Chancellor. But the impetus to new thinking and new policies provided by Bad Godesberg enabled the SPD to win four successive elections and to dominate West German politics in the 1970s.

In the 1980s, after two successive election defeats, the SPD is once again taking stock. A draft party programme (the Ilsee draft) was drawn up in 1986 and a definitive programme will be discussed and adopted at Lübeck in 1989. As a revisionist party, the SPD is very much aware that it needs to come to terms with recent changes in West German society and to adapt its direction and policies, especially on the environment and the economy,[20] to the new world of the 1990s.

Almost all the major European Socialist parties have brought out a new statement of aims within the last fifteen years. After their 1979 election setback the *Spanish Socialists* (PSOE) had an intense debate about the future direction of the party. At an extraordinary party congress in September, Felipe Gonzalez, who had resigned as leader following the defeat of his amendment at the May party congress, persuaded his party to drop Marxism from its statement of aims. The way was thus open for the Spanish Socialists to present themselves as a democratic reform party and to build up an electoral majority by attracting new support beyond PSOE's traditional base. PSOE won both the 1982 and 1986 elections with large majorities, and is now the predominant party in Spain.

In 1980, the *French Socialists* (PS) brought out the *Projet Socialiste* on which François Mitterrand based his presidential manifesto, the 110 propositions, in his successful bid for the Presidency in 1981. The Mitterrand approach was a blend of Keynesian expansion, French-style public ownership and industrial intervention, and policies of redistributive social spending characteristic of Scandinavian Social democracy but less well known in France.

A critic could argue, with some justice, that the 1981 Mitterrand programme, with its emphasis on 'Keynesianism in one country' and its extensive social programmes, was inappropriate to the recessionary world of the early 1980s.[21] But what has been remarkable is the extent to which the French Socialists have learnt from their mistakes. The *Propositions pour la France*, put forward by the Socialists at the 1988 Presidential election (won once again by François Mitterrand), was a realistic document which gave priority to selective industrial intervention to boost research and training, without commiting the party to further nationalization or even renationalizing industries privatized by the Chirac government. However, the Socialist minority government, under Michel Rocard, underlined the party's continuing commitment to social justice and solidarity by introducing an increased social minimum benefit and a wealth tax and by its emphasis on democratizing and expanding education.

Both the *Austrian Socialists* and the *Swedish Social Democrats* produced new statements in the 1970s. In 1978, the Austrian Socialist party (SPOe) firmly set out its commitment to Socialist values and to Keynesian policies to combat recession; its resolve was justified by the triumphant election victory of 1979 and its continuing strong position in Austrian politics during the 1980s. Even so, the Austrian Socialists, as the 1987 Party Congress showed, are once again reconsidering their direction in the fiercely competitive world of the late 1980s. The Swedish Social Democrat party document, which confirmed the party's support for full employment and the welfare state, was followed by the election defeat of 1976. But defeat led to fresh thinking and i

1982 Olof Palme, the Social Democrat leader, put forward the
so-called 'third way', a new economic strategy, designed to
stimulate production, investment and employment, which not
only assisted the party to win the 1982 election but also restored
economic growth. In the late 1980s, after two further election
victories, the party is once again reassessing its policies, particularly on taxation.

The circumstances in which these revisionist statements were
made were often different. Some were responses to electoral
defeat; others were put forward on the threshold of power; yet
others were produced by parties in power to reassert the
relevance of their policies. But, whatever the circumstance in
which they were conceived, all have certain features in common.
Each analyses current economic and social trends and provides
a coherent intellectual and ideological framework. Within that
framework, each describes the most important means and
methods and outlines a few key policy areas. Above all, each
statement seeks to establish for its party a clear political identity
in the light of changing conditions.

*   *   *   *   *

THE PRICE OF PRAGMATISM

Unlike most of our European sister parties, the British Labour
party has never officially been a 'revisionist' party. This is partly
because, in contrast to these other parties, Labour's origins
owed little to Marx. Clause IV (iv) of the party's constitution
and the first statement of aims *Labour and the New Social Order*, both
drafted by Sidney Webb in 1918, ingeniously combined Fabian
collectivism, Guild Socialist cooperation, trade union 'Labour-
ism' and progressive 'Social' liberalism into an attractive new
synthesis which sustained the party for the next forty years.[22]
These key declarations committed Labour not only to 'common
ownership', the establishment of a welfare state, and a fairer
distribution of income and wealth, but also to parliamentary
democracy. From the first, the British Labour party firmly
rejected the revolutionary Marxism which was so attractive to
other Socialist parties, particularly the German Social
Democrats and the Austrian Socialists.

It is this difference which, to a considerable extent, explains why Labour did not follow the 'Bad Godesberg' route. When after the 1959 defeat, the then leader, Hugh Gaitskell, tried to persuade the Labour party to amend Clause IV (iv) in favour of a more selective approach to public ownership, he was defeated, though an anodyne declaration of principles was adopted at the 1960 conference. He was defeated partly because of faulty tactics and partly because he had underestimated the sentimental attachment of his trade union allies to the clause. But perhaps the most important reason for his defeat was that, despite its ambiguous and incomplete nature, Clause IV (iv) was not a revolutionary Marxist statement which simply had to be changed if Labour was to have any chance of victory in the future.

Labour's electoral successes in the 1960s seemed to justify the more pragmatic tactics of his successor, Harold Wilson, who preferred to change the Labour party by stealth. But Labour has paid a heavy price for the victory of pragmatism.

First, in contrast to most other European Socialist parties, it has never officially come to terms with private ownership, the mixed economy and the role of the market, though in practice, of course, it has for many years accepted their existence. The consequence of this confusion is that it has failed to develop a credible model of state intervention and has not benefited as much as it should have done from the overwhelming popular support for the welfare state. It has also been vulnerable to the attacks from the Conservatives and the claims of the fundamentalists that Socialism stands for state ownership.

Secondly, again in contrast to most of the continental Socialist parties, Labour has failed to reassess its direction in the light of changing conditions. After the Wilson attempt to make Labour the natural party of power in the 1960s came unstuck, Labour went through the 1970s on the defensive, even though it was in government for much of the time. The civil war of the early 1980s and the Social Democrat (SDP) breakaway led not to a far-reaching reappraisal but to an uneasy equilibrium which did not convince the electors.

As the 1980s draw to a close, it is more essential than that Labour becomes a fully fledged revisionist party, capable of learning from the past, analysing the changing trends, and carving out for itself a new political identity, which will help create a new majority.

The unpleasant facts have to be faced. The party has suffered three successive defeats: at both the 1983 and 1987 elections it finished far behind the Tories. What is more, the party's declining class base and its disturbing political weakness in the South leaves it in serious danger of becoming a permanent minority party, incapable of mounting a challenge to Conservative supremacy in the 1990s.

Fundamental long-term economic and social shifts are changing British society.[23] The old world of heavy industry and mass production is shrinking rapidly and is being replaced by a far more varied pattern, based on distribution, financial services and computer and information technology industries. Manufacturing today accounts for less than a quarter of the labour force, compared with a third in 1971. In the same period, the proportion in the service sector has risen from a half to over two-thirds.

There have been corresponding shifts in occupation. Significantly, the majority of the employed are now in white collar jobs. Prosperity, home and share ownership have all risen substantially. Britain in the 1990s will be a 'two thirds, one third' society,[24] in which the vast majority of the population will have a stake in the land, while not only the poor but the manual working class will be in a minority.

Profound changes which also affect Britain are taking place in the world outside. The two superpowers are being driven by necessity towards mutual accommodation, with all that could mean for Europe. The balance of economic power is beginning to shift away from the Atlantic towards the Pacific basin. Within Europe, the drive towards a single European market and closer economic and monetary integration has major implications for national decision-making.

Labour has to come to terms with this rapidly changing world. The truth is that Labour's pragmatism, which is at one and the same time complacent, defensive and confused, is no longer enough. The party can no longer hope to muddle through. It has to have the intellectual honesty and courage to face up to change, to be clear about its objectives and to explain how it intends to achieve those objectives. Labour has to become a *revisionist* party, prepared to rethink, reassess and revise. Only a clear, unequivocal and up-to-date statement of what the party stands for will provide the intellectual basis for victory in the 1990s.

*   *   *   *   *

A REVISIONIST PARTY?

At the 1987 Brighton conference following its election defeat, the Labour party, for the first time since the early 1960s, began to look as though it might become a revisionist party. It committed itself in principle to a rigorous review of its main policies. If there were those who argued that more would be required than a policy review,[25] it was good news that Labour was to reexamine its policies in order to make them relevant to the world of the 1990s.

In the period since the Brighton conference significant progress has certainly been made. For the first time since the adoption by the party of Clause IV (iv) in 1918, Labour has published a statement of 'Democratic Socialist Aims and Values'. Reports were produced by the seven review groups under the title 'Social Justice and Economic Efficiency'. Leading figures in the party have given their commitment to the process of review and reassessment. Neil Kinnock himself called on the party to shape and develop policies 'to match new times, new needs, new opportunities, new challenges' and, in a major speech at the 1988 Blackpool conference, courageously argued that Labour had to come to terms with the market economy.

But, as after the 1959 election, the process of revision has aroused some hostility in the party, a hostility expressed most vocally by the far left but not confined to it. The unsuccessful campaign for the leadership by Tony Benn and Eric Heffer in 1988 was specifically designed to exploit this hostility.

In part the discontent comes from the old confusion to which Crosland referred in *The Future of Socialism* between ends and means. To many Labour party activists, the review process amounted to a frontal attack on what they believed to be the central tenet of Socialism – the commitment to public owner-ship. Yet privately the same activists would freely admit that public ownership, at least in the old Morrisonian style, had not been uniformly successful. Long ago, Bernstein warned the SPD against the danger of 'cant' – using words as a substitute for thought.

The second reason for the discontent was the fear that the review would be used to change the party's unilateralist defence policy. On this score, some trade union leaders, particularly Ron Todd, leader of the Transport and General Workers' Union, have been prominent in voicing criticism of the leadership, especially at the 1988 Blackpool conference. Yet it would have been manifestly absurd to exempt defence alone from the review process. It is not only that defence remains the most unpopular of Labour's policies. What is equally important is that, since the INF agreement, the prospects for multilateral disarmament and arms control agreements have been transformed.

Despite the hesitation, hostility and conservatism[26] of some sections of the party, it is essential that the leadership does not allow itself to be deflected from a fundamental reappraisal of Labour's direction and policies. For there is some way to go before the party can be satisfied that it is in a position to put forward a credible alternative agenda which will set the stage for the 1990s.

The overall message from the statement 'Democratic Socialist Aims and Values' and the policy reviews is still confused. The statement of aims' principled commitment to the importance of freedom as a value as well as the more grudging acceptance of the mixed economy is certainly a step forward. From the policy reviews, there is the recognition that market processes 'spur competition, stimulate innovation and widen consumer choice', that straightforward renationalization of privatized companies will be inappropriate, and that Labour will have to adopt a more realistic policy towards Europe. But there is as yet no decisive answer to the question 'What does Labour stand for?'

Over the next two or three years, the Labour party must decide on its overall direction if it is to mount a serious challenge for power in the 1990s. It will have to begin by recognizing that economic and social change has significant implications for the way in which Labour interprets its values, draws up its strategies and revises its policies.

The growing disparitybetween individual, groups and regions in Mrs Thatcher's Britain makes Labour's traditional commitment to social justice and fairness more than ever relevant. But the fact that, in contrast to the 1930s and 1940s, the disadvantaged groups are in a clear minority means that an appeal based on social justice alone is unlikely to be successful. Hence the need to emphasize Labour's commitment to the greater freedom and opportunity which prosperity undoubtedly brings, while stressing that there will be no lasting security for the majority unless they recognize their common obligation to the depressed minority. A balance of values will be required.

Drawing on an idea which, since R. H. Tawney, has always had an important role in Socialist thought,[27] Labour should champion the concept of citizen rights – in politics, in welfare, at work and in the market. Rights challenge the inequalities, disparities and division of a 'two thirds, one third' society. They help humanize the process of change and civilize the workings of the market. At the same time, because they give all citizens (including those who may be more prosperous but cannot be certain of high quality education or good health provision or basic rights at work or in the market) an instrument of empowerment, they provide the basis for a programme which is likely to appeal not only to the impoverished minority but also to the aspiring majority.

Labour must also have the honesty to come to terms with the market and admit that, in many areas, the competitive model, provided it is adequately regulated, works well in the allocation of goods and services. Once the party has demonstrated clearly and unequivocally that it supports a properly regulated and effectively functioning market in large parts of the economy, it is in a far stronger intellectual and political position to point to those areas in which the market system performs so imperfectly that, in the interests of the community, there has to be selective collective intervention. The case for a basic 'floor' of rights will also become more powerful.

It will also be important for the Labour party to reassert its commitment to and support for democratic institutions. Even John Nott, a former Conservative Cabinet Minister, has warned that the Conservatives, under Mrs Thatcher, are revealing an increasingly authoritarian streak. So Labour must champion the cause of democratic reform – strengthening individual rights, providing new checks on the executive and reinvigorating parliamentary and local democracy.

There are two other issues, which, like those already outlined above, must also be tackled by the Labour party. The first is to ensure that the welfare state is efficiently managed and that services are run in the interests of consumers. The second is to develop an external policy which is based on a realistic assessment of British power and interests and which takes seriously our obligations as neighbour and partner.

If Labour is to get the full political benefit from its review of policy, it has to be certain its reappraisal has been rigorous and honest. The party cannot afford any 'no go' areas. That is why later sections of this book consider the merits and shortcomings of Keynesianism, the case for incomes policy and the strengths and weaknesses of the welfare state. There must be no 'sacred cows'. That is why I examine defence policy, trade union legislation and the relationship between the unions and the party itself. Policy options should not be ruled out because they are supported by people outside the Labour party or even by other political parties. It is for this reason that there is a discussion in this book of the case for a Bill of Rights, a written constitution, proportional representation and the integration of tax and benefits. The only valid test is whether or not policies are in line with basic values and will, at the same time, be relevant to the Britain of the 1990s.

For if Labour is to become electable in the 1990s it must be a revisionist party, capable of producing new ideas and strategies – and, above all, of setting a fresh political agenda which will help to create a progressive majority over the next decade.

Part I

The Conservative Supremacy

1 Labour's Decline

Over the last decade the Labour party's fortunes have been at a low ebb. Its direction has been uncertain; its divisions have been only too obvious; and, in 1981, it suffered its biggest split since 1931. Intellectually, it has been on the defensive; not only have some of its most prominent policies been unpopular but, more generally, its approach has appeared old fashioned and out of tune with the concerns of the majority of the British people. Above all, Labour has been rejected by the voters at three successive general elections.

In 1979, Labour, then in government, was badly beaten by the Tories. The party finsished 7 percentage points behind the Conservatives and its share of the vote (37 per cent) was its lowest since 1931. If 1979 was a major defeat, 1983 was a total rout. A divided Labour party deeply discredited by the internecine party warfare of the early 1980s, seriously weakened by the breakaway of the Social Democrats, poorly led and with unpopular policies, finished a catastrophic 14 percentage points behind the Tories and a mere 2 percentage points ahead of the new-formed Alliance between the Liberals and the Social Democrats.

Most Labour supporters believed that, even if Labour failed to win the 1987 election, it would do far better than in 1983. The party had elected an attractive young leader, Neil Kinnock, and was more united. With the notable exception of defence, its policies were more appealing and, in marked contrast to 1983, it fought an energetic, slick election campaign. Yet the Labour party was once again crushingly defeated by the Tories, only improving by just over 3 percentage points on its appalling 1983 performance (from 27.6 to 30.8 per cent) and finishing more than 11 percentage points behind the Conservatives. The only silver lining in an otherwise disastrous result was that Labour finished clearly ahead of the Alliance which still, however, polled 22 per cent of the total vote.

Why has Labour done so badly? This chapter attempts to chart Labour's decline and explain the reasons for it.

* * * * *

19

THE 1970s: LABOUR GOVERNMENT UNDERMINED

One theory that has been advanced is that the Labour party has been in secular decline since 1951.[1] It is true that, taking the 1951 share of the vote (48.8 per cent) as the high water mark, the Labour vote has decreased dramatically. But the 'long-term' decline argument conveniently ignores the fact that the 1951 election (which Labour lost) was an exception because the Liberals put up only just over 100 candidates.[2] It also omits to mention that Labour won two elections in a row during the 1960s and that in 1966 its share of the vote was only marginally lower than in 1945 (47.9 per cent compared to 48.3 per cent). Even in 1970, when Harold Wilson lost to Edward Heath, Labour's share of the vote was 43 per cent.

It is more plausible to see the roots of Labour's decline in the 1960s and in the failure of the Wilson administrations to establish the Labour party as the predominant force in British politics. Despite its creditable social record,[3] the Labour government did not achieve the economic growth that it needed. Growth was vital to the government's plans. If output had been greater, there would have been more for both public spending and consumption. Sustained growth would also have strengthened the economy at a time when the opportunities for British industry in world markets were potentially promising. Last but not least, it would have substantially improved Labour's electoral prospects. But the Prime Minister's refusal to devalue until it was too late fatally undermined his government's prospects. In the 1960s, Labour was presented with a historic opportunity which it did not take.

But if it is possible to trace back the party's decline to the 1960s, the fact is that Labour was offered another chance in the 1970s. It is true that Labour won the two elections of 1974 almost by default. Its share of the vote (37.1 per cent and 39.2 per cent) dipped below 40 per cent for the first time since the war. But in democratic politics, it is relative position that counts; the Tories, under Heath, did even worse than Labour. The result was that for much of the 1970s, Labour was in power, albeit for some of the time on a minority basis.

Indeed, from the vantage point of the mid-1970s, it seemed as though it was the Labour party which was more likely to be able to provide the intellectual and political framework within which the difficult problems of the recession years could be tackled. It was true that the Labour government, like other Western governments, was experiencing difficulties in continuing to apply full-blooded Keynesian policies in an era of oil shocks, high inflation, and floating exchange rates. But if, as was then generally accepted, it was possible through the application of incomes policy to bring down inflation without resorting to wide scale unemployment, then the Labour party's close relationship with the unions gave it the edge. After all, Heath's Conservative government had foundered on its inability to 'get on' with unions and Labour's 'social contract' approach appeared likely to offer a more successful alternative.

The 'social contract' concept seemed to be a highly promising addition to the key ideas of full employment, redistribution and welfare which were at the heart of the post-war consensus which had been accepted by both major political parties. The social contract was based on a compact with the unions and was an ambitious attempt to link together social welfare, tax policy, output, employment and incomes in a coherent whole.

Its initial phase (until July 1975) took too little account of wage increases. But in its later stages it had considerable success in reducing inflation. Inflation was brought down from $27\frac{1}{2}$ per cent in July 1976 to 8 per cent in July 1978. The Labour government also introduced significantly increased benefits for pensioners and large families, as well as extension of rights for employees and trade unionists at the workplace.

Yet, despite these undoubted achievements, support for Labour ideas and Labour governments were undermined by two crucial episodes. The first was the 1976 IMF crisis. In late October, after a desperate rearguard action against international pressure on the pound, the Labour government was forced to go to the International Monetary Fund for a loan.[4] As part of the terms on which the loan was provided, the IMF demanded substantial reductions in public spending plans. On 2 December, after intensive debate, skilfully handled by the Prime Minister, James Callaghan, the Cabinet agreed to cuts of $1\frac{1}{2}$ billion pounds in 1977–8 and $2\frac{1}{4}$ billion pounds in 1978–9.[5]

In the event, the IMF-imposed constraints turned out to have been largely academic. As a consequence of cash limits on public spending introduced in 1975, the volume of public spending was $3\frac{1}{2}$ per cent lower in 1976–7 than in 1975–6. So that at the time when the IMF and the government supposed the public sector-borrowing requirement for 1976–7 to be 9 per cent of GDP, it had actually fallen to 6 per cent. And in 1977–8, public expenditure was 6 to 7 per cent below the level demanded by the IMF, while the PSBR fell to 4 per cent of GDP, well below the 6 per cent agreed with the IMF.

Even so, there was a general recognition that the Labour government had suffered a severe psychological setback over the IMF crisis. It had succumbed to the pressure of the international financial community and hardliners in the United States. It had been forced to abandon its initial Keynesian strategy of attempting to maintain activity by keeping up internal demand. And it had accepted that, as set out in Denis Healey's letter of intent to the IMF, there would have to be 'a continued and substantial reduction over the next few years in the share of the resources required for the public sector'.

The Labour government's humiliation in 1976 brought into question two of the key elements of the post-war consensus – the belief that government could maintain full employment and the commitment to high levels of public spending. It also gave credence to views and policies associated with the new Conservative leader, Margaret Thatcher. In the months immediately following the IMF crisis, there was some indication from opinion polls that Mrs Thatcher's 'new' Conservatism was beginning to strike popular chords. In June 1977 a Chequers meeting of Labour Cabinet Ministers was advised that public opinion had shifted to the right on some issues and that there was strong support in particular for cuts in taxation.[6] Certainly at the May 1979 general election, the Tories had leads on taxation, law and order and council house sales.[7]

But the decisive factor in the defeat of the Labour government was not so much any underlying shift in popular attitudes but the 'winter of discontent' of 1978–9. Ironically the Labour party, assisted by Britain's improved economic performance, staged a remarkable recovery during 1978 and until late autumn ran the Tories neck and neck in the polls. It was the breakdown of incomes policy and the highly publicized strikes which followed which torpedoed Labour's electoral chances. The rubbish in the streets, the piles of unwashed hospital sheets and the dead left unburied removed at a stroke Labour's most potent electoral card – its claim to be able to manage the unions. In those bitter winter months, not only Labour's authority as an actual and potential government but also its most effective and relevant political idea was fatally exposed.

*   *   *   *   *

THE 1980s: LABOUR'S CIVIL WAR AND THE SDP SPLIT

It was the nature and circumstances of Labour's 1979 election defeat which shaped everything that followed – the civil war inside the Labour party, the formation of the SDP and the rise of the Alliance, and Mrs Thatcher's dominance over British politics. Even if James Callaghan had gone to the country in October 1978, as most Labour MPs expected and preferred, Labour might not have won the election. But at least it would have been a 'close run' affair and Labour would have gone into opposition with some credibility left. Instead, Callaghan delayed the election and the winter of discontent ensued.[8]

The collapse of the Labour government's authority during the bitter winter of 1978–9 gave the Conservatives their decisive victory. They not only won 70 more seats than Labour but their lead over Labour was bigger than that of Harold Macmillan in 1959. Labour's share of the poll was at its lowest since 1931, with many working class voters, particularly amongst the skilled employees, deserting to the Tories. The defeat of 1979 also fatally discredited, as much within as outside the Labour party, the old Social Democratic orthodoxies, particularly the ideas of Keynesian economic management and trade union based incomes policies.

Into the intellectual and political vacuum stepped Anthony Wedgwood Benn. Following Labour's defeat, Tony Benn, although he had remained a Cabinet Minister throughout the Wilson and Callaghan administrations of the 1970s, speedily made his bid for the leadership. As part of his prospectus, he put forward an alternative strategy based on import controls, withdrawal from the common market, more public ownership, planning agreements and workers' control.[9] To this primarily economic programme was added the notion of internal party reform. The Callaghan government, according to Tony Benn and the left wing activists who supported him, had betrayed the party. To prevent this happening again, the leadership and Labour Members of Parliament needed to be made more accountable. Hence the argument for giving the extra-parliamentary party a predominant say in electing the leadership, for reselection of members of parliament and for taking control of the manifesto away from the leadership.

At its zenith in 1980–1, the Bennite cocktail was a heady brew, appealing not only to the hard left and Trotskyite elements (which following the abandonment of the proscribed list in 1972 had grown more influential within the party) but also to younger, idealistic party members who wanted to see change.[10] Certainly for over two years after Labour's election defeat and until his bid for deputy leadership was defeated, the initiative inside the party lay with Tony Benn.

In face of the Bennite onslaught, Labour's Social Democratic wing was thrown very much on the defensive. Their economic policies had been discredited by the winter of discontent, and, until their conversion during 1980 to one person, one vote, had no organisational proposals of their own. They could certainly argue that the Bennites were proposing what amounted to a siege economy at a time when the Western industrial economies were becoming increasingly interdependent. They could also say, with considerable justice, that the Bennite organisational reforms were motivated as much by Benn's drive for power as by democratic considerations.

Even so, very few Labour party activists were listening to them. The Bennites won a series of important victories. Reselection was carried at the 1979 party conference and, at the Wembley special conference in January 1981, an electoral college composed of trade unions (40 per cent), constituency parties (30 per cent) and MPs (30 per cent) was set up to elect the leader. The 1980 Blackpool conference pledged itself both to unilateral nuclear disarmament and to withdrawal from the European community without a referendum. At a time when the voters were shifting to the right, the Labour party seemed to be lurching irretrievably to the left.

It was in an atmosphere of defeat, disintegration and despair that the fateful decision was taken by a group of right wing MPs to set up a breakaway party – the Social Democratic Party (SDP). Roy Jenkins, the retiring President of the EC Commission and former Chancellor, Home Secretary and deputy leader, had already raised the possibility of a centre grouping in his Dimbleby lecture in November 1979. But before a new party could get off the ground, it needed the support of a number of influential Labour MPs, particularly the so-called 'Gang of Three', Shirley Williams, Bill Rodgers and David Owen. On 1 August 1980, greatly alarmed by the Bennite surge and by the prevarication of the Callaghan leadership, these three ex-Cabinet ministers issued an 'open' letter in the *Guardian* which gave a clear hint that they were considering leaving the Labour party.

The crucial event, however, in the decision to defect was the election in November of the candidate of the left, Michael Foot, as leader of the Labour party following the resignation of Jim Callaghan. Once Michael Foot had narrowly defeated Denis Healey by 139 votes to 129, in the last purely parliamentary election for leader, the 'Gang of Three' concluded that the Labour party was a lost cause and began preparations for the formation of a new party.

The creation of the SDP significantly strengthened the 'third force' in British politics. During the 1970s, the Liberals had already begun to increase their share of the national vote. At the February 1974 election they won 19.3 per cent and, though their vote fell back to 13.8 per cent in 1979, the successful experiment of the Lib–Lab pact, the increasing volatility of the electorate and the marked decline during the 1970s in identification with the two major parties all gave the Liberals fresh hope. Their leader, David Steel, determined to manoeuvre the Liberals in a permanent and pivotal power-sharing role in British politics but aware that a new party could be more attractive to Labour defectors, had advised Roy Jenkins not to join the Liberals but to work with dissident Labour MPs to set up the SDP. An electoral pact between the Liberals and the SDP was negotiated; and, during 1981, the newly formed Alliance, greatly assisted by the bruising struggle for the deputy leadership of the Labour party (in which the incumbent, Denis Healey, narrowly beat the challenger Tony Benn) won three spectacular by-election victories – at Croydon, Crosby and Hillhead.

The SDP breakaway and the formation of the Alliance was an unmitigated disaster for Labour from which the party has not yet recovered. The moderate group inside the party was gravely weakened, even if their decline was masked for a time by an

entente cordiale with the so-called 'soft' left, who had been deeply
disturbed by the dubious tactics of Tony Benn and the unsav-
oury nature of some of his allies. What was more important was
that the departure of the 'Gang of Three', particularly of Shirley
Williams, was taken as a portent by a significant proportion of
the progressive middle classes, which had previously leaned
towards the Labour party. As a consequence of the SDP
breakaway, Labour lost as much as 5 per cent of potential
support, and its image as an alternative government was crucially weakened.

Although the Falklands triumph and limited economic recovery were clearly factors in the Tory recovery after 1981, the
combination of a badly split and badly led Labour party and the
emergence of a Liberal – SDP Alliance backed by a quarter of
the electorate stacked the cards in Mrs Thatcher's favour.
Indeed, such was the distorting impact of an almost equally
divided opposition in a first past the post electoral system that,
although the Tory vote declined slightly compared to 1979, the
Conservative overall majority in terms of seats actually increased from 43 to 141.

The key factor at the 1983 election was the collapse of the
Labour vote. The Labour vote fell by over 9 percentage points to
27.6 per cent – the sharpest fall by any party since the war and
its lowest share of the poll since 1918. In June 1983, Labour was
driven back to its bedrock support in its heartlands of the North
of England, Scotland and Wales, in the big cities and among the
unskilled working class. It lost its majority backing among the
skilled workers and trade unionists, and failed even to carry a
majority of the unemployed. The affluent, skilled and house
owning working class deserted the Labour party in droves.[11] In
1983, Labour became, to a greater extent than ever before, the
party of declining Britain.

The reasons for Labour's lamentable performance in 1983
were fairly obvious. Michael Foot was not able to convince even
the majority of Labour voters that he would make a good Prime
Minister. The party presented an image of a divided, quarrelling
rabble, deserted by some of its most prominent leaders. It was
also felt that there were too many activists whose real commitment was to the doctrines of Leon Trotsky rather than to the
Labour party. It was clear that some of Labour's policies,
particularly on defence and housing, were profoundly unpopu-

lar. With respect to the economy, the majority of the electorate did not believe the Labour party when it said it could bring down unemployment (then over three million) to one million within five years. In any case, too many voters even among the unemployed (some of whom did not vote at all) did not believe there was an alternative to the Thatcherite strategy. Unemployment was blamed not so much on the government but on other factors, particularly the world economic situation. However, what damaged Labour more than the specifics of its policies was the general unattractiveness of its image as a party. In 1983, Labour was basically unelectable.

*   *   *   *   *

THE ROAD TO 1987

After the 1983 *débâcle*, the task of the newly elected Labour leader, Neil Kinnock, was to see off the Alliance (which had finished a mere 680 000 votes behind Labour) and then overtake the Tories. For much of the parliament, Labour seemed to have staged an impressive recovery. At the 1984 European election Labour, with 36 per cent, was a respectable second and the Alliance was relegated to a poor third. Although the miners' strike held Labour back for most of the following year, Neil Kinnock courageously reasserted his leadership at the 1985 Bournemouth conference over both the intransigent miners' leader, Arthur Scargill, and the Liverpool Militants, whose 'impossibilist' tactics had threatened the future of that city.

From the 1985 to the 1986 conference, the Labour party usually led the Conservatives in the polls, with the Alliance third; made gains in both the 1985 and 1986 local elections; and in April 1986 won the Fulham by-election. But Labour's recovery was always somewhat brittle, depending more on Tory weakness (as over the Westland crisis) than on Labour strength. Its position in the polls rarely touched 40 per cent, usually hovering around a 36–37 per cent ceiling.[12]

Then, from the end of 1986, Labour's challenge began to fall apart. Neil Kinnock made two trips to Washington (including one just before the election) which, far from persuading the Americans, merely had the effect of highlighting Labour's unpopular defence policies. In February 1987 the selection of a hard left wing candidate for the Greenwich by-election, won by the Alliance from Labour, underlined the extremist side of London Labour politics which was so cordially disliked throughout the rest of Britain. The result was that all the effort which the leadership had put into persuading the voters that Labour had changed from 1983 was cast into doubt. Maybe Labour could never have won the 1987 election. But a combination of faulty tactics in the pre-election period, an unpopular defence policy, and the reminder of the unattractive nature of London Labour politics ensured that Labour was not in a position to offer a serious challenge for power.

Indeed, after the Greenwich by-election, the 1987 election was, like 1983, merely a race for second place between the two oppositions. Labour went into the election not only 11 percentage points behind the Tories but neck and neck with the Alliance. The effect of Labour's energetic campaign was to win $1\frac{1}{2}$ million extra votes over 1983 and to put Labour comfortably ahead of the Alliance parties (which still polled over 7 million votes). But Labour still finished over 11 percentage points behind the Tories, who, with 42.3 per cent of the vote, won a massive majority of 101 in terms of seats. In 1987, as in 1983, a divided opposition and a first past the post electoral system exaggerated the scale of Mrs Thatcher's victory.

The reasons for Labour's 1987 defeat were, to a limited extent, different from 1983. Labour was more united than in 1983 and Neil Kinnock was a more popular leader than Michael Foot. In the polls, Labour impressively outscored the Tories on the so-called 'people's agenda' of unemployment, health and education.[13]

But Labour's negative points (in public attitudes) which included the trade union connection, the reputation for extremism, its defence and economic policies, still outweighed the positive. On the negative side, defence (as in 1983) and the issue of managing the economy were probably the most important. Polls indicated that defence alone cost the party over one million votes,[14] while a 2 to 1 margin of voters thought that the Tories were more likely to deliver higher living standards than Labour.[15] The *Sunday Times*'s verdict was probably a fair summary of the 1987 election: 'Those old political standbys, prosperity and security, won the day for Mrs Thatcher'.[16]

The 1987 defeat left Labour in an unenviable position. It may have gained 1½ million extra votes and 20 additional seats but the result was still its second worst electoral performance and its second lowest return of MPs since 1945. What is more, it finished over 11 percentage points behind the Tories. To win a majority at the next election it needs a swing of over 8 per cent and an extra 97 seats – what the Nuffield election survey has called 'an electoral Everest'.[17]

Geographically, the 1987 election result revealed two distinct political nations. In Scotland, Wales and the North of England, there was a 4.5 per cent swing from Conservative to Labour.[18] In the rest of the country there was little if any swing at all. The Conservative vote held ominously solid in the Midlands and the South, while in London and the surrounding metropolitan area there was a swing to the Tories.

If Conservative support is becoming increasingly concentrated in the Southern half of the country, then Labour's vote is similarly concentrated in the North. Over three-quarters of Labour MPs represent constituencies in Scotland, Wales and the North of England. In the Southern part of England, Labour has only 26 MPs altogether and only 3 MPs outside London. (As recently as October 1974, Labour held 80 seats in this area and 29 seats outside London.) The problem for Labour is that the part of Britain where it has been doing relatively well has nearly a 100 fewer seats than the part where the Conservative party has been consolidating its strength. Even more disturbing, Labour is no longer a credible challenger in most of the 250 Southern seats. Labour's weakness in the South is a crippling handicap for a party with pretensions to national power.

Politicians, journalists and political scientists generally agree that social class remains an important underlying determinant of voting behaviour. Although both major parties have normally received considerable across-class support, Labour has traditionally been the party of the manual working class, while the Conservatives have been the party of the white collar, middle class. A striking feature of the last three general elections, especially those of 1983 and 1987, is that Labour has lost a large slice of its working class support.

A fierce academic controversy has arisen over differing sociological explanations of the decline in Labour's working class vote. One school of thought maintains that Labour's decline is accounted for by an erosion of class solidarity.[19] It is argued that Labour can no longer rely on working class support in the way it could a generation ago and that a new breed of affluent, home owning, skilled workers in the South of England have swung decisively to the Conservatives. Another school rejects this explanation and believes that 'in focusing on class dealignment political scientists have concentrated on minor rearrangements of the furniture while failing to notice a major change in the structure of the house.[20] What is crucial is the change in the size of the working class.

In the Oxford study of the 1983 election, the authors assessed the change in the class distribution of the electorate between the 1964 and 1983 general elections. They showed that the manual working class had declined from half of the electorate in 1969 to less than a third in 1983. Over the same period, the salariat (administrators, supervisors, professionals and semi-professionals) had increased from 18 to 27 per cent. According to this account, Labour's decline is caused not so much by the changing nature of the working class but by its diminishing size.

My view is that the two arguments are not mutually exclusive. Clearly, whether the working class is defined as 'rank and file manual employees' (as in the Oxford study) or more widely as in the 'social grade' definition (used in market research and opinion polling), it has significantly shrunk in size since the 1960s. On the other hand, it is also plain that a declining proportion of the working class is now voting Labour. In 1959, 62 per cent of the working class voted Labour: in 1987, the proportion had fallen to 42 per cent.[21]

A significant feature in the decline in Labour's hold on the working class seems to be the voting behaviour of affluent workers, particularly in the South. According to the *Guardian* 1987 Election Survey, the Tory party actually had a larger lead amongst Southern manual workers (by 46 to 28 per cent) than it did in the electorate as a whole.[22] Whether the Conservative strength in the Southern working class is explained more by the so-called 'neighbourhood' effect (through which Southern workers are likely to adopt the voting habits of their increasingly predominant middle class neighbours)[23] than by Southern prosperity is difficult to say.

My own (admittedly unsystematic) investigations in two Southern seats which Labour lost revealed that prosperity was a major factor. 'Everybody feels more prosperous now' was a fairly general reaction. What is clear is that the main growth in Conservative support has been amongst manual workers who live in the South, own their own houses, work in the private sector and are not members of trade unions. The 'new working class' is voting Tory.

So viewed from the perspective of the 1987 election, the Labour party seemed in danger of becoming a permanent minority party. It not only finished far behind the Conservatives. Even more disturbing, its declining class base and crippling political weaknesses in the South left it in a weak position to mount a serious challenge for power in the 1990s.

* * * * *

SUMMARY

The seeds of the Labour party's decline can be traced back to the 1960s when it failed to establish itself as the party of government. Even so, Labour was given another chance in the 1970s. But the crumbling of the Social Democratic orthodoxies in 1975–6 and, more decisively, the undermining of the Callaghan administration by the 'winter of discontent' paved the way for Mrs Thatcher. At the beginning of the 1980s, a prolonged bout of civil war, the adoption of unpopular policies, and, most damaging of all, the SDP split, made the party virtually unelectable for much of the rest of the decade. Its third successive defeat in 1987 left a question mark over Labour's future as a governing party.

2 The Thatcherite Triumph

One of the most perceptive books on the Conservative Prime Minister is significantly entitled *The Thatcher Phenomenon*.[1] To justify this title, the authors remind readers that Mrs Thatcher's position is such that she 'has given her name to the age in which we live'. Thatcherism is unique, they point out, not so much as a set of ideas but as the only 'ism' attached to the name of a British Prime Minister. For anyone who is concerned to challenge those ideas and to bring an end to Conservative rule, it is important to understand both the evolving nature of Thatcherism and its strengths and limitations.

To a political opponent, what has been striking about the 1980s is the extent to which Mrs Thatcher has set the agenda for discussion and debate. It is not so much that Mrs Thatcher has a carefully worked out political philosophy. A more accurate assessment is that she draws on an assortment of firmly held but loosely linked right wing ideas or nostrums. But the force of her personality has meant that it is her views which have inspired Conservative party policies and her policies which her Conservative governments have introduced.

Of course, like all successful politicians, Mrs Thatcher has been remarkably lucky. The 1978–9 'winter of discontent' wave of strikes, which discredited not only the Callaghan government but Labour's whole approach, could not have come more opportunely for the Tories. The 1982 Falklands War enabled Mrs Thatcher to display her undoubted qualities of courage and determination and to appeal to British patriotic fervour at a time when she most needed a boost. And the contribution of North Sea oil and a split opposition has provided the ideal economic and political conditions in which Thatcherism could flourish.

But good fortune is not a sufficient explanation for Thatcher's success. Opposition politicians have become only too aware of the appeal of Mrs Thatcher and some of her ideas. There is now majority support for Conservative policies on trade union reform and on the sale of council houses and significant backing for

32

Tory views on the role of private enterprise and the importance of competition and profit in economic affairs.[2] The basic Thatcherite values of thrift, value for money, reward for effort and enterprise are popular. Although the welfare state still receives overwhelming adherence from voters, on a number of issues Mrs Thatcher has succeeded in capturing public opinion.

The appeal of Mrs Thatcher's leadership, ideas and policies has helped the Tories to win three general elections in succession. It is true that the Conservative share of the vote has declined slightly since 1979 and that their percentage of the poll, which led to victories of such landslide proportions in 1983 and 1987, was actually smaller than the proportion which the Labour party received at the 1959 election when it lost so disastrously. But in a 'first past the post' electoral system in which *three* parties get over 20 per cent of the vote, any party which gains over 40 per cent of the vote is likely to win comfortably. In a three party race, Mrs Thatcher's remarkable ability to keep her party's support solidly over 40 per cent has ensured Tory political dominance.

1979–83: THE THATCHER FACTOR

When in 1976 Mrs Thatcher captured the Tory leadership in a brilliant *coup d'état*, she brought to the position steely ambition, profound anti-socialism, and a moral agenda which 'could have been written on a sampler'.[3] She believed passionately in self-improvement, the family, free enterprise, the creation and acquisition of wealth, 'sound' money and patriotism. She detested socialists, trade unionists, 'wet' Tories, collectivism and consensus.

In comparison with her immediate predecessors as leader of the Conservative party, Mrs Thatcher adopted a decidedly right wing stance. In a series of speeches between 1975 and 1979 she advocated a number of ideas and principles which challenged the post-war settlement. These included a substantial reduction in the role of the state, a strong commitment to market forces and private enterprise, and big cuts in public spending and income tax.[4] Encouraged by Sir Keith Joseph, her close colleague and intellectual mentor, and by other 'gurus' of the New Right, Mrs Thatcher also lent her support to the increasingly fashionable doctrine of monetarism. According to this theory, Keynesian policies to stimulate economic growth were self-defeating. While their impact on unemployment was merely temporary, their real and lasting effect was to increase the rate of inflation. Instead of trying to spend their way out of recession, governments should confine their activities to controlling the rate of inflation by squeezing the money supply and balancing the budget.

Mrs Thatcher's special contribution to this revival of right wing Conservative ideas was the conviction and fervour with which she espoused them. No matter that, as Secretary of State for Education in the Heath government, she had been one of the big spenders. Like Sir Keith Joseph, she had seen the light and was determined to use her considerable gifts of communication to ensure that the voters saw it too.

The main reason for the Conservative victory in 1979 was the 'winter of discontent' and the subsequent breakdown of the Labour government's authority. But the sizeable switch of working class votes to the Tories shown up by the BBC election day survey (a 6.5 per cent swing amongst semi-skilled and unskilled workers, 3 per cent among trade unionists and 11 per cent among skilled workers) revealed a deeper shift of attitudes. Following the 1979 election, I wrote that 'Tory ideas are in the ascendancy – Tory ideas on the role of the state, on taxation, on the position of the unions, on law and order'.[5] There was already a sense that Mrs Thatcher was beginning to win the underlying battle of ideas.

After her 1979 election victory, Mrs Thatcher quickly asserted her ideological dominance over the new Tory government by appointing her supporters to the key economic posts. Over the next two years she crushed dissent by sacking or marginalising so-called 'wet' Ministers who questioned her policies.[6] By the end of 1981, Mrs Thatcher had established a firm grip over her Cabinet and government.

From the start, the policies of her government were decidedly Thatcherite, particularly in economic policy. In his first budget in 1979 when he cut public expenditure plans, reduced direct taxes but increased indirect taxation, her Chancellor, Sir Geoffrey Howe, gave priority to controlling the money supply and squeezing public spending. The most characteristically monetarist budget was that of March 1981. Although the economy was already plunging into deep recession during 1980–1, the government actually tightened its fiscal stance – the Prime Minister's economic adviser called it the biggest fiscal squeeze of peacetime'.[7] At the same time, the value of the pound was forced up by high interest rates. No wonder that British output and employment declined more sharply than any of the major industrial countries and that 20 per cent of our manufacturing capacity was destroyed.

In 1981 Mrs Thatcher and her ideas were at their most vulnerable. It was one thing repressing opposition within her government. It was quite another to persuade the voters that it was sensible to pursue policies which clobbered manufacturing industry and deliberately increased unemployment. Unfortunately the Labour party, damaged by the SDP breakaway and distracted by the struggle for the deputy leadership, was simply not in a position to exploit the government's unpopularity. At the time of maximum weakness, Mrs Thatcher was let off the hook by the lack of effective opposition.

Though the government had been regaining a little ground, chiefly at the expense of the Alliance parties some months before, the Falklands War in the spring of 1982 transformed the political scene. Mrs Thatcher unashamedly cashed in on the victory of British troops in the Falklands: 'We have ceased to be a nation in retreat. We have instead a new-found confidence . . .that confidence comes from the rediscovery of ourselves, and grows with the recovery of our self respect'.[8] Linking her leadership with military success in the Falklands, she told an interviewer: 'I think people like decisiveness, I think they like strong leadership'.[9] So the Falklands factor became the Thatcher factor. The Tories, running third in the polls at the end of 1981, went into the 1983 election with an unassailable 18 percentage points lead.

However, the Tory party's landslide victory in the 1983 election was more a verdict on the state of the Labour party and a consequence of a non-Conservative vote which was almost equally divided between Labour and the SDP–Liberal Alliance than a wholehearted endorsement of Thatcherite policies and ideas. Indeed, despite Mrs Thatcher's Falklands triumph, the Tory share of the vote actually declined slightly compared to 1979. There was certainly strong support for Tory policies on the unions, on the sale of council houses, on defence and on bringing down inflation. In line with Thatcherite doctrine, there was also a growing scepticism about how much governments themselves could achieve in the economic sphere. Even so, according to opinion surveys, supporters of government intervention to reduce unemployment outnumbered opponents. And, in contrast to 1979, a clear majority favoured increased taxes to pay for greater expenditure on health, education and welfare.[10] In 1983, Mrs Thatcher and her party may have won a landslide victory but it would be an exaggeration to call it an unconditional triumph for Thatcherism.

*　　*　　*　　*　　*

1983–7: THATCHERITE PROSPERITY

Between 1983 and 1987 there were modifications and developments in the nature of Thatcherism. If pre-1983 Thatcherism was primarily a doctrine of restraint and lowered expectations, by 1987 it had evolved into an optimistic message of expansion and prosperity.

In the 1983–7 parliament, 'the Thatcher factor', so potent in the aftermath of the Falklands War, was not always a plus for the Conservative party. In January 1986 the fiasco of the Westland affair, over which two leading Cabinet Ministers, Michael Heseltine and Leon Brittan, resigned, and which nearly destroyed the Prime Minister herself, was Mrs Thatcher's nadir. The combination of high-handedness, lack of candour and, above all, uncertainty of touch revealed by the Westland crisis was a prelude to a slump in both Mrs Thatcher's personal ratings and in the fortunes of her party. After the government's bad results in the May 1986 local elections, John Biffen, the popular and respected Leader of the House of Commons, openly questioned Mrs Thatcher's style of leadership on television: 'To assume that because a party has one dominant figure it thereby benefits is not necessarily true at all'.[11]

The government also allowed itself to be diverted, throughout much of the parliament, into a running battle with local government which was, to a considerable extent, Labour dominated. A series of Acts increased the powers of central government. The powers of local authorities were restricted by cuts in spending and by rate capping. In 1986, the government also abolished the Greater London Council and the Metropolitan County Councils, all Labour controlled. The Thatcherites saw nothing reprehensible in this attack on Labour's strongholds. Norman Tebbit argued that the GLC was typical of a new and divisive version of Socialism: 'So we shall abolish it'. But the former Conservative Prime Minister, Edward Heath, warned that to get rid of democratically elected councils was to invite reprisals if Labour was returned to power.

The third ingredient in the government's mid-term difficulties was the growing public reaction to the squeeze on public spending, particularly in education. Sir Keith Joseph, Secretary of State for Education, understood the need for educational reforms and for raising the standards of what he called the 'bottom 40 per cent'. But, as a committed monetarist, he was not prepared to ask the Treasury for the necessary extra resources. As a consequence, spending on education as a proportion of total public spending fell. There were cuts in resources going to higher education and the civil research budget declined in real terms. In addition, Joseph drifted into a damaging dispute with the teachers' unions. By 1986 the government had lost support amongst academics, teachers and parents.

It was economic growth and the prosperity it brought with it which turned the tide for Mrs Thatcher. In this sense, it was the Chancellor, Nigel Lawson, who was the real architect of the Conservative victory at the 1987 election. Lawson had helped devise the Medium Term Financial Strategy (MTFS), the bible of monetarist orthodoxy, but by the end of 1985 he had virtually abandoned monetarism. It had proved almost impossible to measure the money supply, while the connection between growth in the monetary aggregates and the rate of inflation was hard to discern. As Mr Lawson, with characteristic insouciance, told the Lombard Association in April 1986, 'no economic relationship is perfect'.[12] In his autumn statement that year, Lawson relaxed spending curbs. Public spending was now to be allowed to grow in real terms, provided it fell as a proportion of GDP. The government, after years of preaching the merits of cutting public spending, now took credit for public expenditure increases, especially in education and health.

As the election drew closer, so Lawson abandoned monetary and fiscal orthodoxy and encouraged an old fashioned consumer boom, fuelled by a remarkable drop in the savings ratio, a fall in the exchange rate, disguised fiscal relaxation and earnings rising faster than inflation. In the eighteen months before June 1987, real GDP grew at a rate of 4 per cent and credit and consumption rose sharply. Even the unemployment figures, considerably assisted by changes in methods of calculation and by special programmes, fell significantly. In his 1987 budget, the Chancellor pressed home the political message by reducing the basic tax rate to 27 per cent.

Mrs Thatcher claimed that her 1987 victory was the result of a historic 'change of culture and attitude' in the British people.[13] But if there had been such a revolution then the Conservatives should have easily been able to ward off the Labour offensive both before and during the election on health, education and unemployment. In fact, the polls showed that, on the contrary, Labour was able to establish a lead on these issues. Even more telling, according to *British Social Attitudes*, support for the welfare state had grown rather than decreased during the Thatcher years.[14] But backing for Labour on health, education and employment was not nearly sufficient to overcome the general feeling, clearly shown by the polls, that in 1987 both the economy and family living standards were improving. According to a Gallup survey, the balance of perceptions on the economy moved from a minus 32 per cent in September 1986 to a plus 15 per cent on election day. On family finances the comparable figures were minus 12 per cent in September 1986 to plus 2 per cent by the election.[15] Prosperity much more than a revolutionary 'change of culture' won the day for Mrs Thatcher.

*   *   *   *   *

POST-1987: TRIUMPHALIST PHASE

After the third successive Conservative victory, Thatcherism entered a triumphalist phase. Making her leader's speech to the 1987 conference, Mrs Thatcher not only promised the Tory faithful that 'the third election was only a staging post on a much longer journey' but accused the opposition parties of 'feverishly packaging their policies' to look like those of the Conservatives. Thatcherite ideas and Thatcherite policies, she crowed, now dominated British politics. There was a new pride in Britain, she told a *Sunday Express* interviewer. Victoriously she proclaimed the death of British Socialism: 'People know that we have led the world in trying to reverse the tide of socialism, and not merely in Western countries'.[16] At the 1988 conference, she held out the prospect of ten more years of Conservative government.

But, over the more humdrum business of introducing legislation and running the economy, the Conservatives encountered difficulties. The government was forced on the defensive over welfare issues. In the winter of 1987–8 there was an outcry over the National Health Service, which led to the setting up of a government inquiry. In the spring of 1988, withdrawal of and reductions in housing benefit for some previous beneficiaries aroused public and parliamentary protest, including many Conservative MPs. Though the Education Reform Bill passed through parliament virtually unscathed, it was unlikely that the proposals to permit schools to opt out of local authority control would receive the massive support which the sale of council houses had achieved in Mrs Thatcher's first term.

The most controversial piece of legislation in the first session (1987–8) of the 1987 parliament was the Bill introducing the Community Charge, almost universally known as the 'poll tax' Bill. The poll tax, designed to replace local domestic rates on property, is a fixed charge on individuals, unrelated to ability to pay. Polls showed that it was unpopular with a large majority of the electors. There was also some opposition amongst Tory MPs as well as a sizeable revolt in the House of Lords, which, largely because of self-interest of Conservative hereditary peers, was unsuccessful. In the second session (1988–9) the two most important Bills were those to privatise water and electricity. Once again, there was considerable public hostility which the government, protected by its impregnable parliamentary majority, attempted to ignore.

But perhaps the government's greatest problem was the economy. By the autumn of 1988, it had become clear that the Lawson 'boom' which had been such an important factor in the Conservatives' third election victory had run into trouble. The autumn statement forecast massive balance of payments deficits for 1988 and 1989 of £13 billion and £11 billion respectively. It also predicted a significant rise in prices, bringing the British rate of inflation above that of her main competitors. In both August and November, the government was forced to raise interest rates, following the announcement of bad current account figures. On 25 November interest rates were raised to 13 per cent, the highest of any major industrial country. Relations between the Prime Minister and her Chancellor, Nigel Lawson, which earlier in the year had been strained over exchange rate policy, grew cool. There was a marked decline in general optimism about economic prospects.[17]

A MORI poll, published in the *Sunday Times* in June 1988, revealed a more deep seated ambivalence about Thatcherite values.[18] There was support for people being allowed to be able to make and keep as much as they could. On the other hand, nearly 4 in 5 said they would like to live in a society where caring for others was more highly rewarded than the creation of wealth and a considerable majority still backed collective as opposed to private welfare.

The findings of the MORI poll confirm those of other surveys on attitudes. *British Social Attitudes* reveals overwhelming support for the state providing the 'core' welfare services – adequate health care for the sick, more funds for education and a decent standard of living for the elderly. But there is less enthusiasm about more public resources to help the poor, the unemployed and single parent families and there is a marked tolerance of private medicine and private schooling. The same ambivalence is also noticeable in public attitudes towards government economic intervention. Overwhelming majorities believe that it is the government's responsibility to take action on unemployment. But a majority also believes that reducing unemployment could cause inflation. And although more people consider unemployment should be a higher priority for *government* action than inflation, for most inflation represents a more serious *personal* threat than unemployment. With regard to the frontiers between the public and private sectors, a majority want to leave things as they are. There is little support for more nationalisation. And while backing for more privatisation is on the wane, there is enthusiastic endorsement of industry being efficient and profitable.

An accurate summary of public attitudes is that there is significant support for Thatcherite views on thrift, making and keeping money, and enterprise. But a decade of Thatcherism has failed to shake adherence to notions of fairness, backing for collective provision of welfare and selective intervention in the economy. To that extent, support for Thatcherism is conditional and limited.

*   *   *   *   *

THATCHERISM'S STRENGTHS AND LIMITATIONS

In any assessment of Thatcherism, it has to be acknowledged that Mrs Thatcher's most remarkable political achievement is to have built up a solid bloc of voting support – 'a real plurality'[19] which, with a divided opposition, has been enough to give the Conservatives a big electoral majority throughout the 1980s. The special factor is the increase of Tory working class support. The British Conservative party has usually had the backing of a substantial section of working class voters. What is significant about Mrs Thatcher's strategy is the way she has aggressively targeted particular groups and shaped Conservative policies to winning their votes. The 1983 and 1987 elections demonstrated how successful she had been.

Ironically the Tories lost support amongst the middle classes (particularly among the university educated intelligentsia and public sector employees) to Labour and the Alliance parties. Only the petty bourgeoisie remained solid. But Mrs Thatcher compensated for this decline in middle class backing by strengthening Tory working class support. In 1987, the Conservatives won 36 per cent of the working class vote, their highest proportion ever.

Throughout her period in office, Mrs Thatcher has deliberately targeted her appeal to upwardly mobile working class voters. Norman Tebbit, Conservative party Chairman at the 1987 election, described Tory populism in the following terms: 'We have been identifying the things that the chap in the pub and his wife always had a feeling were going wrong and trying to deal with them'.[20] He highlighted the lack of confidence in nationalisation and government control, to being bossed around by shop stewards, to home ownership ambitions and to 'sharp resentment at the amount of money which disappeared from their pay cheques'.

Apart from the traditional emphasis on law and order, the main elements in the Conservatives' populist appeal to working class voters have been Council house sales, privatization and rising living standards. The 1980 Housing Act introduced the right to buy for Council house tenants at discount rates. This proved a popular innovation. Over 1 million of the $2\frac{1}{2}$ million new home owners between 1979 and 1987 were tenants who had bought their own Council houses.

Privatization was a major feature of Mrs Thatcher's second and third terms. By February 1987, 14 major public sector companies had been privatized, 600 000 employees had been transferred to the private sector and 90 per cent of these employees had become shareholders in companies for which they worked. Individual share ownership expanded from under three million in 1979 to more than eight million in 1987. Peter Jenkins has suggested that privatization has had a symbolic impact far greater than the aggregate efforts of wider ownership: 'The sales of British Gas and British Telecom were highly publicized events which served as powerful earnests of the idea that Thatcherism stood for owning things while Socialism did not'.[21] Even the 1987 stock market crash and the failure of the BP flotation were insufficient to undermine the symbolism of privatization. British Steel shares were floated successfully in the winter of 1988, while the flagships of Mrs Thatcher's legislative programme in the 1988–9 session were water and electricity privatization.

Underpinning the spread of home and share ownership was increasing prosperity, particularly in the South and the Midlands. As we have seen, the combination of a relatively long period of economic growth, substantial increases in earnings (real earnings increased by at least a fifth between 1979 and 1987) and politically judicious, if economically dubious, cuts in income tax was enough to convince many working class voters that things were getting better.

The contribution of Thatcherite ideas has been to justify her policies and attract working class support. The rhetoric in favour of enterprise, incentives, wealth creation and freedom provided an intellectual underpinning for Conservative policies on tax cuts, sale of Council houses, wider share ownership and private medicine and education. There is little doubt of the appeal of Thatcherism to the aspiring, the ambitious and the upwardly-mobile – what Hugh Thomas has called 'the lively elements in the nation'.[22] In an interview at the start of her third term, Mrs Thatcher made it clear that her first priority was 'to make certain that anybody who has the talent, who wants to build up something for themselves, wants to take responsibility, wants to get out of the Socialist queue approach, shall be able to do so'.[23] The Thatcherite message is simple, 'If you want to get ahead, vote Tory'.

But for all its success in the 1980s, Thatcherism is a remarkably limited philosophy – economically, socially and politically.

Thatcherites can point to Britain's record of improved economic growth and productivity in the 1980s. It is certainly the case that the combination of a tough attitude towards inflation (at any rate between 1981 and 1984), better utilization of labour and the benefits of North Sea oil has allowed Britain to grow faster than in the 1970s. There has also been a marked rise in productivity. But the massive and growing current account deficits, the big trade imbalance in manufacturing goods and the persistently high level of unemployment indicate that there are still deep seated economic and industrial problems. The Thatcherites, with their dogmatically *laisser-faire* attitude, do not have convincing solutions to such crucial problems for Britain's future as the poor record in civil research and development, the alarmingly inadequate system of education and training and the relative weakness in high technology industries.

The Thatcherite approach to the welfare state and public services is also deeply flawed. It is one thing to stress the need for value for money. It is quite another to argue for reducing public spending, whatever the circumstances, to attack welfare benefits as encouraging dependency, and to support market solutions, opting out and private services as a matter of principle. The run down of health and education services, the cuts in welfare benefits, and the deterioration in public services generally graphically demonstrates the paucity of Thatcherism. As a leading journalist has accurately put it 'Filth and shoddiness prevail in the public realm'.[24] No wonder that the British public so decisively rejects social Thatcherism and continues to believe that health, education and social security should be provided by the state.

But perhaps the most glaring indictment of Thatcher's Conservatism is its failure to create 'One Nation'. Whereas the brand of Conservatism associated with former party leaders, such as Harold Macmillan, stressed the need to unite the country, Mrs Thatcher has shown little concern for bringing people together. In part this is because of her combative and authoritarian temperament. Anybody who is not for her is against her. Indeed, she barely recognises the right of the opposition to oppose her, let alone occupy a crucial and respected place in democratic politics. As demonstrated by the pressure on the BBC, the abolition of the Greater London Council and the Inner London Education Authority, and the attempt in the name of national security to curtail freedom of speech, her respect for democratic norms and conventions has grown increasingly attenuated in other areas as well.

In part, the limited approach of Thatcherism is a question of political tactics. In the 1950s, the Conservative party had to win at least 46 per cent of the vote to stand a reasonable chance of winning an overall majority. This meant that it had to appeal beyond the Conservative party's natural constituency to the semi-skilled and unskilled working class, to the cities, and to Northern Britain. Mrs Thatcher, well aware that, with a divided opposition, a solid 40 per cent is probably enough to give the Conservatives an overall victory, can afford to ignore the North, the inner cities, the unskilled working class and the poor.

There is, however, a more fundamental philosophical flaw. The competitive individualism characteristic of Thatcherism is so unbalanced that it scarcely recognises one person's obligation to another or the existence of society as a whole. It cannot provide a comprehensive and cohesive philosophy in which all citizens, irrespective of their circumstances, have a place. It has nothing to say to the unemployed, the poor or the sick. It has nothing to say to the inner cities or to the ethnic minorities. It has nothing to say to the whole Northern half of the British Isles. It cannot offer convincing answers to poverty, crime, racial tensions and discrimination, inner city deprivation or regional inequalities. It is therefore incapable of uniting the country.

*   *   *   *   *

SUMMARY

In the 1980s, Thatcherism has been the predominant political force. From 1979 it was a doctrine of restraint and lowered expectations; from 1983 onwards it became a message of economic expansion and prosperity. To a considerable extent, it has been in tune with the times – the changing, enterprise minded, individualistic 1980s. It has appealed especially to the aspiring and upwardly mobile. It has succeeded in keeping together a new plurality – a solid bloc which, when combined with a divided opposition and a 'first past the post' electoral system, has been enough to ensure large parliamentary majorities. However, as a guide to the 1990s, the limitations of the Thatcherite approach are apparent. It cannot provide answers to such crucial issues as Britain's appalling record in research and development, its totally inadequate system of education and training, and its relative weakness in high technology industries. The paucity of social Thatcherism is only too vividly demonstrated by the increase in relative poverty and the run down state of public services. Above all, it has divided the nation.

The verdict on Thatcherism is, therefore, likely to be that, despite its successes, it was too limited an approach to maintain its relevance beyond the 1980s. The big political question is what will replace it. Will it be a modified Conservatism or can the Labour party recover and relaunch itself?

3 Must Labour Lose?

In a Penguin Special, sponsored by *Socialist Commentary* and published immediately following Labour's third successive defeat in 1959, Rita Hinden remarked that the tide of history, which Socialists were once convinced was working in their favour, now seemed to be turned against them. She continued 'Short of some unforeseen catastrophe, conditions may well continue to improve, technological advances will mean that the middle classes will go on expanding at the expense of the working classes, young people are ambitious to "get on" and improve their status – the ideas of their fathers, reared in a different school, seem to have little attractions. What is there now to draw new recruits to Labour?'[1] If serious commentators could ask 'Must Labour lose?' after the 1959 defeat, then it is not surprising that the same question is being asked with even greater emphasis following that of 1987.

One answer is to point out that, following the 1959 defeat, Labour recovered to win two successive elections in 1964 and 1966 and four out of the following five elections. But Labour is now in a far weaker position than it was in 1959. In 1959, Labour took 43.8 per cent of the vote and finished only 5 percentage points behind the Conservatives. In 1987 Labour won only 30.8 per cent and was over 11 percentage points behind the Tories. What is even more important is that underlying changes seem to be against Labour.

Even the most cursory survey of political, social and economic trends shows that, in the electoral conditions of the late 1980s and early 1990s, the Conservatives enjoy considerable advantages, while Labour suffers from a number of crucial handicaps. Conservative advantages include a strong leadership whose approach appears to 'go with the grain of the time'; the benefit of North Sea oil until at least the mid-1990s; a divided opposition and a secure electoral base in those social groups and geographical areas which are expanding and prospering. Labour's disadvantages are to some extent the mirror image of Tory advantages. They include an image of uncertainty, disunity and extremism; lack of credibility on defence and the economy; a crippling political weakness in the South; and an electoral base amongst those groups and in those geographical areas which are in decline. An objective observer must conclude that, on existing trends, Labour will find it as difficult to win in the 1990s as it has done in the 1980s.

*   *   *   *   *

THE UNFAVOURABLE TRENDS

As has been noted, the 1987 election revealed two distinct political nations, but Labour's problem is that the Northern part of Britain where Labour has been consolidating its strength has nearly 100 fewer seats than the Conservative areas of strength in the South. Looking ahead, changes in demography are likely to aid the Conservatives. The population shift from North to the South and from the cities to the more rural areas which have been a feature of the last twenty years[2] will continue into the 1990s. As a result when seats are redistributed after the next Boundary Commission Review, those areas in which the Conservatives are strong are likely to gain seats at the expense of the areas in which Labour is strong. On present trends, the political geography of the country, already skewed to Labour's disadvantage, will go on favouring the Conservatives.

Changes in industrial and occupational structure are also working against Labour and for the Conservatives. Traditionally, the Labour vote has been concentrated amongst manual workers in the manufacturing industries and the public sector.

Since 1979 there has been a loss of over $1\frac{1}{2}$ million manufacturing jobs. Manufacturing now accounts for only 22 per cent of the labour force, compared with over a third in 1971. The numbers employed in manufacturing are likely to continue to fall. Employment in the public sector has also declined from 30 per cent of the workforce in 1979 to 26 per cent in 1986. Perhaps the most dramatic change of all has been in the composition of the labour force. In 1971, 59 per cent of workers were in manual jobs. By 1985 the proportion had fallen to 46 per cent. The majority of the employed are now in white collar occupations. Over the next decade, the white collar majority is likely to grow.

Other trends in the economy are also potentially damaging to the Labour party. In 1987 Labour had a 12 point lead amongst trade unionists but trade union membership had fallen from a high water mark of 13 million in 1979 to below 11 million. During the same period the numbers of self-employed, traditionally Conservative supporters, have risen sharply. In 1979 the self-employed accounted for 7.4 per cent of the labour force: in 1986 the proportion had climbed to well over 11 per cent.

Three further developments, more problematic in their political impact, must also be born in mind. First, unemployment rose from 1.2 million in 1979 to nearly 3 million in 1987, though it had fallen back to a little above 2 million by the end of 1988. More than a million have been out of work for over a year. Although the majority of the unemployed voted Labour in 1987 the proportion of the unemployed actually voting was probably below the national average. Another development is the increasing participation of women in the labour force; the overall increase of 1.8 million in the labour force between 1971 and 1986 was entirely attributable to the increased number of working women. By 1991, nearly half the labour force will be women – this could have a major political effect. The third significant change is the dramatic rise in share ownership. In 1979, only 4.5 per cent of the population owned shares. In 1987, share ownership, overwhelmingly because of privatization, had risen to nearly 20 per cent.[3] By 1991 the figure is likely to be as much as 25 per cent. The Conservatives believe that increased share ownership will help them.

There are also a number of major changes in the social field which could be to Labour's disadvantage. First, there is a long standing trend towards home ownership: in 1971 46 per cent of the population owned their own houses; by 1987, it had reached 62 per cent, and by 1991 it will be 67 per cent.[4] While it does not follow that increasing owner occupation by itself necessarily implies an increasing Conservative vote, it should be remembered that at the 1987 election 50 per cent of house owners voted Tory, compared to only 23 per cent for Labour.[5] Although Labour took 56 per cent of the council tenant vote, that sector, thanks to Conservative policy, was in decline. The proportion of the population living in council houses had fallen from 30 per cent in 1979 to 26 per cent in 1987. By 1991, it is likely to be down to 22 per cent.[6]

The second social change has been the expansion in educational qualifications. The proportion achieving O level (now GCSE) and A level grades has risen significantly. There has also been a growth in those achieving higher education qualifications. According to the Oxford study of the 1983 election, the beneficiary of this development appeared to have been the centre parties. The authors concluded that if 'class is the basis of the Conservative and Labour parties, education is the basis (albeit a weaker one) of the Alliance'.[7]

As we have seen, a factor in Labour's decline has been the changing class composition of the electorate – the decline in the proportion of manual workers and the increase in the proportion of professional and managerial employees. This shift is likely to continue. Early in the 1990s, the 'salariat' will outnumber the manual workers.

In the 'two thirds one third' society, the long term trends are working to Labour's disadvantage and to the Conservatives' advantage. Labour's traditional support in manufacturing industry, in trade unions, amongst manual workers and on the council estates, is being eroded by economic and social change. The Labour party has already acknowledged that it faces considerable problems. A report produced in November 1987 for the Shadow Cabinet and the National Executive Committee of the Labour party warned that both class structure and housing tenure were moving in favour of the Conservatives, that the composition of the labour force was changing rapidly and that there would be growth in the consumption of private services to which Labour was seen as hostile.[8] It also predicted that the shift in population from the inner cities to the suburbs and the countryside could lose Labour seats at the next Boundary Commission review.

In contrast, the Conservative core among the 'salariat', those not in unions and home owners has grown. The Conservatives now have an electoral bedrock in those groups which are expanding and prospering. A common estimate of the 'natural' level of support in 1987 (that is to say the level of support that might be expected from underlying trends) was about 39 per cent for the Tories and only 35 per cent for Labour.[9] In the 1990s, the gap is likely to widen in favour of the Conservative party.

*   *   *   *   *

LABOUR CAN WIN

A Labour victory in the 1990s is essential. There are certainly some activists who may pay lip service to the need for a Labour government but who really prefer permanent opposition. Opposition enables them to engage in the activities to which they are temperamentally suited – criticism, condemnation and attack. So they are less concerned with electoral victory than they ought to be. They apparently forget that perpetual opposition means that Labour will be unable to bring support and succour to the poor, the unemployed and the aged – the groups whom the Labour party is in business to help. Without power, or its prospect, Labour's *raison d'etre* will gradually wither away. As with the French Communist party, a life of opposition will condemn the British Labour party to terminal decline.

Labour has to win – and, despite the unfavourable trends, it can do so. A glance at what is happening in other democratic societies experiencing similar modifications in their social structures suggests that there is no inexorable trend which prevents parties of the Left gaining and holding power.

The Social Democrats (SAP) continue to dominate Swedish politics. Though they were in opposition from 1976 to 1982, the Social Democrats have been in power since 1982. In the 1976 and 1979 elections they were beaten by the so-called 'bourgeois' coalition parties but still managed to win about 43 per cent of the vote. In 1982, the Social Democrats won with 45.9 per cent and were returned in 1985 with 45 per cent to form a minority government. In 1988, they won again with just under 45 per cent.

The Austrian Socialist party (SPOe) has the most consistently successful record of any Western European Socialist party over the last twenty years. Under Bruno Kreisky, it won three successive elections in the 1970s, each time with more than 50 per cent of the vote. In the 1980s, the Socialists lost their overall majority and from 1983 to 1986 were forced into coalition with the small Freedom party (FPOe) and from 1986 into a 'grand coalition' with the People's Party (OVPe). Even so the Socialists have remained the largest single party, receiving 47.8 per cent at the 1983 election and 43 per cent at the 1986 election.

In the 1980s, the Socialists (PS) have become the foremost party of France. Their candidate, François Mitterrand, has won two successive presidential elections – in 1981 with 51.7 per cent and in 1988 with 54 per cent. In 1981, the PS won a large majority in the National Assembly (with 37.5 per cent on the first ballot) and, in 1988 failed by only 12 seats to win an overall majority (with just under 38 per cent on the first ballot). Even when the Socialists were defeated in the 1986 parliamentary elections, they won over 32 per cent of the vote and remained the biggest single party in France.

The Spanish Socialist party (PSOE) under Felipe Gonzalez is now the governing party of democratic Spain. It won the 1982 election with 48 per cent of the vote and was returned again in June 1986 with a slightly reduced majority but still with over 44 per cent. The verdict of a leading foreign correspondent on what was happening politically in Spain during the 1980s was unqualified: 'The Socialists are the undisputed masters of the political scene'.[10]

In the 1980s the German Social Democrats (SPD) have been less successful than they were in the 1970s. After leaving office in 1982, they lost the 1983 election with 38.2 per cent of the vote and lost again in 1987 with 37 per cent of the vote. Like the Labour party, the SPD is now in a situation in which it has once again to rethink its overall strategy. But its relative failure should not be exaggerated. It is still polling in the high 30s per cent and has retained sufficient cohesion and vitality to be a potential challenger for power in the 1990s.

Politics in Australasia may not be strictly comparable with that of Western Europe. But the Australian and New Zealand Labour parties both won general elections in 1987, with 45.8 per cent and 47 per cent of the vote respectively.

So the argument that there is some irresistible world wide force which is a barrier to the Left is refuted by the political success of Socialists, Social Democrats and other parties of the democratic left. Despite changes in the industrial and social structure, such parties have been able to gain and hold power throughout Europe and elsewhere in the world.

The truth is that Labour's electoral performance is significantly worse than most other Socialist parties. Indeed, if it is the case that the party's natural support is now about 35 per cent of the electorate, it follows that Labour substantially underpolled in 1983 (28 per cent) and in 1987 (30.8 per cent). So, even taking social trends into consideration, Labour is doing far worse than it should be doing. The Labour party report already quoted estimated that structural changes in class composition between the 1983 and 1987 general elections accounted for only between 6 and 8 points of the 13 percentage points loss in support over the period. Another account of Labour's decline also argues that it has lost more votes through political fluctuations than through social change.[11] Labour's poor showing should, therefore, be attributed not only to a failure to adapt to changing social conditions but also to more specific political mistakes and failures.

If it is true that at least some of the party's loss of votes is explained by political factors, that at least offers some grounds for hope in the future. Indeed, it could reasonably be argued that provided political mistakes could be avoided, Labour's support might be substantially increased. In this context, it is worth recalling that in the summer of 1986 Labour was hitting the 40 per cent mark in the public opinion polls. On this line of argument, a sensible Labour party can still win an election in the 1990s.

It is certainly healthy for Labour to have to concentrate on its short-term political failings. There is little doubt that a Labour party which was more united, more in control of its 'extremists' and generally more effective and competent would make a more formidable challenge for power. But I do not believe that such changes, necessary though they are, will be enough.

To have a real chance of victory, Labour will also have to show that it has come to terms with economic and social developments and that it understands the problems and opportunities of the 1990s. Indeed, the distinction made by some commentators between the effect of Labour's political errors and the impact of long-term social trends as explanations of the party's decline is only partially convincing. If a party fails to adapt to change, then that adds up to a major political error – perhaps the biggest political error of all. In politics, the prizes go to those who keep abreast of the times. The penalty for failing to adapt is decline and eventual extinction. The lesson for the Labour party is that it can win in the 1990s only if it changes itself.

*   *   *   *   *

BEWARE BLIND ALLEYS

The party must, therefore, decisively rule out any strategy which fails to take social, economic and political change into account. Labour cannot afford to adopt a purely class approach. This is partly a question of political arithmetic. As we have seen, the working class has declined, while white collar groups have expanded.[12] In the 1990s, white collar voters will be a clear majority of the electorate.

Certainly Labour needs to retain, and if possible, increase its share of the working class vote. We have already seen that a sizeable minority of the working class, particularly in the South, are voting Conservative. But, while keeping – and, if possible, expanding – its working class base, it will also have to widen its appeal to other groups. Significantly, this is precisely the course that Labour has always followed when it has won elections. In 1945, 1964, 1966 and 1974, Labour won because, at the same time as rallying its traditional working class vote, it was also able to attract support across the class divide.

A similar strategy has also been adopted by successful parties of the left in other countries. At almost every election since the war, the Swedish Social Democrats have won backing *both* from a high proportion of the manual workers *and* from white collar voters. The success of the Austrian Socialists in the 1970s, owed much to the so-called 'Kreisky' voters – the extra 5 or 6 per cent of the electorate, mostly professional and white collar workers, which, when added to their working class support, gave the Socialists three successive election victories with over 50 per cent of the vote. The coming to and retention of power of the French and Spanish Socialists in the 1980s has been to a considerable extent due to the ability of Mitterrand and Gonzalez to appeal beyond the ranks of their traditional support on the basis of their parties' values, policies and overall credibility and competence.

But rejecting a political approach based on class alone is not only a matter of electoral calculation. It is also fundamentally alien to democratic socialist values. Labour works for an open society in which *all* individuals, irrespective of class, race or gender, are able to develop, achieve and fulfil their abilities and potential. Of course, many of those who are likely to benefit from the election of a Labour government – whether over education, health or pensions or jobs – are likely to consider themselves

'working class'. But they will be able to obtain access to better
education, a better health service and better pensions and more
secure employment, not because they are working class but
because as citizens they are entitled to basic social rights.
Labour should stand, not for the victory of one class or group
over another, but for a genuinely classless approach to politics
and society.

Nor can Labour find salvation as a purely trade union party.
A large proportion of trade unionists will continue to vote
Labour. But numerically a Labour victory cannot now be based
on trade union votes alone. In any case, it would be wrong in
principle for Labour to allow itself to be dominated by an
interest group, however influential and powerful. Obviously the
party will continue to have close links with the unions (though,
as I argue later, the shape of the relationship should now be
reviewed).[13] It will also respect trade union views. But, as a
national party, seeking national solutions to national problems,
it must be seen to represent the community as a whole.

The so-called 'rainbow coalition' idea which some argue
should replace a class strategy is nothing more than a 'red
herring'. The intellectual origins of this concept go back to the
1960s 'New Left' gurus like Marcuse and Gorz, who sought to
revivify revolutionary Marxism by bringing in new radical
groups, including women, ethnic and sexual minorities and
students, to reinforce a declining industrial proletariat.[14] In the
later 1970s and early 1980s, the Bennite left attempted to forge
an alliance of a number of heterogeneous elements – feminists,
blacks, peace campaigners, gays, militant trade unionists and
Trotskyites – to win power *within* the Labour party. The most
prominent exponent of the 'rainbow' coalition as an internal
party device has been Ken Livingstone who took over the
leadership of the Greater London Council by a *coup d'état* in 1981
and fought an expensive, high profile and ultimately unsuccessful campaign to save it from extinction.

It is now argued that the 'rainbow coalition' can help Labour
win power nationally. Hilary Wainwright tells us that 'there is a
socialism emerging which is more than the sum of these movements, though it has been influenced and in part produced by
each one of them – feminism, peace and ecology, black organisations, militant and political workplace trade unionism and a

multitude of community and cultural campaigns' and predicts a big electoral potential for this 'new Socialism'.[15]

Of course it is right that Labour should be committed to equal rights and opportunities for all, irrespective of class, race and gender. Of course it is right that the party should be prepared to campaign for equal rights. Of course it needs the support of as many groups as possible. But the idea that the Labour party can win power nationally by a crude appeal to a ragbag of minority interests is frankly absurd.

The impact of such policies has already proved politically disastrous. The crass behaviour of the Labour controlled Brent Council over the McGoldrick case; the insensitive tactics of Haringey Labour councillors over the introduction of teaching about homosexuality into schools; the self-indulgent gestures of too many London Labour councillors over the IRA in particular and the police in general, not only contributed to the poor election results in London in 1987 but were also highly damaging to the Labour party nationally.

As the Democrats found out over the McGovern *débâcle* in the 1972 presidential election, the basic problem with a 'coalition of minorities' strategy is that it turns off the majority. Labour will never be able to ensure a fair deal for oppressed minorities unless it gets the support of those who are not oppressed. Alienating the white and heterosexual majority is no way to help the blacks, gays and Lesbians. The 'rainbow coalition' is a half-baked idea which Labour is right to discard as electorally damaging and against the best interests of those it seeks to aid.

The Labour party should not attempt to be a class or trade union dominated party, nor try to construct a 'rainbow coalition' of minority groups. Instead, it should be a people's or citizens' party, seeking to represent the whole community. The emphasis should be not on seeking to satisfy particular interests but on defending and promoting the general good. The most credible basis for a modern definition of the general good is the idea of democratic citizenship. Labour's project should be to secure that common framework of rights and obligations, resources and opportunities, which guarantees citizenship and within which individual citizens can pursue their own goals. In other words, the new Labour party should be about citizenship and citizen rights.

THE WAY AHEAD

If Labour is to win, it must not only be a people's or citizens' party: it must also be capable of putting forward a positive programme which will set the agenda for the 1990s.

Labour cannot expect that merely by opposing the government it will be returned to power. It is already clear that over such issues as the introduction of the poll tax, social security charges, the National Health Service and the handling of the economy the government has run into considerable difficulties. But there is no guarantee that disaffected Tory supporters will return to Labour. They may either abstain or decide, as so often over the last twenty years, to turn to the third party.

The point for Labour supporters to grasp is that, despite the collapse of the Alliance immediately after the 1987 general election and the undignified squabbling between the newly-formed Social and Liberal Democrats (SLD) and the rump SDP, the probability is that the centre has now managed to carve out for itself a distinct political base. It is strongest amongst highly educated professional and semi-professional salaried workers. The authors of the Oxford Study of the 1983 election commented: 'The Alliance vote is not, as previous interpretations have suggested, an amorphous protest vote drawn evenly from the different social classes. Its base, though small, is an expanding one and thus its share of the vote might be expected to have an underlying upward trend'.[16] Alliance voters also tended to support political positions which were neither Labour nor Conservative. For example, they backed both private enterprise and welfare – David Owen's 'tough and tender'. So, while the centre will take time to recover from internecine warfare between the SLD and the SDP, it would be unwise for Labour to write it off as finished for ever. It would be quite conceivable for the SLD or a centre alliance in a new form to recover enough support to win up to 20 per cent of the total vote, thus providing an alternative vehicle for protest against the Conservatives. So exposing the government is unlikely to be enough to convince waverers to vote Labour.

It is only a half truth that governments lose elections. Oppositions have to earn victory as well. When the Labour party won in 1945 and in the 1960s it had a positive message which captured the national imagination. Clement Attlee put forward a comprehensive programme of reconstruction and social reform, while Harold Wilson presented Labour as a modernizing force which would open up British society.

In contrast, in 1983 Labour had no message to give the British people, unless 'it was the longest suicide note in history'.[17] The party was in decidedly better shape in 1987 and managed to persuade the voters that at least its heart was in the right place. But, although it was convincing on health, education and unemployment, the electorate still doubted whether it had the vision, capacity and competence to shape the future. Labour will win in the 1990s only if, like Clement Attlee in 1945, Harold Wilson in the 1960s and Margaret Thatcher in the late 1970s and the 1980s, it is able to set out a credible alternative agenda which will address itself to the needs and moods of the times.

The prerequisite, as I argued in the Introduction, is that Labour has the moral and intellectual courage to become a fully fledged *revisionist* party – revisionist in the sense of being prepared to rethink, reexamine and reassess.

Rethinking does not imply the abandonment of Labour's values and policies. Nor does it mean that Labour should forget its history. But, as Aneurin Bevan once wrote, 'Democratic Socialism is a child of modern society and so of relativist philosophy. It seeks the truth in any given situation'.[18] Labour has to be prepared to look again at values, strategies and policies in the light of changing conditions. That is also the purpose of this work.

The remaining sections of this book attempt to set out the revisionist alternative. Chapters 4 to 6 consider aims and objectives – the balance between values, rights and obligations, and the relationship between state and market. Chapters 7 to 11 examine strategies and policies on such vital issues as the economy and industry, industrial relations, the welfare state, democracy, and foreign and defence policy.

* * * * *

SUMMARY

Despite the unfavourable trends, Labour can still win. To do so, it will have to adapt to economic and social change and become a people's or citizens' party capable of representing the whole nation. Strategies which do not take change into account should be decisively rejected. There is no future for Labour as a class or trade union dominated party or as a 'rainbow coalition'. Nor can the party rely on negative opposition to unpopular Conservative measures. If Labour is to mount a serious challenge for power in the 1990s, it will have to set out a credible alternative agenda which will reflect the needs and moods of the times.

Part II

The Revisionist Alternative: Aims and Objectives

4 A Balance of Values

Central to the revisionist approach is the emphasis placed on values and on the need to distinguish between values and methods. Thus Crosland warned against defining Socialism in terms of a particular method: 'The worst source of confusion is the tendency to use the word [Socialism] to describe, not a certain kind of society, or certain values which might be attributes of a society, but particular policies which are, or are thought to be, means to attaining this kind of society, or realising these attributes'.[1] He argued that the only constant element consisted of certain moral values and aspirations and, as we have seen, went on to define Socialism in terms of welfare and equality.

The 1959 Bad Godesberg programme of the German Social Democrats was a good illustration of the kind of approach which Crosland had in mind. It began by a bold proclamation of what is called the 'fundamental values of Socialism – freedom, justice, and solidarity'. Although it set out the main outline of the SPD's post-war policies, the real significance of Bad Godesberg is that, for the first time in the history of the SPD, it not only drew a distinction between ends and means but also put policies within an ethical framework.

In contrast, the British Labour party has been content, at least until the publication of 'Democratic Socialist Aims and Values' in 1988[2] and its subsequent adoption by the party conference, to muddle along without a statement of values. Clause IV (iv) of the Labour constitution requires the party 'to secure for the workers by hand or by brain the full fruits of their industry and the most equitable distribution thereof that may be possible upon the basis of the common ownership of the means of production, distribution and exchange and the best obtainable system of popular administration and control of each industry or service'. As one would expect from its author, Sidney Webb, Clause IV (iv) is an ingeniously drafted sentence but it cannot seriously be regarded as providing an adequate framework of values. For one thing, there is no attempt to distinguish between ends and means. Common ownership is so central an objective

that, though only a means, it takes on the status of a value.
Equally important, values are nowhere overtly identified,
though ethical principles such as fairness, community and
democracy are to some extent implied in the clause.

The pragmatists in the Labour party, always a powerful
tendency, argue that to set out the values for which the party
stands is a meaningless enterprise. Yet, in politics as in everyday
life, behaviour is governed by assumptions and beliefs. So called
'realists', who deny the importance of values, are often lazy
thinkers who are not prepared to work out and question their
own assumptions. It was John Maynard Keynes who wrote:
'practical men, who believe themselves to be quite exempt from
any intellectual influences, are usually themselves the slaves of
some defunct economist'.[3]

Those who say that any attempt to define the party's principles will stir up more trouble than it is worth have a slightly
stronger case. The furore over Hugh Gaitskell's attempt, following the 1959 election defeat, to amend Clause IV (iv) is a
warning of what happens when such an enterprise is hasty and
ill-prepared. But a policy of masterly inactivity has even greater
disadvantages. It has permitted an unholy alliance of Trotskyite
infiltration and right wing Conservatives to make up the version
of Socialism which suits their particular cause. So far from
avoiding trouble, 'safety first' pragmatism ends up by damaging
the Labour party.

Roy Hattersley has rightly argued that a clear definition of
Labour's ideological position is essential for the party's own
good.[4] As we have seen with the Bad Godesberg programme, a
statement of values forces a party to be unequivocal about its
objectives. It helps it face up to economic and social change. It
inspires and informs new thinking about means and policies.
Above all, it assists a party to carve out for itself a distinct
political identity which enables it to appeal to new support. A
Gallup poll carried out in October 1987 for the *Sunday Telegraph*
revealed that over 60 per cent of voters did not know what the
Labour party stood for. If this is the case it is hardly surprising
that so many voters do not support the Labour party. 'Paradoxically, unless we stake out our ideological boundaries and
defend them against external assault and internal subversion, we
will not attract to our cause the millions of unideological
supporters who are necessary for our victory'.[5]

*   *   *   *   *

VALUES ARE INTERDEPENDENT

The 1988 Labour party statement of values, drafted by Neil Kinnock and Roy Hattersley, is a major step forward for those who believe that it is crucial for Labour to commit itself to an overall ethical framework. What is refreshing about the document is the emphasis which is placed on individual liberty as a Socialist goal. In *The Future of Socialism*, Crosland had scarcely referred to liberty, on the grounds that this political assumption was shared by British Conservatives.[6] By contrast, the first sentence of 'Democratic Socialist Aims and Values' boldly states: 'The true purpose of democratic socialism, and, therefore, the true aim of the Labour party, is the creation of a genuinely free society, in which the fundamental objective of government is the protection and extension of individual liberty, irrespective of class, sex, age, race, colour or creed'. It then goes on to draw distinction between the Socialist and the Conservative definition of freedom: 'To Socialists, freedom is much more than an absence of restraint or the assertion of the rudimentary rights of citizenship . . . When so many men and women cannot afford to make the choices which freedom provides, the idea that all enjoy equal and extensive liberty is a deception. Unless men and women have the power to choose, the right to choose has no value.'

A distinction is also drawn between values and means. Public and social ownership takes its place as one, albeit important, method amongst others, such as regulation, supervision, redistribution and intervention, by which government seeks to compensate for market inadequacies and imperfections. In this sense, 'Democratic Socialist Aims and Values' is Labour's first revisionist statement, and, as such, must be warmly applauded by those who want to see a modern Labour party.

The document has, however, one major defect. It does not show enough regard for the interdependence of the three central Socialist values – freedom, equality and community. There is certainly an eloquent section on equality; there are two brief paragraphs on community; there is recognition of the connection between equality and liberty. But there is no explanation of how, in a Democratic Socialist approach, all three themes have to be linked together. Bernard Crick puts the point in this way: 'Liberty, equality and fraternity are the specifically socialist cluster of values – if one treats "cooperation" and "community" as closely related to fraternity. Only equality is specifically socialist in itself: liberty and fraternity, however, take on a distinctly socialist form when the three are related to each other'.[7] A Socialist definition of freedom in which people are genuinely able to choose implies greater equality of wealth, opportunity and power. Otherwise freedom is merely an empty promise. 'Democratic Socialist Aims and Values' rightly declares: 'freedom and equality . . . are inextricably linked'. A similar argument can also be made about community (as I shall call it). Without underlying notions of fairness, justice and mutuality, community becomes a conservative justification of existing privileges, inequality and power structures.

There is also another sense in which the socialist 'cluster of values' has to be considered together. None of the three values is an absolute; each of them is balanced by each other. Absolute freedom would lead to anarchy: 'Clearly when liberties are left unrestricted they collide with one another'.[8] In order to preserve or increase the freedom of the majority, the liberty of some has to be limited. Murderers, violent aggressors and criminals have to be restrained, the strong have to be prevented from maltreating the weak, the few from exploiting the many. Liberty has to be mediated by equality and community; rights have to be balanced by obligations.

Similarly, equality cannot be an absolute. Absolute equality is neither realisable nor desirable. A society which attempted to achieve this objective would have to engage in a form of personal or social engineering which would be highly detrimental to the aim of preserving and extending freedom. Although (as is argued below) a whole number of unjustified inequalities still mar British society and ought either to be eliminated or reduced, at some point there is a trade-off between equality and freedom which Democratic Socialists, committed to liberty, have to make.

Neither can community be unrestricted. If a society was all obligation and no rights, the outcome would be a most repressive despotism, while a community without justice and fairness would at best be a latter day feudalism.

It is also important to understand that the balance between desirable values can change over time. In the 1950s Anthony Crosland asserted that Socialism was about equality, while in the 1980s Roy Hattersley and Bryan Gould have argued that socialism is about freedom.[9] There are a number of reasons for this new emphasis on freedom. The first is technical. The arguments associated with the American philosopher, John Rawls, have provided Socialists with analytical tools to put forward a more convincing Socialist definition of freedom[10] The second is political. Mrs Thatcher has succeeded to a considerable extent in changing the terms and meaning of the debate so that the emphasis is far more on freedom than equality than it was in the 1960s and 1970s. The third, and perhaps most important of all, is that society itself has changed. In a 'two thirds, one third' society, it becomes more essential than ever before not only to challenge Conservative notions of freedom but to show that the Socialist definition is preferable.

In this chapter, I also explore the third in the Socialist triad of values – the concept of community. In the past, prominent Socialist thinkers like R. H. Tawney, G. D. H. Cole and the Webbs have attached importance to the sense of community or the notion of sharing in common purposes, activities and obligations. In more recent years, however, the theme of community has been strangely neglected. It is now essential that the Labour party pays more attention to this idea. For Thatcherism, with its unbalanced stress on competitive individualism, has done much damage to community. If Britain is to be a healthy society in the 1990s, there will need to be a far greater sense of common purpose.

*   *   *   *   *

REDUCING UNJUSTIFIED INEQUALITIES

As we have seen, Anthony Crosland proclaimed that socialism was about equality.[11] R. H. Tawney wrote his magisterial work *Equality*[12] because he was convinced that reducing and, as far as possible, eliminating unjustified inequalities, ought to be the main aim of British Socialism. Bernard Crick has written: 'Anybody who can honestly call themselves a Socialist must agree that equality is the basic value in any imaginable or feasible Socialist society'.[13]

For all that, equality is undoubtedly a controversial idea which has been attacked by its opponents from Plato onwards as unrealisable, unjust and dangerous. Plato's argument against equality was that it would be excellent if human beings were equal; but since they are not and cannot be made so, equal treatment would be unjust.[14] The modern apostle of inequality, F. A. Hayek, has added that, as the market process is impersonal, it is 'absurd' and 'unjust' to demand justice from it.[15]

A powerful reply to the inegalitarians was made by Rousseau: 'I conceive that there are two kinds of inequality among the human species; one, which I call natural or physical because it is established by nature, and consists in a difference of age, health, bodily strength and the qualities of mind or of the soul; and another, which may be called moral or political inequality, because it depends on a kind of convention and is established, or at least authorised by the consent of man'.[16]

Rousseau's distinction between 'natural' inequalities and those created by the way society is organized is a useful point of departure because it underlines that many inequalities are socially made. But it does not answer those, particularly Conservatives, who are prepared to accept some kind of 'equality of opportunity', or the removal of inequalities established by social convention, provided everybody then has the opportunity to become unequal again through the exercise of differing natural abilities. Most Socialists, while conceding that a society in which there is a degree of 'equality of opportunity' has decided advantages over an immobile and stagnant society, would argue that 'equality of opportunity' by itself was not enough.

For one thing, there cannot be genuine 'equality of opportunity' without a considerable reduction in existing inequalities – whether of income, housing conditions or of education provision. In other words, for there to be an equal start in life there must also be a good deal of equality of condition already – a crucial point which Conservatives almost always ignore. But an even more serious objection is that a formulation based only on equality of opportunity has the consequence of excluding those who fail to win life's prizes. Mrs Thatcher's hymn to inequality 'Let our children grow tall'[17] is splendid for those that can but not so good for those that cannot. In one of his finest passages, Tawney devastatingly refuted this line of argument: 'So the doctrine which throws all its emphasis on the importance of opening avenues to individual advancement is partial and one-sided. It is right in insisting on the necessity of opening a full career to aspiring talent; it is wrong in suggesting that opportunities to rise which can, of their very nature, be seized only by the few, are a substitute for a general diffusion of the means of civilisation, which are needed by all men, whether they rise or not, and which those who cannot climb the economic ladder, and sometimes, indeed, do not desire to climb it, may turn to as good account as those who can.'[18]

In view of the glaring shortcomings of the 'equality of opportunity' definition, Roy Hattersley proposes that Socialists should argue for 'equality of outcome'.[19] The problem with this attractively positive formulation, as Hattersley himself admits, is that it immediately raises the objection that it is neither fair nor practical for everybody to have precisely identical material circumstances. A large family will need a bigger income than a small family. Some might choose to increase their leisure while others might prefer working to save up money for the future. Incentives may be needed in order to ensure that people work and save – though how great those should be is a matter of opinion. There is also a case for specially rewarding those with special responsibilities and skills – though how great the rewards should be is again a matter of opinion. There is also the cost to liberty which a literal interpretation of 'equality of outcome' involves. A closer examination of Roy Hattersley's position reveals that he is not arguing for 'equality of outcome' at all but a fairer distribution of resources and reduction in unjustified inequalities.

The basis of the Socialist position should be that all human beings are worthy of equal treatment. What people have in common as human or moral beings is such that by comparison the differences fade into insignificance. From this assumption of equal worth it follows that no one has claim to preferential treatment in absence of compelling reasons.

Paradoxically, the egalitarian position becomes more persuasive if the argument is put in negative terms.[20] Thus, according to John Rawls's 'difference principle', inequalities are justified only if they benefit the least advantaged.[21] Indeed, it can be persuasively argued that socially established inequalities, be they of wealth, power or status, should be justified only if a clear public benefit can be demonstrated. In other words, socially established inequality should always be called into question.

In Britain today there are a whole range of inequalities which

are hard to justify on any grounds. The top 1 per cent of the
population owns one-fifth of the total marketable wealth of the
country, over half of company shares and nearly two-thirds of
the land. The bottom 50 per cent owns only 7 per cent of total
marketable wealth.[22] Although the position shifts somewhat if
pension rights are included (the top 1 per cent then owns 12 per
cent of total wealth compared with 19 per cent for the bottom 50
percent) this disparity – which has, if anything, increased under
Mrs Thatcher – is difficult to defend. Unequal shares of wealth
have been perpetuated by the inheritance of large fortunes, a
transfer between generations which has little economic or any
other justification. And though most people get their income
from wages, salaries and pensions, the top 1 per cent derive a
third of their income from private investment – a substantial
proportion of which is inherited. Under Mrs Thatcher, inequality of incomes has grown sharply. In 1976 the top tenth of
households had five times more disposable income than the
lowest tenth: in 1984 they had seven times more. The number of
lower income families has also increased substantially.

It is not only a question of unjustified inequalities in wealth or
income (between groups, classes, and regions as well as individuals); disparities in health and education, working conditions, status and economic and political power are just as
indefensible. Why should money be able to buy superior health
care or better education? Why should the female majority and
the Black and Asian minorities continue to be discriminated
against? Why should there be different treatment of blue and
white collar workers? Why should British employees have
less rights at work than their European counterparts? Why
can only the better off be certain of obtaining their rights at law?
Britain may have become a more prosperous society in the 1980s
but, if anything, it has become more unequal. Indeed, in the 'two
thirds, one third' society, the moral case against unjustified
inequality is, if anything, stronger than it has been in the past.

*   *   *   *   *

LIBERTY AND PROSPERITY

The emphasis which Labour leaders and the party statement
'Democratic Socialist Aims and Values' have put on freedom has

already been noted. Neil Kinnock has proclaimed: 'We want a state where the collective contribution of the community is used for the advancement of individual freedom'.[23] Roy Hattersley has written 'Socialism exists to provide – for the largest number of people – the ability to exercise effective liberty'.[24] 'Democratic Socialist Aims and Values' states that 'the true aim of the Labour party is the creation of a genuine free society'.[25]

It should, however, be admitted that, despite the basic strengths of the Socialist position, the Thatcherites have forced Labour on the defensive on this issue. Put briefly, the Conservative arguments runs like this.[26] Freedom should be defined negatively as absence of restraint. The free society is one in which a few basic citizen rights are guaranteed but thereafter government should intervene as little as possible. If there should be intervention in the free working of the market on grounds of justice or for social ends, there will inevitably be less rather than more freedom. Isaiah Berlin has eloquently warned of the dangers involved in 'positive' definitions of freedom. Followed to its logical conclusion, so Berlin argues, the notion of 'freedom to' or self-realization can result in a person being forced against his and her will but for his and her own good to be 'free'.[27] In that way, according to Berlin, the doctrine of 'positive freedom' leads on to the totalitarian state.

In common with other democrats, Democratic Socialists have always believed in the central importance of the classical political freedoms. Indeed, arguably their parties and supporters have gained most from them. Certainly, without democracy and the rights that went with it, there would have been no Socialist governments and no welfare states in Europe. Socialists also know from bitter experience that, unless there is respect for these freedoms, government rapidly becomes an instrument of oppression – whether in Nazi Germany, in Eastern Europe, or (Conservatives please note) in Chile and South Africa as well.

The basic rights of citizenship cannot be taken for granted. The price of freedom is not only eternal vigilance but also their effective exercise. On paper, Stalin's 1936 Soviet Constitution was one of the most advanced in the world. Yet, as Mr Gorbachev has publicly admitted, the reality was a highly repressive and cruel dictatorship. On the other hand, most of the West European democracies have written constitutions or bills of rights which, when combined with support for democratic norms, effectively guarantee the rights of individual citizens.

In Britain, these freedoms are protected not by a Bill of Rights but by individual laws and democratic convention. However, as is described in more detail in Chapter 8, under Mrs Thatcher rights have been flouted and diminished, independent organizations have been attacked and the government has behaved in an increasingly authoritarian way. Clearly the Conservatives are not in a strong position to claim exclusive rights to liberty or to lecture the Labour party about their alleged indifference to freedom from political oppression. As I argue later, Labour has been given a marvellous opportunity to demonstrate that, contrary to Thatcherite propaganda, they take the so-called 'negative' freedoms far more seriously than the Tories.

While being among the foremost champions of the classic freedoms, Democratic Socialists also assert that, without the right to certain basic social 'goods', such as educational opportunity, health care, decent housing, a reasonable level of income, freedom cannot be fully enjoyed. As Bryan Gould puts it, 'economic deprivation can be an important constraint on freedom . . . What this means is that, in order to determine the degree of freedom in any particular society, we must look at substantial inequalities in social and economic power, as well as the familiar constraints upon physical movement and political and civil rights'.[28] The argument of Conservatives that, because the market is an impersonal process, it can be absolved from responsibility is flawed because the reality is that markets are themselves established by human agency. If all citizens are to be in a position to exercise their freedoms, then government has to intervene to remove the restraints imposed by markets or by other social arrangements and to guarantee access to certain welfare rights.

In his *A Theory of Justice*, John Rawls has attempted to construct a modern social contract which would set out the principles on which free and rational people might agree to enter society and arrange their affairs within it.[29] He assumes that everybody starts from a 'veil of ignorance' as to the relative disposition of natural advantage and to his or her place in society. He goes on to argue that, from that original position, the overriding principle that shall be adopted is that everyone should have an equal right to the most extensive liberties, *provided* that they are compatible with a similar set of liberties for other people. So, by showing that an equality of freedoms is what free and rational people would demand, he demonstrates that, for freedoms to be more extensively exercised, they need to be equally distributed.

The Socialist counter to the Conservative charge that any intervention in the market process involves loss of freedom is that by enabling the majority to exercise their rights more effectively it actually extends rather than limits the total amount of freedom. Tawney's comment is apposite here: 'In so far as the opportunity to lead a life worthy of human beings is needlessly confined to a minority not a few of the conditions applauded as freedom would more properly be denounced as privilege. Action which causes such opportunities to be more widely shared is, therefore, twice blessed. It not only subtracts from inequality but adds to freedom'.[30]

While strongly supporting the validity of the Socialist case on freedom, I would add these comments. First, although government intervention to ensure that the majority of citizens are in a position to exercise their rights adds to the freedom of the majority, there is no disguising that the freedom of some has to be reduced. Socialists need therefore to make it quite clear that the only ground for restraining the freedom of some is to expand the freedom of the many. For freedom's sake, there also have to be limits to the amount of state interference in the market. The Bad Godesberg programme spoke up boldly for the free competition of consumer goods and services, free choice of working place and freedom of employers to exercise their initiative. Politically, as well as economically, the formula 'as much competition as possible – as much planning as necessary' has much to recommend it.

Secondly, in the 'two thirds, one third' society, the Labour party has to underline that its firm commitment to the expansion of freedom, opportunity and choice includes enthusiastic support for higher individual standards of living, for home ownership, for wider share ownership (discussed in more detail in Chapter 6) and above all for a more general provision of the conveniences and good things of modern life – cars, telephones, washing and washing up machines, video recorders, foreign holidays and so on. Socialists need to begin by saying loudly and clearly that prosperity is beneficial because it increases the freedom of the majority – and then go on to argue that it should be more widely shared. Indeed the Socialist definition of freedom is far more relevant to the age of prosperity than the narrow Conservative version because it helps bridge the divide between the prosperous majority and the poorer minority.

*   *   *   *   *

STRENGTHENING COMMUNITY

As I have argued above, Socialists now need to give greater attention to community. In Britain today there are already a number of disturbing signs that community has been weakened to the detriment of national and social cohesion. Indeed, if Britain is to be a healthy society in the 1990s, it will have to develop a greater sense of common purpose. Thatcherism, with its unbalanced emphasis on competitive individualism and its unconditional commitment to the market, does not offer an effective basis for unity. Democratic Socialism is far better placed to provide the moral and intellectual underpinning necessary for a modern version of community.

Cooperation has always been essential to human societies. Although we seek the maximum possible individual freedom, it has to be compatible with the freedom of others. Otherwise, there is anarchy, chaos and disintegration. Indeed, without a minimum degree of working together, we would not be able to survive at all. In short, community is the glue which binds society together.

But, if many would agree on the importance of community, there is far less agreement on how community is to be defined and what is needed to strengthen and develop it. Curiously, despite its importance, the concept of community has been relatively ignored. Indeed, of all the key political concepts, community has been the one most neglected by social and political philosophies. In a valuable study of community, Raymond Plant points out that one of the difficulties of the concept is that it is both a descriptive and an evaluative term.[31] Thus when we use the word 'community' we can be either describing existing units of social organisation or commending aspects of social life which we believe to be of value. While there may be agreement on whether the village, the neighbourhood, the school, the group, the factory or the local football club constitutes a community, there will be much more dispute about which aspects of social life are to be commended. It will depend on our assumptions about human nature, its capacities and powers, and about the possibilities inherent in human life.

For example, the view of community taken by traditional Conservatives is likely to be very different from that of the Marxists. The traditional Conservatives favour a conception of community which assumes a pessimistic view of human nature and an acceptance of the ineradicable differences in human capacities and powers. Community is based on hierarchy, place and mutual obligation between groups in different places in the hierarchy. The problem with this Conservative model is that it is essentially backward looking, resistant to change and closely linked to existing inequalities of wealth, status and power.

The Marxists argue that the community cannot exist in capitalist society because people interact not as social beings but as isolated individuals in the market, each seeking to maximize their own advantage. Community can come only after the creation of a post-revolutionary socialist society without exploit-ation or class. However, there is little evidence that Marxist solutions would lead to a strengthening of community. The concentration on conflict and violent change in the Marxist model is incompatible with the democratic persuasion that is necessary for people to work together in modern society. And the belief that a change in ownership is enough to create a greater sense of community, either at enterprise level or in society as a whole, is mistaken. It is difficult to argue that human relations have been transformed by a change of ownership or that social cohesion is greater in Eastern than in Western Europe. It has been shrewdly remarked that for both Conservatives and Marx-ists the notion of community is somewhat of an embarrassment; 'the conservative locates community in a cherished past and the radical in the longed for future'.[32]

The New Right Thinkers associated with Thatcherism hardly acknowledge the existence of community at all.[33] Although they accept that community may have relevance in small scale societies, they are deeply sceptical about its value as an overall concept which, they argue, is likely to be antagonistic to modernisation and change. The idea of community presupposes shared ends and values which do not exist in modern society. If there is a common good in society, it includes little more than the

framework of law within which individuals preserve their private
ends, and the market mechanism which is the best institutional
means for securing this.

Mrs Thatcher has never shown that she understands the
importance of community. In a celebrated interview in *Woman's
Own*, she even denied the existence of society: 'There is no such
thing as society: there are only individual men and women, and
there are families'.[34] But it is very difficult to derive any notion of
common obligation or responsibility to others from such an
atomistic, market dominated approach. Hence Mrs Thatcher's
dilemma when faced with antisocial behaviour so characteristic
of modern Britain such as football hooliganism, inner city
vandalism, or riots by drunken youths in prosperous Southern
towns. Hence her difficulty when, after years of preaching the
virtues of individualistic materialism, she then urges those who
have done well out of the Thatcher years to become more 'active'
in aiding the less successful, helping their neighbours and
contributing to charities.[35]

The nearest surrogate to community which Mrs Thatcher
recognises is the unattractively strident form of insular nationalism which has been such a feature of her leadership, especially
over the Falklands war and in her approach to the European
Community. But nationalism of this type can so easily dege-
nerate into the appalling behaviour of English football supporters abroad (as well as at home) which has led to the banning
of football club teams playing on the continent of Europe.

The Britain of the 1990s will need a stronger basis of common
purpose than is provided either by an unbalanced individualism
or by a blind faith in the efficiency of markets or by an unrealistic
and potentially dangerous jingoism. A greater and more sustained investment in research and development, in education
and training and in labour policies than the market can generate
will certainly be needed. If welfare services are to continue to
meet the needs of the majority, then a long-term commitment to
high quality, collective provision will be required. If the environment is to be protected, then, as even Mrs Thatcher now
belatedly recognises, it will have to be on the basis of community
planning. If those groups and regions whose interests have been
so neglected over the Thatcherite decade are to achieve a
stronger position, then a more comprehensive framework for
national cohesion than individual self-aggrandisement must be

created. Modern Britain badly needs a modern social philosophy.

The starting point for a Democratic Socialist approach to community must be that we are not the atomistic, separate, sovereign individualists of liberal theory: 'We are not egoistic calculating machines which decided to form a society, because, after careful scrutiny of the evidence, we came to the conclusion that it would be in our interests to do so'.[36] On the contrary, we live in society because we are social creatures, genetically programmed for sociability. And we choose our purposes, not in solitary ratiocination but 'through a constant, never-ending process of communication with other members of our society'.[37]

The belief that human beings have the capacity for cooperation is not only a more generous assessment of human nature than is made by Conservatives. It is also more realistic. It explains why people rescue strangers from drowning or give their blood to save the lives of others. It puts into perspective the comradeship of those who do difficult and dangerous work, like miners, fishermen and shipyard workers. Above all, it accounts for the everyday examples of collaboration and mutual assistance which make society tick. The recognition that human beings have common values, purposes and obligations is not some utopian dream but is rooted deep in human behaviour and experience.

How then do we strengthen community? A number of political and social thinkers and commentators have stressed the point that the first loyalty of men and women is to their primary groups – the village, neighbourhood, town, school, hospital, work group or occupation – and that it is here that the sense of community is most strongly felt and participation most meaningful. Both Emile Durkheim and R. H. Tawney emphasized the importance of occupation, while more recently Alisdair MacIntyre has argued for building local forms of community. Writing at the end of the 1970s,[38] I argued that, in order to encourage community, Socialists should back participation in small scale organizations.

However, even the most flourishing primary groups, important though these are as the initial communal building blocks, do not by themselves lead to a stronger overall sense of cohesion.

By definition, these are partial communities. Like liberties, communities can collide – neighbourhood against neighbourhood, work group against work group, and even, as in Northern Ireland, community against community. If society is to work at all, some way has also to be found of asserting the common good.

This is by no means a simple task. Liberal theorists have warned of the dangers of the idea of overall community, on the grounds that personal freedom presupposes moral diversity, disagreement about ends and social and political pluralism. It is certainly essential to be aware that community can be a repressive rather than an enabling concept. On the other hand, to suppose that there are no shared assumptions or common purposes in society is to fly in the face of both experience and common sense.

It is these shared assumptions and common purposes which must now be affirmed and expanded. The most fundamental shared assumption is that political differences are settled not on the streets but by the ballot box and that there are basic democratic rights and procedures which must include the right to criticize those in power, to organise opposition to them and to replace them by others. It is one of the underlying arguments of this book that these democratic rights and procedures need to be strengthened to make government less arbitrary, more accountable and, where appropriate, more decentralized and to ensure that politics becomes more open and participative.

Secondly, we need to strengthen the system of citizen rights not only in political life but also at work, in welfare and in the market. Giving citizens a greater formal stake in society also makes it more likely that they will have a greater sense of obligation to others in society. As I argue in Chapter 5, if people believe that their rights are secure, then they are more likely to be law abiding.

Thirdly, there are the collective activities and services themselves – by definition a matter of common concern. Although the polls show strong and persistent support for the welfare state and selective government intervention, there is little doubt that the Thatcher years have sowed doubts about the efficacy of collective action. One of my main contentions is that the idea of collective or community action can be revitalised only if Labour is prepared to accept that, in many areas, properly regulated markets work well. Paradoxically, the conditional acceptance of the role of the market is likely to make the case for collective intervention more rather than less compelling.

Finally, political leadership will also be required. After years of Thatcherite attack on collective institutions and even the idea of society, Socialists and other progressive democrats must reassert the case for common purpose. And, as a counter to the bombastic jingoism of Mrs Thatcher, they will also need to put forward a more realistic and constructive vision of Britain. This vision will have its share of pride. But it will be a pride based not on outdated flagwaving but on confidence in our economic, social and democratic achievements and in our contribution as a good neighbour and partner.

* * * * *

SUMMARY

This chapter has stressed the importance for revisionist Socialism of a framework of aims and values. It has argued for a balance or mix of the key Socialist values – for that combination of equality, freedom and community which is applicable to the modern world. It concludes that Socialists should warmly welcome the increase in freedom that prosperity has brought with it but insist that it is more widely shared. This formulation is vastly preferable to the narrower Thatcherite definition of freedom because it helps bridge the gap between the prosperous majority and poorer minority. Although it is unrealistic to aspire to equality of outcome, the case against the unjustified inequalities which so disfigure Thatcherite Britain is stronger than ever. In contrast to Mrs Thatcher's unbalanced individualism, Socialists should now give higher priority to community and to the need to strengthen the common assumptions, obligations and purposes so vital for national cohesion.

5 Rights and Obligations

Debates about rights and obligations, about the entitlement and duties of citizenship, have involved some of the finest minds of the past. However, such questions are not only matters of historical or academic interest. As we can see from what has happened under Mrs Thatcher, they are vital issues which go to the heart of the relationship beween human beings in society and between the citizen and the state. They are therefore highly relevant to Britain's future as a democratic society. In this chapter, I shall seek to establish a modern Socialist perspective on rights and obligations.

*   *   *   *   *

THE LEGACY OF THATCHERISM

The record of Mrs Thatcher's governments on rights is, by the standards of the most advanced western democracies, decidedly shabby. I describe in Chapter 10 its appalling record on rights and in particular judgements against the United Kingdom at the European Court of Human Rights.[1] The Conservative government has also increased the powers of police over the citizen and narrowed the rights of accused persons. It has attempted, in the name of national security, to restrict the freedom of the press and the media. Thatcherites argue that the introduction of Council tenants' 'rights to buy', the balloting rights of trade union members, employee rights to share in privatised industries and parents' rights in education have significantly augmented social rights. But the squeeze on resources going to services such as health and education has, in practice, made it difficult for citizens to obtain their rights in vital areas. Under Mrs Thatcher the unhappy combination of authoritarianism and prejudice against public spending have put rights under threat.

As we have seen, there is also evidence that the strands of civic obligation, so crucial to the effective working of society, are becoming frayed. It is not merely the rising crime figures, disturbing though these are. It is the scandal of football hooliganism, the vandalism in the inner cities and the drunken riots in country towns. It is the unedifying spectacle of city dealers bending and breaking the law in order to make a 'fast buck'. Above all, it is the lack of concern shown by those who have done well out of the Thatcher years for those who have not.

One possible counter to this criticism of Mrs Thatcher's Britain is to argue that this country is merely suffering from a more general malaise, common to most industrial countries. Thus Bell mourns the 'loss of civitas, that spontaneous willingness to obey the law, to respect the rights of others, to forgo the temptations of private enrichment at the expense of the public weal – in short to honour the "city" of which one is a member'; Ionescu warns of the erosion of fraternity by a hedonistic and short-sighted materialism; and MacIntyre predicts a Dark Age, bereft of any belief in a common good.[2] It is certainly intuitively plausible that it should be more difficult to engender a sense of civic obligation in an open than in a closed society, in a mobile than in a stable society, and in a larger rather than in a smaller society.

But, as we have seen, the special problem of Thatcherism is that it scarcely recognises the need for community or that there is a common good as distinct from particular interests. Indeed trying to erect a convincing theory of political and social obligation on the basis of an extreme version of market individualism is like trying to build a castle on sand. If, as Mrs Thatcher has claimed, there is no society, then why should people behave in a socially responsible way?

The truth is that under Mrs Thatcher, the basic common framework of rights and obligations, the social contract that lies at the heart of citizenship, is in danger of being undermined.

*   *   *   *   *

TOWARDS A MODERN SYNTHESIS

It is essential that Labour develops a modern theory of rights and obligations. It has been argued earlier that Labour should be the party not of sectional interest but of the general good; that it should embrace the idea of citizenship; and that a crucial project for the party must be the establishment of a common framework of 'citizenships' in terms of rights and duties.[3]

A brief examination of the ways in which the concepts of rights and obligations have been discussed by social and political philosophers provides a useful starting point.

The seventeenth and eighteenth century advocates of 'natural rights', like Locke, Rousseau and Paine, were concerned to discover a basis for the relationship between the citizen and the state which would protect individual freedoms. Locke's 'Life, Liberty and Property', the natural freedom of Rousseau, Paine's 'Rights of Man', the 'natural and imprescriptible rights' of the Declaration of the French Revolutionary Assembly, the 'self-evident' truths of the American Declaration of Independence were all assertions that there were certain 'natural' rights above, independent and separate from government and civil law. These 'natural' rights were derived from man's nature as a human being. As one commentator has put it 'Every man is human "by nature"; no human being is "by nature" a slave of another human being. There must then be an essential human nature which determines that state and a law governing the relations of human beings as such, independently of the laws of all particular societies concerning their artificial relationships'.[4]

The 'social contract' device, used by Hobbes, Locke and Rousseau, was an attempt to link these theories of natural rights to theories about political and social arrangements. The Hobbesian model, with its pessimistic assumptions about human nature and about life without government ('nasty, brutish and short'), was a special case. To Hobbes there was but a single natural right, that of self preservation, and that natural right could be assured only when individuals accepted the sovereignty of the all powerful Leviathan. The purpose of Locke's 'social contract' was somewhat different. It was not only to secure 'Life, Liberty and Property' but also to establish a new basis for government – that of consent: 'Freedom for man under government is not for everyone to do as he lists but to have a standing rule to live by, common to everyone of that society, and made by the legislative power erected in it; to have a liberty to follow his own will in all things where the Rule prescribes not, and not to be subject to the inconstant, uncertain, unknown, arbitrary will of another man.'[5] The implication of the doctrine of consent was that, in the last resort, people were entitled to resist an unjust and arbitrary ruler.

Rousseau's objective in his *Social Contract* was to reconcile natural rights and the common good: 'The problem is to find a form of association which will defend and protect with the whole common force the person and goods of each associate, and in which each, while uniting himself with all, may still obey himself alone, and remain as free as before'.[6] Rousseau's solution was the general will, a will which was more than the sum of group or partial interests: 'The general will ... must be general in its object as well as its essence; it must both come from all and apply to all ... what makes the will general is less the numbers of voters than the common interest uniting them'.[7] In Rousseau's scheme, each individual puts his person 'under the supreme direction of the general will, and, in our corporate capacity, we receive each member as an indivisible part of the whole'.[8] Thus, Rousseau attempted to dissolve the perennial tension between freedom and order.

It is easy enough to criticize theories of natural rights and social contracts. Bentham called natural rights and doctrines 'nonsense on stilts',[9] while Hume pointed out that most governments had been founded on usurpation or conquest 'without any pretence of a fair consent or voluntary subjection of the people'.[10] Certainly assertions about rights which human beings enjoyed in a 'state of nature' as opposed to rights established by law or about 'social contracts' as opposed to legal constitutions are strange propositions, as there is simply no evidence of states of nature or freely agreed social contracts prior to the establishment of societies and government. But, despite the artificiality of these stage props, there is something of lasting value in what the seventeenth and eighteenth century philosophers were saying.

The importance of the natural rights theorists was that they were setting out what they believed to be the principles by which human societies and government ought to operate and against which they should be judged.[11] They argued that citizens ought to be treated as being of equal value; that they ought to be able to think and express their thoughts freely; that they ought to be able to live without arbitrary interference with their persons and property; that they ought not to be governed without some form of consent; and that these basic rights should be observed by good governments and good societies.

In most natural rights models, rights and obligations were

mutually related. Paine wrote: 'A Declaration of Rights is by reciprocity, a declaration of duties also. Whatever is my right as a man is also the right of another; and it becomes my duty to guarantee as well as to possess'.[12] At one level, Paine's formula is persuasive. If there are certain rules or laws from which our rights are derived, then we have an obligation or duty to obey those rules or laws.

In his brilliant modern attempt to establish a just social contract, Rawls sets out more fully the reasoning behind Paine's assertion: 'A person is under an obligation to do his part as specified by the rules of an institution wherever he has voluntarily accepted the benefits of the scheme or has taken the advantages of the opportunities it offers to advance his interests, provided that institution is just or fair . . . the intuitive idea here is that when a number of persons engage in a mutually advantageous cooperative venture according to certain rules and thus voluntarily restrict their liberty, those who have submitted to these restrictions have a right to a similar acquiescence on the part of those who have benefited from their submission'.[13] In other words, we must not gain from the cooperative efforts of others without doing our fair share. According to this view, mutual advantage is the basis of political obligation.

However, there is another version of political obligation which puts the emphasis not on individual rights but on common obligations. Thus Simone Weil opened her celebrated wartime report to the Free French: 'The notion of obligations comes before that of rights, which is subordinate and relative to the former. A right is not effectual by itself, but only in relation to the obligation to which it corresponds, the effective exercise of a right springing not from the individual who possesses it, but from other men who consider themselves as being under a certain obligation towards him'.[14] Weil argued that every human being had a supreme obligation to other human beings on account of their common humanity. This supreme obligation entailed respect for the social collectivities which provided for their material and spiritual needs.

Simone Weil's account of political obligations harks back to an older tradition – the idea of man as, above all, a social animal. It was Aristotle who wrote that 'he who is unable to live in society, or who has no need to because he is sufficient for himself, must either be a beast or a god'.[15] To Aristotle, politics was not about the arbitration of warring private interests (*à la* Hobbes) nor about the protection of individual freedoms (*à la* Locke). It was about the promotion of the common good. Man's social nature meant that his overriding commitment was to the polis, with all the duties and obligations which citizenship involved.

The Aristotelean model is obviously unsatisfactory as a basis for modern society. Indeed Aristotle and his mentor Plato have been subject to devastating attack as forerunners of modern totalitarianism, in that they were concerned solely with the collective and ignored the claims of the individual.[16] Clearly, the lack of distinction between areas of private judgement and public control, so crucial to the open society, marks out both Aristotle and Plato as thinkers in the closed, pre-democratic mould. But, while we should reject the Aristotelian framework as a whole, we should, nevertheless, accept that it contains some crucial insights. There *is* such a thing as a common good or public interest as well as private goods and private interests. Politics *is* at least in part about debating matters of common concern and deciding on common purposes. Common obligations *are* at least in part derived from notions of commonweal.

David Marquand has compellingly argued that a redistribution of resources to the less well off cannot be justified in terms of what he calls the 'reductionist individualism' which originated from seventeenth and eighteenth century natural rights theories.'For a redistributionist must be able to answer the question, why should I make sacrifices for others? The answer, because it is in your interest is unlikely to carry much conviction for long, while the answer, "Because you are a kindly altruist, who feels compassion for those less fortunate than yourself", dodges the problem. However emollient the language in which it is put the answer has to be, "Because it is your duty; because you are part of a community, which existed before you were born, which will endure after your death, which helped to make you what you are and to the other members of which you have obligations; because you are a member of the human race, and no man is an island unto himself" '.[17] In short, obligation cannot solely be derived from individual rights and liberties. Notions of community or fraternity have also to be brought into play.

This suggests that a modern theory of rights and obligations has to reject absolutism in both its garbs – either the unbalanced individualism of the natural rights theorists or the overbearing public philosophy of the Aristotelian school. Instead, it should draw what is valuable from both traditions. On the one hand, the natural rights approach emphasises the importance of consent and provides benchmarks by which we can judge the levels of freedom in a society. On the other hand, the Aristotelian approach reminds us of the importance of community, the need to assert the common good and the link between the common good and obligation. There will, of course, be tensions between the two positions. But these tensions are inherent in any democratic society and not even the passion of a Rousseau can smooth them away. The aim must be to provide a constructive synthesis, a viable balance between rights and obligations, between private interests and the common good, and between the citizen and the state.

*　　*　　*　　*　　*

NEGATIVE AND POSITIVE RIGHTS

The Democratic Socialist case on rights encompasses but goes beyond the liberal position. It asserts that welfare is a basic human right which should be ranked with the more traditional rights such as the right to life and liberty.

It was noted in Chapter 4 that Democratic Socialists have always believed in the central importance of the classical political rights and that arguably their parties and supporters have gained most from them. This cluster of rights includes the right to liberty and security of person, the freedom from arbitrary arrest, degrading punishment or imprisonment without fair trial, freedom of thought, conscience, religion, expression, information and of peaceful assembly and association. It also includes the rights to criticize those in power, to organize opposition to them and replace them through the ballot box by others.

To underline the importance which they attach to these fundamental rights, most Western European democracies have not only signed the European Convention on Human Rights but also enshrined them in Bills of Rights or in their constitutions. The United Kingdom, as one of the few democracies without a written constitution or a Bill of Rights, has been content to rely on respect for democratic norms and individual Acts of Parliament to guarantee rights. Despite this country being one of the original signatories of the European Convention, both the Conservative and Labour parties have continued to support the conventional wisdom. But our relatively poor record on human rights casts doubt on the old orthodoxy. There is now a strong case, as I argue in Chapter 10,[18] for incorporating the European Convention on Human Rights into British law. Such a symbolic decision, which should be advocated by the Labour party, would be a clear signal that British governments were at last taking rights seriously.

Market Conservatives, like Hayek, Freedman and Nozick, have asserted that rights can be defined negatively only as an absence of restraint and interference. The sole purpose of rights is to ensure freedom from restraint by imposing constraints on interference by others. Only 'negative' rights of this sort are capable of being protected by law and are compatible with the rule of law. According to this view, poverty or the lack of sufficient resources or opportunities is not a restriction on liberty, because it can be defined only as freedom from coercion. Market outcomes, because they are the result of a process and not the deliberate intention of individuals, cannot be said to be coercive even to those who are least well off. The market Conservatives then go on to argue that action taken to reduce poverty or provide sufficient resources is itself coercive and, therefore, a restriction on freedom.

In contrast to the market Conservatives, Democratic Socialists believe that, in addition to 'negative' rights, rights should also be defined *positively*.[19] This is because, in order to be able to exercise freedom, individuals need to be able to act. Without the availability of certain basic resources and opportunities, the ability to act is constrained. 'Effective agency' therefore requires not just restrictions on coercion defined by negative rights but positive rights to those resources and opportunities which are necessary conditions to the effective exercise of freedom. Hence the case for welfare rights, including a minimum level of income, health care, education and housing.

In a general sense, the idea of 'positive' rights provided the moral underpinning of the Welfare State. The 1942 Beveridge Report, with its attack on the five giants of Want, Disease,

Idleness, Ignorance and Squalor, was based on a new concept of citizenship. The assumption (if not always the practice) was that citizenship involved equal social rights as well as equal legal and political rights. Everybody was entitled to protection against unemployment, injury and sickness, a minimum level of income, health care and education.

I do not intend to provide a comprehensive list of 'positive' rights. Welfare rights and rights at work are, in any case, discussed in Chapters 8 and 9.[20] My purpose is briefly to consider some of the problems and limitations as well as the advantages of the 'positive rights' approach.

The problem with 'positive' rights of this kind is that they are more difficult than negative rights to enforce at law. It is clearly possible for a person to press home the claim that he or she is being wrongly deprived of a pension or being illegally denied access to health care. Where the dilemma arises is when a citizen asserts a claim for a particular level of pension or particular standard of health care. At that point, the question of scarce resources comes in. Of course, a pensioner might claim that his or her contributions represent an entitlement to a particular level of pension. But what if the pensioner believes that his or her needs require a higher level of pension? This claim, particularly if other pensioners followed suit, would quickly run against a resource barrier. The claim of a patient who demands access by right to all of the most up-to-date medical technologies is likely to meet with a similar fate. This line of argument has been used by Conservatives in an attempt to undermine the 'positive' right case.

One way to tackle the resource problem could be to concentrate, in the first instance, on procedures rather than resources. Thus I advocate in Chapter 9 that patients should be entitled to a contract with their local health authority which would stipulate minimum standards of provision, while parents would be entitled to a similar contract with their local education authority. In this way, meaningful rights would be guaranteed, power would be put into the hands of citizens, bureaucracies made more accountable and the level of standards raised.

Statutory rights at work represent a mixture of 'negative' and 'positive' rights. A right to protection against unfair dismissal can be considered as an example of a 'negative' right, because it gives employees protection against arbitrary interference by the employer. A right to sickness or maternity pay is a 'positive' right, amounting to a claim on company resources. Rights to information, consultation and participation are more like the procedural rights which are proposed for health care and education.

From the Left has come the argument that it should be a limiting planning condition for mixed economies that there should be a job available for each individual who chooses to work.[21] In other words, there should be a right to work. But establishing a right to work raises problems. Clearly the state should have the responsibility, through economic and labour-market policies, to provide the conditions under which everybody is able to find a job. But even in countries like Sweden which have comprehensive labour market policies, there is no statutory right to work. In an effective market economy, it is simply not feasible to make such a guarantee. A more practical approach is to provide rights to a minimum level of income when unemployed, to assistance in finding a job, and to training and retraining. In this way, respect for individual rights and priority for employment can be combined with the flexibility which the effective operation of the market requires.

The Right, particularly in the United States, argued that unemployment benefits should be conditional on performing corresponding obligations of a 'workfare' type.[22] Obviously, in Britain today, with continuing high levels of unemployment, inadequate regional and labour market policies and unsatisfactory level of training, attempts to make welfare rights conditional should be strongly resisted. However it should be noted that in Sweden, with virtually full employment, effective regional and labour market policies and a highly developed system of training, those who refuse work or training lose benefits for themselves (though not for their dependants). In a vastly different context to Mrs Thatcher's Britain, there may be a case, in carefully defined circumstances, for linking entitlements with fulfilling obligations.

Whatever the problems and limitations, there is little doubt that the concept of citizens' rights is potentially among the most promising Socialist ideas to emerge in recent years. First, it is expressed in terms of the individual, thus underlining that a major purpose of Democratic Socialism is to maximize individual empowerment. Secondly, it serves to limit the market process and humanize the process of change. Thirdly, if properly applied, it is an instrument for the improvement of efficiency as well as for social advance. Fourthly, its application is widespread, covering as it should 'positive' as well as 'negative' rights, work as well as private life, society as well as politics. Finally, it provides the basis for a credible definition of the general or common good, so crucial for modern government. It is likely to have both a major impact and considerable appeal.

OBLIGATIONS AND DUTIES

If rights are usually popular, obligations are far less so. People are quick to demand their rights but often have to be reminded of their duties. Yet, unless citizens accept their responsibilities and respect the rights of others, society ultimately breaks down. As we have seen from the earlier discussion, there are two kinds of obligation. There are those which correspond directly to rights such as obeying the law, paying taxes and (in some societies) conscription and even compulsory voting. There are also those which derive from notions of community or fraternity or fellow-feeling, and which are usually grouped under the heading of common obligation. Examples include one's duty towards one's neighbour, the obligation of the rich and powerful to the poor and the weak and, more generally, the necessity of doing one's fair share and pulling one's weight. It should be a Labour priority to strengthen the ties of obligations of both types.

The first point that needs to be made is that there is a positive connection between the protection and extension of rights and the recognition of obligations. As we can see from the examples of the Scandinavian democracies, societies in which rights of both the negative and positive varieties are respected tend also to be the societies in which the sense of obligation and duty is most fully developed. If citizens genuinely believe that their rights are secure, then they are likely to be law abiding and socially responsible. In this sense, the extension of rights is likely to strengthen obligation.

Democratic rights are of special significance. Without a say, there can be no responsibility. Hence the case for ensuring that individuals are able to participate in every aspect of their lives, that decision-makers are accountable, and that decisions are taken at the lowest possible level.

It will also be essential to reincorporate into the national community those groups and areas whose interests and needs have either been neglected or ignored under recent Conservative governments. People cannot be expected to have any sense of obligation if they do not feel that they have been fairly treated. Thus government action to help the poor and disadvantaged, to provide jobs and training programmes for the unemployed, to prevent discrimination against blacks and Asians, to bring assistance to run-down inner cities and to promote regional development is not only vital for its own sake but also because it strengthens national cohesion and common purpose by giving alienated groups their rightful share of citizenship.

Even Mrs Thatcher accepts that those who have done well out of her administrations have a responsibility to the less fortunate. But her reluctant admission of this responsibility only comes after her governments have already very substantially diminished the obligations of the better off. Despite the astonishingly unequal distribution of wealth in this country, taxes on capital have either been decreased or removed. The rate of income tax paid by the rich has been drastically reduced. Labour's Policy Review notes that the rate at which people in Britain start to pay tax is amongst the highest in the world, while the top rate is now lower than any other European country except Switzerland.[23] In addition, the government is introducing a local poll tax which is largely unrelated to ability to pay.

Any meaningful definition of common obligation must include a recognition that the richest and most powerful have a special obligation to the other more vulnerable members of society. This assumption, which is the guiding principle of family life, should be equally relevant in the organization of society. There is also the argument that those who have gained most from society ought to give most back. It is considerations such as these which underpin the case for income tax which varies according to ability to pay and rises as income rises and for taxes on capital gains and on inherited wealth. Of course, in deciding on particular levels of taxation a Labour Chancellor of the Exchequer has to take into account levels in other countries. But, unless tax systems contain the element of fairness, in the longer term they are likely to fall into general disrepute, thus further weakening the sense of obligation.

As important as the specific measures described above are the general ideas and aspirations to which political leaders give their backing. As had already been noted, Mrs Thatcher's strong espousal of materialistic individualism and her attacks on collective institutions have undoubtedly had some impact on attitudes. By contrast, the years of Social Democratic government have strengthened support in Sweden for solidaristic, communitarian values. A key part, therefore, in any strategy to strengthen common obligation in Britain will be for politicians to reestablish and reinforce support for collective values and action. For without a sense of common purpose, there will be no common obligation.

* * * * *

SUMMARY

This chapter has argued that questions about rights and obligations are not only matters of historical and academic importance but, in view of the legacy of the Thatcher years, are central to the future of British society. Drawing on both the 'natural rights' and Aristotelian traditions, a modern synthesis should attempt to strike a balance between rights and obligations, between individual interests and the common good, and between the citizen and state. Labour must champion citizen rights of both the 'negative' and 'positive' varieties. It should also seek to strengthen the ties of obligation. In stressing the importance of citizen rights and duties, the Labour party would not only be attacking Thatcherism at its weakest point but also laying the basis for an alternative Socialist approach.

6   State and Market

One of the most important tasks facing the Labour party is to decide on the relationship between the state and the market. Once Labour has officially accepted that the market can perform a valuable function, it is in a far stronger position to press home the case for government intervention in those areas where the market either works imperfectly or does not operate in the common interest. This chapter considers the proper role of the market, examines the grounds for state intervention and seeks to establish a balance between state and market which both maximizes efficiency and ensures respect for justice and community.

*   *   *   *   *

STRENGTHS AND LIMITS OF MARKETS

In previous chapters, I have argued that Labour's failure to come to terms with the role of the market has been a major handicap to the party. It has enabled Conservative politicians to make the voters' flesh creep by claiming that Labour's ultimate objective was to establish the kind of authoritarian and arthritic command economy which is now being abandoned both in Communist China and the Soviet Union. At the same time, Trotksyite infiltrators have been able to taunt the party leaders with the charge that they were betraying the party's constitutional commitment to massive nationalization. And its ambivalence over the market has meant that Labour has found it difficult to develop a credible model of state intervention and to benefit politically from the overwhelming popular support for the core welfare services.

The starting point for Labour's reappraisal must, therefore, be the admission that, in many areas of the economy, the market can work well. Markets represent a means of disseminating information which is transmitted mainly in the form of signals through the pricing mechanism.[1] Crucially, they provide a means of stimulating a productive response to unsatisfied needs.

In this sense, the market is a 'discovery' procedure, a way of signalling new demands, techniques and resources. The market is also a vast coordinating mechanism, adjusting the activities of millions of people, allocating resources and solving problems without a vast bureaucratic apparatus. In these respects – coordination, allocation and dissemination – markets are vastly superior to any substitute.

The Labour party should therefore accept the role of markets in the economy not as an unfortunate necessity to be endured for a limited period but on principle. It should do so for two main reasons: 'One is that the efficiency costs of abolishing all market forces far outweigh any possible moral gains . . . The other reason is that markets can actively facilitate the exercise of consumer choice. The freedom of people to spend their incomes as they wish, and to change their spending patterns, can only be realised if markets are allowed to function. A non-market system would require not only phenomenally complex planning, but a degree of control over consumption patterns which most people would, with reason, find unacceptably oppressive'.[2] In other words, on grounds both of efficiency and liberty, there is a strong case to be made out for an economy which is, at least in part, based on the market.

But an acceptance of the role of the market does not imply for a moment that Democratic Socialists have also to believe the absolutist claims of the New Right and market Thatcherism.[3] Conservatives claim that markets always work well, that markets are capable of solving most of society's problems, that the inequalities of outcome associated with markets are essential to improving the lot of the poor, that markets always work in the public interest, that the market has a superior moral basis, and that the market can replace government as the key institution in society. But these claims do not stand up.

The imperfections and limitations of markets are examined in more detail later in this chapter. Some general points about these Conservative claims need, however, to be made at the outset. First, markets cannot exist without government. There is no evidence that markets are in any way more 'natural' than government. If anything governments preceded markets. As David Marquand neatly puts it, 'at the door of the auction room stands the policeman'.[4] Moreover, the state has played a key role in the development of virtually all industrial economies. Even in nineteenth century Britain, which was the nearest to a pure market economy, the state played a crucial enabling role in putting through the enclosure Acts and the canal, transport and railways Acts in ensuring that enough land was available for expansion and in insisting that the appropriate company and banking structure was in place.

Since the Second World War, the rise of the highly successful 'developmental' states (government led ones in Japan and France, and more consumer orientated ones in Scandinavia and Northern Europe) has produced a new balance between state and market, with states guiding and manipulating markets in order to ensure that economies adjusted to change: 'Like surfers riding a turbulent sea, they harnessed the inevitable short-term logic of the private, profit-seeking entrepreneur, seeking to make the most efficient use of his existing inputs, to a national logic, in which the future weighed more heavily than the present. And although they worked through the market, they did so by rigging it'.[5] In other words, in the modern state it is the government which has called the strategic shots.

This leads on to a second consideration. As we have seen, the market provides an effective means of disseminating information and coordinating and allocating economic activities. But it is subject to what Fred Hirsch called 'the tyranny of small decisions'.[6] In the market, individuals are free to choose what they want in the here and now but there is no way in which either the long term or strategic consequences of these decisions can be taken into account. The outcome may be one which the individual would not have desired if these consequences had been known. It may also be contrary to the common or general interest. If politicians, legislatures and governments did not exist, they would have to be invented in order to give guidance on these broader issues. In the real as opposed to the ideological world there has to be a mixed economy.

Thirdly, so far from markets having a superior basis in morality, 'there are substantive moral limits beyond which we do not want a market mentality to go'.[7] A market in human organs, for example, is deeply repugnant. A market is no more than a technical device for buying and selling and coordinating economic activities. As such it is morally neutral. Indeed, it is the market system itself which requires the support of morality. That is to say that free exchange depends upon a background of accepted values and attitudes, which themselves must not be undermined, if the market system is to be sustained. The only answer to the self-interested person who wants to know why he should not seek monopoly, subsidy or other special privileges is that it is against the public interest. In other words, some notion of community is needed to sustain markets. Again, if the market tries to take over areas such as education and health which, on grounds not only of efficiency but also of social justice, are inappropriate, the market process itself is brought into disrepute. In other words, markets have to operate within a framework of civic responsibility and values.

So while Democratic Socialists should accept that markets have a role, the overweening claims about the supremacy of markets made by the new Right should be firmly rejected. The reality is that, without the intervention of governments, markets would either not be able to function at all, or would work imperfectly, or would operate against the public interest. For the sake of both efficiency and morality, there is a powerful case for selective collective action, mediation and intervention. It is this case which the Labour party should now make. Indeed, one of Labour's main projects for the 1990s must be to revitalise the concept of collective action.

*   *   *   *   *

RULES FOR SELECTIVE INTERVENTION

However, the argument for collective action needs to be made with care. Labour's shortcomings in the 1970s and Conservative supremacy in the 1980s have had the effect of sapping public confidence in collectivism. If there is still widespread support for the welfare state, there is also considerable scepticism about what governments can achieve.[8] Labour will not succeed in persuading public opinion unless it starts again from the beginning, assuming nothing, and testing all proposals for government intervention against the simple question 'What is the best solution for the community as a whole?' In other words, Labour will have to abandon its instinctive presumption in favour of government intervention and argue cases on their merits.

This is not to say that a Labour government should resort to a defensive pragmatism or to making it up as it goes along.

Overriding values such as community and reducing inequality have to be taken into account, as well as the realities of markets. On this basis, it should be possible to formulate some guiding rules. At the outset, we need to distinguish between three categories in which some form of state intervention is required. First, there is the situation where markets are the most effective means of coordinating and allocating resources and activities. Secondly, there is the situation where markets work imperfectly and need to be supplemented or guided. Thirdly, there is the situation where markets are so inadequate that they have to be set aside either in whole or in part.

As we have seen, in many parts of the economy, the market is an effective mechanism of coordination, allocation, and dissemination. But even where markets operate effectively, there will be a need for state intervention in the form of rules, regulation and supervision. Competition is the vital element which ensures that the market system works in the public interest. But not all producers favour competition. Indeed, as Adam Smith pointed out long ago, they 'rarely meet together even for merriment and diversion, but the conversation ends in conspiracy against the public on some contrivance to raise prices'.[9] J. K. Galbraith has convincingly demonstrated how, in modern economies, producers often succeed in manipulating markets.[10] If markets are to be preserved, competition promoted, and consumers protected, governments have to intervene. Hence the case for a tough competition, mergers and monopolies policy.

Where it is impracticable or impossible to break up monopolies, intervention will be required. The major utilities (including water, gas and electricity and rail, post and telecommunication industries) are obvious examples. These are vital both to the individual consumer and to the economy as a whole and some form of public surveillance will be needed to protect the consumer and safeguard the national interest. The Labour party policy review has adopted a refreshingly open position as to whether nationalisation (considered more fully later in this chapter) is necessarily always the best answer to a monopoly.[11] An interesting proposal which is being considered is a new category of 'public interest' company, whose targets on consumer service, investment pricing policy will be monitored by powerful regulatory authorities. Public regulation rather than public ownership may sometimes be the most appropriate solution.

Even where competition is working reasonably effectively, rules will be required in order to ensure that the consumer receives adequate information and is protected against sharp practice and fraudulent or exaggerated advertizing. There are other considerations. In a series of powerful speeches[12] Jacques Delors, President of the European Commission, has argued that the completion of the European internal market in 1992 needs to be accompanied by a 'social dimension' to ensure that the benefits of increased competition to the consumer are not achieved at the expense of employees. He has therefore proposed the establishment of a platform of guaranteed social rights based on the European Social Charter, the right to permanent training and the introduction of legislation on European companies which would provide for information and consultation rights. In short, if markets are to operate to the benefit of consumers and workers, there will need to be rights for both groups.

I now consider the second category where markets need to be supplemented or guided. In the British economy, the most obvious examples are in research and development, education and training and in labour market and regional policies. As I discuss later, the future development of industry depends to a considerable extent on new processes and products. Yet the British record on research and development is woefully poor. A disastrous combination of industrial and financial 'short-termism', escalating costs of investment and an inadequate response by government has put Britain at the bottom of the league of all the major industrial countries. If Britain is to compete successfully in the future, governments will have to intervene more actively in research and development.

In education and training, also of vital national importance, the market again fails to deliver effectively. British employees are markedly less well qualified and well trained than their counterparts in competing economies. Too many firms see education and training and research and development as an overhead to be cut when profits are under pressure; in better times, they hope to poach or borrow from their more prudent rivals. They put the quick buck before more lasting profitability, the short term before the long term. If the national interest is to be protected, government has to take corrective intervention.

Despite the rhetoric, even Thatcherite governments have preserved labour market and regional policies. This is because, left to themselves, markets fail to provide enough jobs in the right place at the right time and widen rather than reduce regional disparity. The purpose of labour market policies is to help those without jobs to find them, to reequip the unemployed with more employable skills, and, where necessary, provide transitional employment. The aim of regional policy is to promote economic development in the less prosperous regions, to reduce the unhealthy regional imbalances and spread growth around. Yet again, markets have to be supplemented by government action.

The emergence of the 'developmental state', in which government guides and bends markets to promote economic and industrial change, has been noted above. The prime example is that of Japan. Since the end of the Second World War, the Japanese economy has shifted first in the 1960s from labour intensive to export orientated capital intensive industries, and then in the 1970s to the knowledge based industries. At the end of the 1980s, with the increase in the value of the Yen, the Japanese economy was being restructured to give a greater emphasis to the home market and the service industries. This amazing process of adaptation was led by government which used a wide variety of instruments to push firms and industries in the required direction, including credit, tax incentives, subsidies, licensing, research and development, discussion and persuasion.[13] Most other advanced Western economies have some form of industrial policy through which governments have tried not so much to replace markets as to influence them by encouraging and cajoling the market players to take a longer term view than dictated by narrowly defined market requirements.

At the macro, economy-wide level, markets also need supplementing, guiding and managing. The primitive monetarist position that economies were basically self-stabilising has long since been abandoned even by the Thatcher government. As we have seen, it was the former architect of monetarist orthodoxy, Conservative Chancellor, Nigel Lawson, who in 1986 formally abandoned monetarism and encouraged a consumer boom, fuelled by disguised fiscal relaxation, an expansion in credit, a fall in the exchange rate and earnings rising faster than inflation. This produced a surge in output and falling unemployment, though latterly at the cost of a massive and growing balance of payments deficit. So after all, the old Keynesian insight that governments must manage demand in order to ensure that it is neither deficient nor excessive remains relevant. Governments need to use all the instruments at their disposal (including fiscal and exchange rate intervention as well as monetary policy) to iron out fluctuations in demand, and to ensure that demand does not stick at a level which either allows high unemployment to persist or the economy to become overheated and inflation to rise and the economy to become unbalanced between internal and external demand.

We now come to the third category where markets have to be set aside either in whole or in part. Most of the apostles of the New Right accept that defence and law and order are 'pure public goods' which have to be provided by the state. Hayek has even gone so far as to admit that 'we find it unquestionable that in an advanced society government ought to use its power of raising funds by taxation to provide a number of services which for various reasons cannot be provided or cannot be provided adequately, by the market'.[14] The question is where the line should be drawn. As we have seen, there is overwhelming public support for the 'core' welfare state services (health, education and key state benefits). But many of the New Right assert that these essential goods could be provided by the market.[15]

The key argument for the collective provision of a basic minimum income and vital services such as education and health is derived from the idea of 'positive' rights and 'effective agency', discussed in Chapter 5. Without the availability of certain basic resources and opportunities, the ability to act is constrained. 'Effective agency' or the ability to act requires positive rights to those resources and opportunities which are necessary conditions to the effective exercise of freedom. Only collective provision of these basic resources and opportunities can ensure that everybody is in a position to exercise freedom.

This is not to say that there cannot also be a measure of private provision. In the housing field, for example, two-thirds own their own houses. There is a flourishing private and company pensions industry. There are significant and growing private sectors in both education and health. There is some support for introducing an element of internal markets and competition within the state sector. But, in any clash of priorities, the overriding consideration must be to ensure that every citizen has equal access to the set of benefits, resources and opportunities which is usually called the welfare state. Significantly it is freely admitted by private providers of health, education and pensions, for example, that they cannot deliver the range and quality of service which collective provision ensures for the majority of citizens. Only where these resources and opportunities are provided overwhelmingly through collective means can these rights be guaranteed.

Another area which is overwhelmingly a 'public good' is the basic 'infrastructure' of roads, sewerage and transport systems. The argument here is that only the government, as the guardian of the public interest, can ensure that these services which are widely used by the general public are adequately maintained and, where necessary, expanded and modernised. Indeed, as the contrast between 'private affluence and public squalor'[16] becomes more glaring, the case for more public investment in these essential public goods becomes more compelling. The Thatcherite attempt to turn the argument on its head by blaming the consequences of their failure to invest on the inadequacies of the public sector has not, if polls are to be believed, convinced the voters.

The threat to the environment, which has become such a major political issue, is a classic case of market failure. The individual company will seek to 'externalize' environmental costs by passing them on to others. Thus, in the competitive model, it will be more profitable for a chemical plant to pump effluent into a river or for a power station to emit sulphur dioxide into the air. The harmful consequences in water or atmospheric pollution will not be a matter for them. If the environment is to be protected and the community interest safeguarded, there has to be government intervention.

Even Mrs Thatcher has belatedly accepted that action is required over such global environmental concerns as the greenhouse effect, the gap in the ozone layer and acid rain.[17] Yet, in fact, the government's performance on environmental protection has been totally inadequate. Britain has the dirtiest beaches and is the largest emitter of sulphur dioxide in Europe, is being taken to court by the European Commission for breach of Community standards in the provision of drinking water (nearly 11 million Britons are drinking below standard water), and is the worst offender in the dumping of untreated sewage and waste materials into the North Sea.[18] No wonder that, under the Conservatives, this country has been called 'the dirty man' of Europe. The government has also been extremely slow to respond to the implications for hygiene and health of changes in food technology, production methods, and marketing and preparation, although notified cases of food poisoning have increased from 14 000 in 1982 to 40 000 in 1988. The resignation in December 1988 of a junior Health Minister, Edwina Currie, over her allegations about the presence of salmonella in eggs and subsequent revelations about listeria bacteria in chilled food have only served to highlight the need for effective regulation of the food industry.

The explosive increase in house and office building in the villages and towns of Southern England over the last decade has triggered off widespread opposition. Part of this may represent an understandable if self-interested NIMBY (not in my backyard) rejection of necessary expansion. But circulars by successive Conservative Secretaries of State for the Environment have undoubtedly undermined the official planning system and given the green light to development, regardless of the impact on the environment.

Eighty-one per cent of the electorate believe that the government ought to be doing more to protect the environment. They are right. It is now generally accepted that uncontrolled market forces may endanger health and lead to hazardous pollution, unsightly dereliction, the destruction of towns and cities, and the rape of the countryside. If pollution is to be stopped, if the environment is to be safeguarded, if the use of land is to be planned in a rational and socially desirable way, then governments have to step in.

Environmental pollution does not respect national boundaries. The fallout from Chernobyl still affects the sheep on Welsh hillsides. British acid rain falls on the lakes and forests of Norway and Sweden. The Sandoz disaster in Switzerland severely polluted the Rhine, killing millions of fish and threatening drinking water in the Federal Republic of Germany and the Netherlands. The United Nations' Brundtland Commission on Environment and Development has rightly called for 'sustainable development' – growth plus protection of the environment – and proposed that action be taken on an international level.

Lastly, there is the hotly debated issue of distribution. Even the market economists and philosophers admit that the market does not distribute rewards in a way which individuals would consider fair. But they argue firstly that this is the result of an impersonal process and secondly that, in any case, there is no agreement on what the appropriate criterion of a just distribution would be. Because of the lack of agreement, bureaucrats who are charged with implementing such a distribution have to behave in an arbitrary and discretionary fashion which is incompatible with the rule of law. In any case, they assert that, for the market to operate effectively, there needs to be considerable inequality to provide the incentives which are required for people to work, invest and take risks. The market will raise the living standards of all, including the poor. Indeed, they believe that the most effective way to help the poor is through the so-called 'trickle down' mechanism whereby what the rich consume today will gradually trickle down to the rest of society.

However, there are serious flaws in the New Right case. First, the market process is not an impersonal lottery. It is quite clear from experience that those who already have the most are likely to do best in a market situation. Secondly, even if the process was impersonal, we do not have to accept its outcome. As we have seen, there are wide inequalities in British society. But inequality on this scale cannot be justified either by the need for incentives or by the 'trickle down' effect.

The effectiveness of the so-called 'trickle down' mechanism is substantially undermined by the fact that some vital 'positional' goods such as education decline in value the more widely they are used.[19] When graduates are scarce, they are in a strong position in the market. When the supply of graduates expands, it raises the threshold of credentials. It is a case of everyone in the crowd standing on tiptoe and no one getting a better view. So, in reality, the 'trickle down' argument amounts to little more than saying that the rich are entitled to the first and privileged bite of the socially scarce goods because they are first in the queue. In any case, under Mrs Thatcher, 'trickle down' is not actually working. The number of those dependent on income support has increased very substantially, while the actual level of their benefits as a percentage of disposable income has fallen sharply. This hardly suggests that the market is effectively relieving poverty.

If it is accepted that for everyone to exercise freedom requires the equal availability of certain basic resources and opportunities, there has to be a fairer way of distributing resources than

through the market. The case for the state having a redistributive function is to ensure that all citizens are in a position to
exercise their freedom to participate meaningfully, not only in
markets but in life more generally.

STATE AND OWNERSHIP

All Western industrial economies are inevitably mixed economies which need the guiding hand of government if they are to
operate at all.

In modern democracies, however, government intervention
has always to be justified. Some Socialists still assume that any
kind of collective activity in whatever the circumstances is *per se*
a good thing. This statist assumption is as wrong as the
assumption of the New Right that all government interference is
bad. There have not only to be strong reasons for intervention
but, as we have seen, intervention has to be carefully tailored to
meet particular requirements. Equally important, as is argued in
later chapters, the citizen has to be able to seek redress against
arbitrary government action.

Where the state provides services, it is essential to demonstrate that the consumer comes first. The main argument for
public health and education is that it is the best solution for the
majority of consumers. That is why Socialists should always
champion value for money, good management, quality control
and a high standard of service. That is why they support an
enforceable system of citizen and consumer rights in public
services and industries. Socialists should always support greater
efficiency in the public sector.

The question remains: is there still any role for public
ownership, or has it outlived its usefulness? The idea that, in the
Marxist sense, wholesale state ownership can transform society
for the better is obviously outdated. On the contrary, as we can
see only too clearly from the experience of the Soviet Union, the
costs of a command economy in terms of crippling inefficiency,
lack of freedom and choice are heavy indeed.

With respect to the natural monopolies, there is a powerfu
argument, as has already been noted, for public supervision and
regulation. Whether this also means that these industries have
also to be in public ownership on the old Morrisonian model i

far more debatable, particularly in view of the extensive nature of this government's privatization programme. The concept of the 'public interest' company with special obligations as regards consumers and the community, and closely supervised by a regulatory authority is an attractive one. In cases where it is necessary to ensure public control, public shareholding (of both the majority and minority kind) and special controlling shares will often be preferable to outright nationalization.

A possible area for exploration may be the role of competitive public enterprise. The idea of state or mixed state and private companies being set up to operate in the market 'to act as highly competitive price-leaders and pace-setters, provide a yardstick for efficiency, support the government's investment plans, and above all produce a better product or service'[20] is not a new one. It has its difficulties. If these industries are going to be profitable, why is private industry not there already? And who is to operate these companies? Clearly, they cannot be run direct by Whitehall.

One answer is to have a state holding company which, on the Japanese analogy, is able to take a longer-term view of economic prospects, say in high technology fields, than British industry. However, if such a holding company is to operate effectively, it must work within strict criteria and, above all, it must not be used, as the old National Enterprise Board too often was, as a casualty ward for ailing industries and companies. Its task must be rather to promote a competitive and profitable presence, including British participation at a European level, in such areas as electronic and information technology which are crucial to Britain's industrial future.

At the local level, 'enterprise agencies', which put together a 'mixed' package of public and private resources and expertise, have often proved extremely successful in helping establish and sustain small businesses. However, the short-sighted and penny pinching approach of the Conservative government is threatening to undermine their value. These institutions should have sustained public financial support, in conjunction with industry, banks and local government. Local government also needs to be freed from the legal restraint that limits their powers to set up local enterprise boards.

Finally, we need to consider the case for dispersing the ownership of capital. As has been noted, privatization has undoubtedly led to wider share ownership, especially among employees. But, if employees are to be given a real stake in their firms, share ownership needs to be spread on a far more systematic basis. Bryan Gould has persuasively argued for an extensive system of employee share ownership schemes, drawing on the lessons of American schemes.[21] There is also the example of the Swedish employee investment funds system established by a tax on excess profits. One possible way forward may be to give all employees rights by which companies are obliged to give them shares according to length of service.

* * * * *

SUMMARY

This chapter has argued that, on grounds of efficiency and freedom, Socialists should accept the role of the market in large parts of the economy. On the other hand, the idea that the market can exist on its own or can be the overriding institution in society is pure fantasy. The guiding hand of government is needed. State intervention will be needed in all three situations – where markets work well, where they work imperfectly and where they work so inadequately that they have to be set aside. If total state ownership in the Marxist sense is clearly an outdated concept, there will be a role for public regulation, supervision and shareholding, competitive state companies and enterprise boards and agencies, as well as a systematic extension of employee share ownership.

Part III

The Revisionist Alternative: Programmes and Policies

7 Economic and Industrial Policies for the 1990s

Throughout the 1980s, the Labour party has been on the defensive on economic and industrial policy. In part, this is because of what happened under Labour governments in the 1970s. In part, it is because of the years of economic growth, improved productivity and increased prosperity in the 1980s. Yet the underlying weaknesses of the British economy and the competitive challenges both from within and outside Europe have given Labour a fresh opportunity to put forward a new synthesis which will be relevant to the needs of the 1990s.

*   *   *   *   *

THE THATCHER RECORD

It is important to understand that a strategy for the 1990s has to be based on a realistic assessment of the 1980s. An honest appraisal of the Conservative record is, therefore, an essential starting point for developing a modern Labour economic and industrial policy.

The two main achievements of the Thatcherite period in office have been faster economic growth compared to the 1970s and an improvement in labour productivity.[1] Since the disastrous recession of 1980–1, the British economy has expanded steadily throughout the decade. Indeed, British growth from 1982 has been faster than most of our European rivals. Average GDP growth in the 1979–87 period also compared favourably with the 1973–9 cycle, though it was still significantly below that of 1968–73.

Equally important has been the surge in productivity. During the 1980s, labour productivity in Britain not only rose much faster than in the 1970s but average productivity growth rates were higher than in any other industrial economy, with the exception of Japan. In part, this improved relative British performance reflected sluggish productivity growth rates in the major West European and North American economies. A similar productivity growth record between 1968 and 1973 left Britain second bottom of the six major industrial countries for that period.[2] Improved productivity also coincided with sharper increases in unemployment rates in Britain than in the other major countries, although there has been a marked relative improvement since mid-1986.

The questions for the Labour party are, first, how far Britain's relatively impressive performance is due to Conservative economic policy, and secondly, how likely it is to be sustained into the 1990s.

It is clear that Britain owes its relatively prolonged period of economic growth since 1982 not to the monetarist policies pursued between 1979 and 1982 but to their gradual abandonment by a more pragmatic Chancellor in the middle and later 1980s.

According to the monetarist theory so fashionable in the later 1970s and early 1980s, economies were basically self-stabilizing. Attempting to stimulate economic activity beyond the level set by the 'natural rates of unemployment' could not have more than a temporary impact. In the longer run, its only effect would be to push up prices. This increase in the rate of inflation could be reversed only by a subsequent increase in unemployment and any attempt to prevent this by further injections of purchasing power would merely lead to a further increase in inflation. So the monetarist prescription for low inflation, sustained economic growth and a return to full employment was for government to limit themselves to controlling the money supply and to balancing the budget.

Mrs Thatcher's first administration was determinedly 'monetarist'. John Kenneth Galbraith remarked that, if there had to be an experiment in monetarism, then what better people to inflict it on than the tolerant, phlegmatic British.[3] Be that as it may, the Thatcherite 'monetarist' experiment was a disastrous flop.

For one thing, it proved almost impossible to measure the money supply accurately. The Thatcher government successively announced different definitions – M3 (in 1980), M1 (in 1982), a redefined M3 (in 1985), M0 (also in 1985). All proved inadequate. And, as Keynesians had always argued, increases in the supply of money appeared to have little direct influence on what happened to inflation. By the end of 1985, Lawson had virtually abandoned monetarism.

It is certainly true that inflation fell from 22 per cent in the summer of 1980 to about 5 per cent by 1984 (though it rose sharply during 1988). But the fall in inflation was caused by a classic 'squeeze' on the economy, by the impact of an overvalued currency and by a drop in international commodity prices, which brought inflation down on a worldwide basis. And the costs in terms of lost output, reduced investment and increased unemployment were catastrophic – sharper than for any other major industrial economy.

The reason for the recovery of the British economy in the middle 1980s was the government's adoption of a more flexible strategy. Assisted by North Sea oil and the proceeds of privatisation, fiscal policies were gradually relaxed and public spending increased. As we have seen, in the eighteen months before the 1987 general election the Chancellor encouraged an old-style consumer boom, fuelled by tax cuts, earnings rising faster than inflation, a dramatic fall in the savings ratio and massive credit expansion. It would be an exaggeration to call Lawson a Keynesian. His determined and successful efforts to eliminate the public sector borrowing requirement as a matter of principle, whatever the economic circumstances, preclude that description. But given his abandonment of firm monetary targets, he could hardly be considered a monetarist either. Perhaps the most accurate portrayal of Chancellor Lawson was that by 1988 he had become a macro-economic pragmatist, quite prepared to depart from monetarist and fiscal orthodoxy if it suited.

The case for Conservative policy is more plausible on the micro-level, particularly with respect to the improvement in labour productivity. The 1987–88 OECD survey on the United Kingdom commented that 'non-interventionist policies, which refrained from bailing firms and individuals out of economic difficulties, may have forced both management and labour to reassess their traditional behaviour and to accept changes in order to avoid bankruptcy and unemployment'.[4] Without accepting Thatcherite propaganda on the alleged benefits of tax incentives, deregulation or privatization, it is clear that the combination of more efficient work practices, improved labour productivity, weakened trade unions, and increased company profits put British management and British companies in a stronger position than they had been in the 1970s. To that extent, the 'sharp shock' imparted by the 1980–81 recession had beneficial, if largely unintended side-effects.

The question is how far the improved growth and productivity rates of the 1980s are sustainable into the 1990s. Significantly, the exceptionally fast growth in 1987 and 1988, stimulated by the Lawson boom was, as we have seen, accompanied by a rise in prices and a sharp deterioration in the balance of payments. The massive current account deficit, which rose to £14 billion in 1988 and was officially forecast to remain at £14 billion in 1989, could in part be explained by the fact that Britain was growing faster than her competitors. However a more disturbing factor was the adverse trend in manufactured goods. In the 1980s, for the first time since the industrial revolution, Britain consistently ran a deficit in manufactured goods. Import penetration in manufacturing increased rapidly throughout the decade. It may be sensible to finance for a period a balance of payments deficit which is caused by temporary cyclical factors. But an external deficit which amounts to as much as 3 per cent of GDP and reflects underlying structural weaknesses cannot be supported indefinitely. Corrective action has to be taken. At the very least, her massive balance of payments problems puts a question mark over Britain's ability to grow faster than her rivals.

There are also doubts over the improvement in productivity. The OECD have noted that this has been linked not to increased investment but to changes in work organization.[5] It concluded, therefore, that a large part of the improvement in productivity may represent what it called 'successive level changes' which, in contrast to shifts in productivity related to new investment, will taper off. Our poor record in civil research and development, the glaring inadequacy in education and training and the relative weaknesses in high technology industries, noted above, all cast doubt on whether, without substantial change, it will be possible to sustain the improvement in British economic performance into the 1990s.

*   *   *   *   *

MODIFIED KEYNESIANISM

In preparing a policy for the 1990s, the Labour party must also draw on the lessons of the last two decades. In terms of macro-policy, it is now clearly understood, even by the most ardent Thatcherites, that monetarism does not work. Indeed, as we have seen, Nigel Lawson, himself once an enthusiast, tacitly abandoned orthodox monetarist policies in favour of more pragmatic and expansionist policies.

On the other hand, it is no use Labour supporters pretending that Keynesianism has survived the difficult years of the 1970s and early 1980s intact. Keynesian policies have been challenged on two main fronts. The first charge is that such policies lead inevitably to accelerating inflation. Critics point to the inflationary explosion of the early 1970s and, in particular, to the massive increase in British prices during 1974–5.

But the inflationary upsurge of the early 1970s was not the inevitable consequence of Keynesian policies but, as the McCracken Committee of independent experts concluded, the result of 'an unusual bunching of unfortunate events unlikely to be repeated on the same scale, the impact of which was compounded by some avoidable errors in economic policy'.[6] 'The avoidable errors' in policy referred to in the McCracken Report were the speed and universality of the 1972–3 upswing which led so quickly to production bottlenecks, shortages of raw materials and steeply rising prices for commodities as buyers scrambled for supplies. At the same time, the breakdown of the Bretton Woods system of fixed exchange rates (and the size of the United States payments deficit) precipitated an exceptional movement of funds into international capital markets. There was a big rise in the prices of property and gold (markets which are traditional havens for footloose funds) and a speculative element was added to commodity dealing, already stimulated by the upswing and harvest failures.

Then, at the end of 1973, came the first oil price rises, following the outbreak of war in the Middle East. Between October 1973 and January 1974 the export price of oil increased by four times. This increase directly added $63 billion to the OECD oil bill, raised OECD prices by 2 per cent and, most significantly, transferred from the OECD area and the non-oil developing countries to OPEC an amount of real income equivalent to about 2 per cent of OECD GNP.[7] The effect of the oil increase was therefore both inflationary and deflationary – and it was hardly surprising that its impact has been described as a 'shock'.

So the inflationary explosion of 1973 cannot be described as the final stage of a progressive trend upwards caused by twenty years of misguided Keynesian policies but the consequence of an uncontrolled economic upswing in 1972–3, an exceptional movement of funds across the exchanges, and the explosive impact of the first oil shock.

The argument that public spending caused the surge in British inflation in 1974–5 is also misconceived. It is certainly true that, as a consequence of increases in transfer payments and subsidies and of public sector pay increases, public expenditure increased sharply from 40.5 per cent of the GDP in 1973–4 to 45.5 per cent in 1974–5 (though by 1979 its share had been cut to 42 per cent). But nearly half of this increase was paid for by buoyant receipts and the remainder was financed in a non-inflationary way outside the banking sector. The rise in British prices (which climbed to 28 per cent by mid-1975) was determined by other factors. What happened was that the inflationary impact of the oil shock and the commodity boom was compounded by a wages explosion. The combination of cost of living increases (provided for in Stage 3 of the Conservative government's incomes policy), the ripple effect of the settlement of the miners' dispute and the general trade union hostility to incomes policy gave an extra twist to an already inflationary situation.

However, if the monetarist explanations of the great international inflation of 1973 and of the British version of 1974–5 are incorrect, the fact remains that, in the early 1970s, Keynesian policies failed to deal adequately with inflation. The ill-fated 1972–3 boom is a severe warning of the dangers of too ambitious expansion by too many countries at once, and the British case demonstrates what can happen when wage increases are allowed to run too far ahead of output and productivity.

The second challenge to Keynesian demand management is the growing interdependence of modern industrial economies.[8] Over the past twenty years, most OECD countries have experienced a sharp increase in the proportion of their GDP represented by imports and exports. By the end of the 1980s, trade represented well over a quarter of the total output of mos industrial economies. There has also been a big increase in international borrowing and lending and the availability of short-term capital has become much greater. The implications of this increased 'openness' of industrial economies is that the ability of governments to influence their own output and employment has, to some extent, been weakened and their vulnerability to outside events and pressure has been increased.

The shift to greater interdependence is of special significance to Keynesians because the international economy, as it operated during the 1980s, had a deflationary bias. When a particular country adopted a restrictive stance, its impact was likely to affect the output of others. On the other hand, when a country adopted expansionist policies, the result was less likely to be the transmission of expansion than the discouragement of those policies by fiscally conservative international institutions and by more orthodox governments.

Medium-sized economies which attempted to expand against the trend, like the United Kingdom in the mid-1970s and France in the early 1980s, were unsuccessful. Both ran up large balance of payments deficits and, because of loss of reserves, were forced by international pressure to change their policies. The unhappy experience of Britain and France certainly shows that 'the growth of interdependence has made it more difficult for a single country to use Keynesian policies to bring down a high rate of unemployment if other major countries are not doing the same'.[9] As has been noted, in the later 1980s Britain, under a Conservative government, was once again experiencing problems in expanding faster than other countries.

However, it would be wrong to conclude that it is, therefore, impossible to operate Keynesian policies. Throughout most of the recession, Austria, under governments pursuing Keynesian policies, combined low inflation with low unemployment and relatively fast growth. Sweden, under a Social Democrat government, successfully pursued a strategy based on devaluation, a voluntary incomes policy and a package of public investment and labour market policies. If there are significant differences between the Austrian and Swedish models, the common factors are the clear strategic direction, the high priority given to sustaining employment within a balanced set of objectives, and the crucial role of the unions.[10] In the post-oil shock world, there was no way that these governments could have successfully

harmonised the varied objectives of full employment, low inflation and high social spending without some measure of trade
union backing for restraint over wage increases.

The expansion of the vastly bigger American economy in the
1980s is also an example of Keynesian policies. Reduction of
taxes and increases in military spending raised the federal
budget deficit from about 2 per cent in 1982 to 5 per cent in 1985.
The economy which had been in the doldrums began to grow
again and unemployment fell dramatically. At the same time,
the rate of inflation also declined significantly.

But American Keynesianism was applied in a perverse and
erratic way. When the economy was fully launched on a recovery
path, the United States administration failed to get agreement
on the necessary steps to reduce the budget deficit. Partly as a
consequence of the continuing deficit, interest rates were kept
high, the dollar became overvalued, the current account deficit
widened and overseas borrowing increased. The subsequent
sharp fall in the value of the dollar during 1986 and 1987, the
turbulence in the international currency markets, and the stock
market crash of October 1987 were caused in part by faulty
American policies in 1984–5.

Flaws in American economic policy do not, however, undermine the case for Keynesianism. It is no part of the Keynesian
argument that budget deficits should continue on a massive scale
when an economy is expanding and unemployment falling
rapidly. Nor is it maintained that economic policy-makers can
ignore for long a deteriorating trade balance.

A more successful case of the application of Keynesian policies
is that of Japan.[11] In the first half of the 1980s, export led growth
provided the motor for the Japanese economy. However, from
mid 1985 to late 1986, the appreciation of the Yen and the
weakening of export markets pushed the economy into recession.
In May 1987 the Japanese government changed course and
introduced an expansionist fiscal package, composed of a balanced mix of increased public investment and tax cuts. This
fiscal stimulus, which was reinforced in 1988, brought about a
vigorous recovery. Residential construction boomed, private
consumption gathered strength, businesses revised upwards
their investment plans and unemployment fell. Domestic output
rose by over 5 per cent in 1987 and even faster in 1988.
Significantly the 1987–8 OECD report on Japan congratulated

the government on redirecting the Japanese economy from export to domestic demand led growth.

From these examples it can be seen that the crucial Keynesian insight is still as relevant as it was in the 1930s. If an economy is to expand up to its productive potential, then governments must manage demand. For, as Mr Lawson discovered, economies are not self-stabilising. Governments need to use all the instruments at their disposal (including fiscal, monetary, and exchange rate intervention) to ensure that demand does not stick at a level which allows high unemployment to persist, and to iron out fluctuations in demand. Labour supporters should note, however, that demand management implies not only budgetary expansion but, in those cases where demand is excessive, budgetary contraction as well. There should also be a balance between internal and external demand, between consumption and investment, and between 'overheated' and 'sluggish' regions. A balanced approach is essential.

*　　*　　*　　*　　*

COUNTER-INFLATION AND COORDINATION

A Labour government, elected in the 1990s, is entitled to have confidence in sensible, moderately applied and well balanced Keynesian policies, provided that it learns the lessons of the last two decades – especially the importance of controlling inflation and the growing interdependence of national economies.

With respect to inflation, Keynes himself recognized the difficulty of trying to combine full employment, stable prices and full collective bargaining. Every British government since the war has tried to square the Keynesian circle by attempting to control wage increases through some kind of incomes policy. Indeed, even Mrs Thatcher's administrations, despite the monetarist rhetoric, have pursued vigorous restrictions on public sector pay, while, in the private sector, after an initial 'hands off' period, they have relied, with scant success, on exhortation reinforced by unemployment. Significantly, through much of the 1980s, average earnings have risen faster than inflation.

The usual criticism of incomes policy is that it has been tried and failed. Not surprisingly, the memory of the appalling 'winter of discontent' is still vivid in the minds of the political class. But the truth about British incomes policy is more complex. A leading economic journalist rightly concluded that 'they have been tried sporadically, have worked for a time and have then broken down'.[12]

Most of the successful industrial economies have for many years operated some kind of incomes policy. The Swedish and Austrian examples have already been mentioned. Other larger countries, such as Germany and Japan, also have a mixture of formal and informal arrangements which have ensured that wages and salaries do not increase at a rate which jeopardizes economic growth. If Britain had done as well as Germany and Japan over the last twenty years in restraining inflationary wage increases, then 'growth would have been significantly faster and contemporary living standards substantially higher'.[13]

Clearly a counter-inflation policy for the 1990s has to be different from the model that succeeded for a time and ultimately failed in the 1970s. For one thing, it has to depend far less on the support of the trade unions. Power in the British trade unions has always been much more dispersed than in the more central-ised Northern European and Scandanavian systems. And the trade unions are, in any case, less important elements in the economy than they were in the 1970s. So it would be both unfair and unwise for Labour governments to expect too much from the unions, though they should recognize the central role of manage-ments in wage determination. At the same time, a policy for the 1990s has to be more balanced and more effective than the unacknowledged one operated through much of the 1980s by the Thatcher governments.

The minimum requirement is a broad consensus between government, employers and trade unions. This does not imply the kind of detailed intervention in the economy so characteristic of the approach of the National Board for Prices and Incomes in the 1960s. Nor should it entail a reliance on norms, as in the 1970s. What is needed is a general agreement on the overall growth of incomes which the economy can afford. The govern-ment will need to back up this agreement by pursuing non-accommodating monetary policies and maintaining, as far as possible, a stable exchange rate. The case for full British membership of the European Monetary System is set out below. In addition, it may need to have reserve powers. There is an argument, for example, for being able, if necessary, to use the tax system to deter strategic employers from conceding inflationary wage increases and passing them on in higher prices. But, whatever the precise details, the truth is that a Labour government, committed to moderate Keynesian expansion and to reducing unemployment, will have to try and reach a consensus on income and wage increases. The Labour party should have the courage and good sense to say so while it is in opposition. Otherwise, it will be wide open to the charge that its economic policies will lead to inflation.

A Labour government in the 1990s is also going to have to learn from what happened to the British Labour government in 1976 and to the French Socialist government in 1982–3. The truth is that economies are now more 'open' and 'interdependent'. Britain is also a member of a European Community which is likely, during the 1990s, to become increasingly integrated at the monetary level. All this means that economic expansion has to be pursued in a moderate and balanced manner.

In this context, the contrast between British and Japanese economic policies in the 1986–8 period is instructive. British expansion, as we have seen, was based on private consumption, boosted by increasing recourse to credit and a fall in the household saving ratio to a thirty year low. In both the 1987 and 1988 budgets, Chancellor Lawson unwisely fuelled this consumption boom by tax cuts which not surprisingly served to worsen an already deteriorating balance of payments. In Japan, the government's approach was far more balanced. The expansion of the economy was based not only on private consumption but also on investment in housing, manufacturing and the service sector. The 1987 budget contained tax cuts but the emphasis was more on increases in public investment and public works. Japanese growth was consequently more soundly based and was therefore more likely to be sustainable than in Britain. The moral of the story is that it is better to begin in a cautious and balanced way than go all out for a big, consumer led expansion and, in the end, be 'blown off course' by a balance of payments crisis.

It is, of course, essential that, in contrast to the Wilson governments of the 1960s and the Thatcher government of the 1980s, a Labour government in the 1990s ensures that its economic policies are not undermined by an overvalued currency. The highly successful Swedish devaluation of 1982 is a good illustration of decisive action by an incoming government determined on growth, investment and employment creation. But devaluation is no panacea. Sweden was able to draw the full benefits from devaluation only because Swedish unions were prepared to accept a squeeze on domestic consumption in favour of profits. And over-reliance on devaluation can lead to a dangerous wage–price spiral, with higher import prices being compensated for by increases in money wages which are in turn passed on in increased prices. If it is essential to prevent the currency from being obviously overvalued, once compensatory moves have been taken there is a strong case for ensuring currency stability by action on the domestic and international fronts, including joining the exchange rate mechanism of the European Monetary System (EMS).

British membership of the European exchange rate mechanism, (though preferably after an initial devaluation) would assist in achieving a more stable exchange rate, help secure lower interest rates and act as a useful counter-inflationary discipline.[14] It is difficult to argue that staying out has brought significant benefits. On the contrary, the operation of an exchange rate policy determined largely by the market has often been both perverse and highly damaging to the economy, particularly in 1980–1. Outside, British interest rates have also remained markedly higher than German rates. Mrs Thatcher and her advisers have argued that a strong currency and high interest rates are necessary to restrain inflation. But joining the exchange rate mechanism and thus tying the pound to the Deutschmark would be a more effective long-term counter-inflationary discipline.

A Labour government must work for sensible international coordination not only on exchange rates but crucially on economic growth. The 1973 experience when too many economies grew too fast is a firm warning against too ambitious an expansion. The 1978 Bonn agreement is a better example of what can be done when major industrial countries agree on a concerted effort. Even if individual countries take only modest steps, the cumulative effect can be significant. The Cecchini report for the EC estimated that, if the completion of the European internal market is accompanied by measures to expand demand, then this would add 3 per cent extra to the

Community's GDP.[15] Sensible, restrained and balanced Keynesianism is certainly still practical on a national basis but it works better if it is also pursued on a European or international basis.

*   *   *   *   *

STIMULATING CHANGE

In the Britain of the 1990s, demand management at the macro-level will need to be complemented by the appropriate policies at micro-level – what John Smith, the Shadow Chancellor, has called 'supply side socialism'. As has already been noted, average labour productivity growth rates in the 1980s were higher in Britain than in any other country, except Japan. But the gap between British productivity and our main competitors still remains wide. Even if labour productivity in UK manufacturing were to rise more rapidly than in Germany by as much as 2 per cent a year, it would still take almost ten years to catch up.[16] Moreover, the improved productivity performance has to be set against a decline in manufacturing which has been far sharper than in other comparable countries. This is not an academic point. As we have seen, import penetration increased during the 1980s and Britain now runs a substantial deficit in manufacturing trade. Sadly, there is little evidence so far that this loss of capacity in manufacturing has been compensated for by a surge forward in high technology industries. Indeed, in comparison with Japan and West Germany, our performance in this sector is still relatively weak.

It is also crucial to understand that the world of the 1990s is going to be even harsher than that of the 1980s. There is not only the challenge of the European internal market which is due to be completed by 1992. There is also the intense competition from the United States and Japan in the high technology field and from the newly industrialised countries (such as South Korea, Taiwan, Hong Kong and Singapore) in consumer durables. More generally, the growing globalization of business activity will continue to put a premium on increasing efficiency.

The only viable strategy for a Labour government in the 1990s is to build on the improved productivity performance of the 1980s by stimulating and encouraging the process of adaption.

The old panacea of import controls, so enthusiastically advocated by some Labour party and trade union members in the 1970s, will simply not be a feasible option in the interdependent world of the 1990s. Nor will it be possible to try and prop up old declining industries. What a Labour government will have to do is support competition, welcome profitability and insist on the need for change. Change cannot, however, be left to market forces alone. Governments will need to intervene both to assist and speed up the process of change and cushion and compensate individuals, groups and regions who are adversely affected by the process. Increasingly, it will also be necessary to take action on the European level.

In the Thatcherite rhetoric (though often not in the practice), there is no case at all for a government having an industrial policy. For example, in his evidence to the House of Lords Select Committee on Overseas Trade in May 1985, Nigel Lawson, the Chancellor of the Exchequer, complacently proclaimed that the relative decline of manufacturing was 'neither new nor unhealthy'.[17] The Treasury argued that the exports of service industries would in time compensate for Britain's decline in manufacturing and that, as North Sea oil production decreased, the balance in non-oil trade, including manufactures, would automatically improve. There was nothing that the government need do to bring that happy state of affairs about.

Significantly, one of the most trenchant critics of the government's *laissez-faire* attitude has been Michael Heseltine, former Conservative Secretary of State for Defence and one of the contenders for the Thatcherite succession. He has argued that, if Britain is to prosper when North Sea oil runs out, an industrial strategy will be required. According to Heseltine, 'the health of British industry depends crucially, in many fields, on it having government as partner'.[18] It is certainly remarkable that countries with political systems as varied as Japan, France, Austria, Sweden and even West Germany, have consistently operated industrial policies, based on a partnership between government and industry. The interventionist powers and effectiveness of the Japanese Ministry of International Trade and Industry (MITI) are legendary. The Japanese have taken a strategic view of world markets, invested in industries which will prosper in the medium term, and captured an increasingly large share of international trade. Since the Second World War, under both right wing and Socialist governments, French government and industry have worked closely together in the national long-term interest. The Austrian economy, with a consistently expansionist policy, well integrated banking and industrial sectors – and, above all, with the justly celebrated social partnership – has survived the recession in better shape than most countries, ensuring that industry is in a good position to adapt to the competitive world of the 1990s.

As we have seen, the Swedish Social Democrats have left industry largely in private hands. But through extensive labour market policies, Swedish governments have encouraged the shifting of resources from declining to expanding industries. In addition, the Social Democrats have expanded government support to research and development, so that Swedish firms and industries can continue to prosper in advanced high technology markets. Despite the 'social market' ideology, the West Germans have also intervened to promote new technologies, to encourage investment in research and development and to develop labour market and regional policies.

It is the idea of partnership between government and industry, so commonplace in most industrial states and so foolishly despised by Thatcherites, that Labour must champion. It is not a question of establishing a large central planning apparatus, of setting up a whole host of bureaucratic structures or of nationalizing firms and industries for ideological reasons. Nor is it a matter of trying to replace markets. Rather, partnership is a means of improving competitiveness and efficiency, in order to promote success in domestic and world markets. The role of government is not to try and run industry or 'second guess' business but to act as an enabler, as a midwife of change.

The institutions necessary for a successful partnership between government and industry are already mostly in place. New life needs to be given to the National Economic Development Council, set up by Harold Macmillan in the 1960s, but inevitably downgraded by the Thatcher government. It has the double advantage of representing both sides of industry and of having built up a considerable body of experience and research on the opportunities and shortcomings of British industry. It could provide, together with a more dynamic and interventionist Department of Industry, prepared to use existing powers more effectively, the essential industrial overview which has been so lacking under Mrs Thatcher.

With the completion of the internal European market of 320 million, an industrial strategy is going to be even more necessary. The official Thatcherite doctrine is that the unleashing of new competitive powers by the breaking down of trade barriers will be enough to ensure that British industry and services benefit. Clearly, if British based companies are able to establish themselves more effectively on a European-wide basis, this should bring substantial economies of scale. But, as is already happening in France, Germany and Italy, the ground needs to be carefully prepared beforehand. There is a strong case for a strategic assessment of the sectors where Britain has a comparative advantage (such as financial services) and those in which Britain could be at a disadvantage (such as electrical and electronic goods, office machinery and data processing) and for deciding what action needs to be taken. Similarly the opening up of public procurement to competitive EC tendering represents both a challenge and opportunity for British industry which needs to be considered sooner rather than later.

In some sectors, particularly those with a high technology content, the appropriate response may well not be a purely national one. A European solution may be the most effective. Cross border mergers, cooperative link ups, technological alliances and, in some cases, the development of fully fledged 'European' companies are likely to become increasingly common over the next decade. Already, for example, it is obvious that, despite the difficulties, the European consortium, Airbus Industries, provides the only effective basis for competition with Boeing and McDonald. In the world of the 1990s, British companies – and British governments – must be prepared to make their contribution on a European basis or risk losing out altogether.

*   *   *   *   *

INTERVENTION POLICIES

In the longer term, the ability of British industry to remain competitive will, to a considerable extent, depend on sustained and effective investment in research and development and in education and training.

Research and development is the key to the innovation in product and process, so crucial to industrial survival. Bruce Merrifield, US Assistant Secretary of State for Productivity, Technology and Innovation, has put the case for R & D in the strongest possible terms: 'A nation that does not accord the utmost importance to R & D has made a decision not to be in business in five to ten years time . . . In any nation, R & D expenditure in excess of 3 per cent of GNP is now required for survival and growth'.[19] Of the main European nations, Britain devotes the lowest share of its gross domestic product to civil R & D.[20] Alarmingly, we now also have a far smaller proportion of industrial output in high research intensive industries (the sector where our future should lie) compared with our main competitors. It is clear that, if the British economy is to compete adequately in the 1999s, a major government effort in R & D is urgently required.

Fundamental scientific research, so vital to technological advance, needs to be put on a more secure financial basis. The cutbacks in university grants and the inadequacy of research council resources has meant that a sizeable proportion of high quality research projects has gone unfunded and that many of our most talented scientists have departed abroad. There is a strong argument for establishing, as the House of Lords Select Committee on Science and Technology recommended, a national Council for Science and Technology to review academic and industrial priorities in basic and strategic research and to relate research to our overall economic performance.[21]

It is also crucial to strengthen links between industry and research institutions. The remarkable recovery of the Massachusetts economy over the last decade demonstrates how effective a constructive partnership between academe and industry can be. At the same time, like other advanced countries, industry needs to be directly encouraged by tax incentives to step up its relatively inadequate investment in R & D. Pressure should also be exerted on companies by a statutory obligation to publish R & D expenditure. However, the scale of what is required, particularly in high technology areas, means that R & D projects will sometimes be beyond the scope of single companies or even national government. Hence the case for collaboration and the development of policy at a European level, now officially supported by member states under the Single European Act.

Looking to the future, it is obvious that the skills and talents of our people are the nation's greatest asset. Yet a series of authoritative studies have shown that Britain's relative under-investment and inadequate standards in training and education inhibit the introduction of new technology, more efficient work practices and the performance of British industry.[22] British workers and managers are less well qualified and less well trained than workers and managers in the United States, Germany, Japan and France. Industry carries out less than half the amount of training undertaken in Germany and Japan and the gap is widening. A National Institute Report concluded that per head of population France is now producing 3 times as many craftsmen and $2\frac{1}{2}$ times as many technicians as the United Kingdom.[23]

In training and education, as in research and development, the market does not deliver effectively. Left to itself, industry as a whole has failed to give workers the required training. There are, of course, brilliant exceptions. But as has been noted earlier, too many firms see training as an overhead to be cut when profits are under pressure; in better times, they hope to poach skilled employees from their more prudent rivals. Short-term interest does not add up to the long-term common good.

So a key priority for the 1990s must be a plan to bring the skills and educational qualifications of our workforce up to the level of at least our main European competitors. The government must have the responsibility for improving educational standards, for ensuring that a much higher proportion of young people stay on at school after 16 and for increasing substantially the proportion of graduates, especially of engineers and technologists. It will also have to improve youth training radically. In 1988 the Youth Training Scheme was criticised in scathing terms: 'For the vast majority of entrants, few of whom have reached GCSE standard in a range of core subjects, the best that can be hoped from present policies in Britain is a form of semi-skilled operator training, leading to qualifications below craft level'.[24] The answer could well be a statutory right to training for all employers, which could act as a stimulus to improvement.

For their part, firms should be obliged to provide training for their workforces. Labour's concept of a National Training Fund, administered by a Manpower Services Commission or training authority and operating on a levy and grant basis, would not only end the 'free-riding' practice of those companies who poach skilled workers from those who take their training responsibilities seriously; more important, it would begin to provide the volume of high quality training which British industry and British employees so desperately need.

I have already argued above that it is a government responsibility to cushion and compensate those individuals, groups and regions who are adversely affected by change. This responsibility has already been recognized at a European level by the decision taken in 1988 to complement the completion of the internal market by increasing substantially the so-called 'structural funds' and by the emphasis which the President of Commission, Jacques Delors, has put on the need to ensure that all Europe's citizens benefit from the completion of the internal market. It is important to grasp, however, that the argument for labour market and regional policies is not only a social one. It is also economically inefficient for people to remain unemployed for long periods, just as it is economically inefficient to allow whole regions to become relatively unproductive.

Indeed, the purpose of labour market policies should be not only to provide temporary work for those who cannot find jobs but to match labour demand with labour supply as quickly and efficiently as possible. While at least two million remain unemployed, special employment measures on a large scale will clearly be necessary. But, as the Swedish experience so conclusively demonstrates,[25] getting those without jobs into employment depends to a considerable extent on training and retraining the unemployed and reequiping them with new skills. Labour market policy in Sweden has always been seen not primarily as a form of 'make-work' but as a means of making the economy more efficient by stimulating labour markets to function more effectively. In the 1990s, comprehensive labour market policies will continue to be essential not just to provide temporary jobs but as a means of promoting economic growth.

The failure of the British economy to provide enough jobs in the right places means that economic and industrial policy has also to be supplemented by regional policies. The case for regional policy is that unbridled market forces accentuate rather than decrease disparities between regions. The simple market model ignores some of the underlying causes of regional differences, such as geographical distance between centre and periphery, the concentration of company headquarters and R & D in the south, and the differing structure of regional economies and markets. Most important of all, it downgrades both social needs and national economic requirements.

Economic growth, which is concentrated in the south, widens regional disparities in terms of unemployment, income and wealth. It is also in danger of being short-lived. In 1988, the Southern economy became overstretched with shortages of skills, leap-frogging wages and spiralling costs, while the Northern economy remained relatively sluggish. If it was possible to spread growth around, this would not only revive the North but also prevent the South from becoming overheated.

In the past, regional policies have had some success. A Department of Trade and Industry study has demonstrated that, because of regional policies, particularly regional development grants, there was an increase of between 350 000 and 630 000 jobs in the assisted areas in the years 1972–81.[26] In the 1990s, the purpose of regional policy will be somewhat different from that of the 1960s and 1970s. Rather than merely to create jobs, the objective should be to help the regions to help themselves by promoting economic growth. The emphasis will be as much on encouraging indigenous firms to expand as attracting outside companies into the area. Regional policy will also concentrate not on propping up declining industries but on stimulating innovation and development.

A comprehensive portfolio of regional incentives, regulated by EC rules and supplemented by EC funds, must still continue to provide the framework for regional assistance. However, a key new ingredient should be the extension to some of the English regions of the Development Agency model as in operation in Scotland and Wales. The agency model has already proved itself to be a flexible and effective means of assisting economic and industrial change in Scotland and Wales. Similar Development Agencies should, therefore, be set up in those English regions like the North and the North West which could benefit from them.

* * * * *

SUMMARY

In the 1990s, the Labour party will strongly support competition, profitable investment and industrial innovation. But change cannot be left to market forces alone. Government will need to facilitate – and, where necessary, speed up – the process of adaptation, encouraging investment in research and development, promoting education and training, and revitalizing the idea of partnership between government and industry. Government will also be required to assist and cushion individuals, groups and regions who lose out. Hence the case for a floor of social rights and for regional and labour market policies. Increasingly solutions will have to be found at a European level.

Learning the lessons of the 1970s and 1980s, Labour will be cautiously Keynesian, prepared to use all the available instruments – fiscal, monetary and exchange rate intervention – to sustain the level of demand at an appropriate level but aware of the need for a moderate, balanced approach. Acutely conscious of the dangers of inflation, it will support the idea of a broad consensus between government, employers and unions on growth of incomes and back this up by pursuing firm monetary and exchange rate policies. It will work for sensible international coordination, including joining the exchange rate mechanism of the European Monetary System.

8 Trade Unions and the Labour Market

With the exception of the Labour party, the trade unions have been the most obvious losers of the Thatcher years. In the 1970s, under both Labour and Conservative governments, they were in an extremely strong position. There was a major expansion of union membership – the biggest since 1945. The Labour government introduced legislation favourable to trade unions and employees. Trade unions played a key role in the Labour government's economic, industrial and social strategy. The public impression, if not the reality, was that the unions had grown all powerful.

In contrast, the 1980s have been a deeply depressing decade for the unions. The membership gains of the 1970s have been wiped out. Changes in the labour market, the adoption of anti-union policies by increasing numbers of employers, and the Thatcher government's industrial relations legislation have combined to tilt the balance decisively against the trade unions. Unlike other post-war Conservative administrations, the Thatcher government has virtually ignored the political views of the labour movement.

As union membership and influence has declined, so has Labour support amongst trade unionists. At every general election between 1945 and 1974, a majority of trade unionists voted Labour. At both general elections in the 1980s, only a minority of trade unionists supported the Labour party. At the same time, a majority of trade unionists believe that trade union links with the Labour party are too close.[1]

It is now essential for the Labour party to reassess the role of trade unions in the harsh conditions of the late 1980s and 1990s; to reexamine the part which legislation should play in industrial relations, especially the case for concentrating on the provision of statutory rights for individual employees; and more generally to reconsider its relationship with the trade union movement.

*　*　*　*　*

SHIFTING THE BALANCE

The 1974–9 Labour government's attitude towards the unions was strongly influenced by the need to gain their support for incomes policy. As we have seen, the Social Contract of 1974–9 was an ambitious attempt to link together incomes, output, employment, tax and welfare policy in a coherent way. If its initial phase (until July 1975) took too little account of wage increases, it had considerable success over the next three years in reducing inflation and there were substantial gains for large families and pensioners, as well as extension of rights at the workplace. Significantly, however, the labour legislation introduced by the Labour government was introduced as much to strengthen collective bargaining and the position of the unions as to guarantee individual rights.

The two Trade Union and Labour Relations Acts of 1974 and 1976 repealed the Conservative Industrial Relations Act of 1971 which put legal restrictions on the ability of trade unions to organise, negotiate and strike. The Employment Protection Act of 1975 bolstered collective bargaining in a number of ways. Under the Act, trade unions were able to refer claims for recognition and for extensions to the scope of collective bargaining to the Advisory Conciliation and Arbitration Service (ACAS). ACAS was an independent but statutory body, designed to expand the role of conciliation in industrial disputes as an alternative to the law. In addition, the Act gave trade unions rights to disclosure of information for collective bargaining purposes and contained provisions to stimulate progress towards voluntary collective bargaining in the wages council industries. The 1975 Industry Act also gave trade unions rights to certain kinds of company information. The Labour government also legislated to provide expanded individual rights in a number of areas, including unfair dismissals, redundancy, equal opportunities, guarantee payments, health and safety, maternity, and time off work and insolvency of a firm, but its emphasis was on extending collective trade union rights.

As noted in Chapter 1, Mrs Thatcher owed her election victory in 1979 in part to the disruptive 'winter of discontent', when trade union popularity plummeted to a post-war low. So her government was exceptionally well placed to introduce measures designed to shift the industrial balance back towards management. Learning from the failure of the all embracing, institutionally based legislation of 1971, the Employment Secretary, James Prior, embarked on what he called a 'step by step' approach.

The 1980 Employment Act banned secondary picketing and withdrew immunity from most other forms of secondary action. It also attempted to weaken the closed shop by establishing an exemption on grounds of conscience or personal conviction and by obliging employers to hold ballots before agreeing to a closed shop. The 1982 Employment Act, introduced by James Prior's successor, Norman Tebbit, restricted the definition of an industrial dispute, made unions liable to damages in a whole range of circumstances, and gave new rights to employers. The 1984 Trade Union Act obliged unions to hold secret ballots for the election of executive committees, for the establishment and maintenance of political funds, and before authorizing industrial action. The 1988 Employment Act gave the right to union members to continue working during a strike (even though it was approved by an authorized ballot) and removed the remaining legal support for a post-entry closed shop.

The Conservatives have also removed millions of especially-vulnerable workers from the protection of statutory rights enacted by the Labour government. The most important change, which affected over three million workers, was the raising of the qualifying period for statutory protection against unfair dismissal from six months to two years continuous employment. The 1986 Wages Act removed minimum pay protection from young workers under 21. The right to maternity pay and maternity leave has been curtailed.

At the same time, the government has resisted EC directives which would have given the growing number of part-time workers the same rights as full time workers and protected temporary employees and those on fixed term contracts. The British government has also been influential in persuading the Council of Ministers to postpone further consideration of the Vredeling–Richards directive which would have given employees right to information and consultation.

However, the only advance in the extension of rights has come under pressure from the EC. The 1983 Equal Pay (Amendment) Regulations gave women the right to claim equal pay for work of equal value, while the 1986 Sex Discrimination Act introduced common retirement ages for men and women. Even so, the overall impact of the Thatcher years has been to make British employees among the least protected in Western Europe.

While Thatcherite legislation helped shift the balance away from the unions, a combination of changes in the labour market and a tougher attitude by employers also reduced their power. A paper prepared in 1987 for a TUC review of the future of trade unionism[2] pointed out that, by the end of the 1980s, the membership gains of the 1970s had been effectively wiped out; that the proportion of the workforce in unions was now only just over 40 per cent (in contrast to almost 50 per cent at the end of the 1970s), and that the loss of union membership in the United Kingdom had been on a greater scale than in other comparative countries. It also stressed that employment growth since 1983 had been concentrated in regions where trade unionism was weakest. It concluded that future employment trends were likely to continue to be unfavourable to the growth of trade union membership because of the limited prospects of any major falls in unemployment, the continued fall in employment in manufacturing, the increase in employment in the largely unorganized private services and in areas of relatively low union organization and membership. As with the Labour party, it seemed that trends were working against the trade unions.

*   *   *   *   *

WHAT ARE WE HERE FOR?

'What are we here for?' The question asked of the trade unions in 1962 by George Woodcock, the then General Secretary of the TUC, badly needs answering anew in the more difficult conditions of the late 1980s and 1990s. Indeed, a prerequisite in the development of a new Labour party policy on industrial relations is a trade union movement which understands the change which have occurred and has the will to adapt.

Writing in the 1970s, I defined trade union purpose as that c 'democratising and humanizing industry'.[3] I argued that it wa necessary to go beyond the Webbs' definition of a trade unio as a 'continuous association of wage earners for the purpose c maintaining or improving the conditions of their employmen because it was too narrowly economic. The definition favoured by the authoritative industrial relations commentator, Allan Flanders, was that the objective of trade unions was to establish a system of industrial rights through collective bargaining. This was an improvement on the Webbs because it stressed the democratic side of trade unionism, but I believed that its emphasis on collective bargaining alone was unnecessarily limiting, and that the function of the unions should be the joint regulation of all strategic decisions.

The arguments in the 1970s for such widely defined trade union objectives were compelling. On the one hand, technological and organisational developments in industry, combined with the growing need of governments to influence collective bargaining, threatened traditional trade union functions. On the other hand, the new power of the shop floor, as well as the growth in trade union membership and coverage, gave the unions an opportunity to develop a more cooperative role. However I warned the trade unions that, if they continued to behave as purely reactive and defensive organisations, there would be 'growing support for anti-union legislation'.[4] My conclusion was that what was required was a positive trade union programme, designed to create a system of power-sharing from shop floor to boardroom.

However, that formulation of trade union function now needs considerable amendment in the light of changed circumstances. Trade unions have to take into account the profound shifts which are taking place in industrial structure, in the composition of the labour force, and in the strategies of employers and concerns of employees. A third of Britain's labour force now work in offices, compared to only 22 per cent in manufacturing. A third of the value of national output is in the distribution sector. The old world, on which trade unionism has been based, is rapidly disappearing. The pace of change is likely to be even greater in the 1990s with the competitive challenge from both within and outside Europe.

The composition of the labour force is also changing rapidly. In the 1990s, half the workforce will be women – and half of those women will be part-time workers. The importance of women employees will be accentuated by a shortage of young employees. A NEDO report published in July 1988 predicted a fall of 1.2 million young people in the labour force between 1987 and 1985 and a decline in the numbers o, school leavers by a quarter compared with the mid-1980s.[5]

The trend towards a more divided and diverse labour force is also likely to continue. On the one hand, there will be a 'core' of skilled workers with access to secure, better paid jobs; on the other hand, there will be a growing army of 'peripheral' employees – that is to say part-timers, temporary workers and freelancers. This development is, to a considerable extent, the result of the expansion of the service sector. There is, however, evidence of changes in company employment policy as well.[6] Employers are increasingly retaining a basic 'core' of skilled employees, while hiring and firing 'peripheral' workers (who are cheaper to employ and have virtually no rights) according to fluctuations in output and demand.

More generally, employers are now putting greater emphasis on a more individualized, less collectivized approach to industrial relations. According to an ACAS report, increased interest in merit payment systems has coincided with a decline in industry-wide and multi-company bargaining[7] and a questioning of the role of traditional collective bargaining. Looking to the 1990s, it has been predicted that employee relations 'will become more and more individualised, with ever greater growth of pay related directly, either in part or wholly, to individual performance, and with the growth of individual contracts struck between an employee and an employer'.[8]

Attitudes of employees are also changing. Growing numbers are now unorganized and unrepresented, while others are more concerned with their own individual preoccupations than with collective relations.

The basic assumption of trade unionism – that employees are human beings with the right to be treated as such – is as valid today as it has been in the past. But, in the conditions of the 1990s, there will have to be considerable modifications in trade union function. Unless trades unions take account of the changing needs of employees, they will find themselves becoming increasingly irrelevant, deserted by members, marginalised by managements, and ignored by governments.

In a perceptive comment on the extent of the reforms that will be needed, John Edmonds, General Secretary of the General Municipal and Boilermakers, has argued: 'When we listen to British working people in the 1980s . . . we find that they wan trade unions which are different both in substance and in style. The new unions which succeed will be more diverse in their policies, more flexible in their methods, and more obviously attentive to the needs of individual members . . . they will be less interested in sustaining a mythology of perpetual conflict and more open in their search for methods which solve problems without causing hardship'.[9]

For a start, trade unions will have to be responsive to the environment within which they are operating. In the highly competitive world of the 1990s, the accent will be on efficiency. Trade unions will have to not only accept but actively promote the joint management–employee interest in profitability, innovation and adaptability. The unions will also have to come to terms with the individualistic emphasis in employee relations which so many employers are now adopting. They will have to recognize that, from the point of view of the individual worker, a more professional management which is prepared to devote time, energy and resources to employee relations is highly desirable. The task for trade unions will be to provide a service relevant to the new conditions – like, for example, drawing up contracts for 'core' employees, helping devise framework agreements for performance pay criteria, and giving advice on a wide range of issues, including pensions, personal finance, and health and safety. Promoting improvements in health and safety will be of crucial importance.

With respect to the 'peripheral' employees, their main problem is that they are highly vulnerable to arbitrary treatment. What they need, above all, is the protection of a system of rights at work. In this context, trade unions must not only put themselves at the forefront of a campaign for such rights but be prepared to act as their monitors and enforcers. Here, trade unions could find employers somewhat more receptive than in the past, because the shortage of young workers will make it necessary for management to pursue policies which give a higher priority to labour retention.

In the atmosphere of the 1990s, the strike weapon is likely to be very much a weapon of last resort, used even less frequently than in the late 1980s. More and more disputes are likely to be settled by arbitration. Unions have much to gain and little to lose from a fair and effective system of arbitration which gives both unions and employers the unilateral right to refer disputes to arbitration. Above all, a trade union movement which is seen to be intent on trying to solve problems without strikes is likely to get the support of employees.

Trade unions have also to face up to the issue of union structure. The spate of 'single union' agreements is an indication that many employers are no longer prepared to put up with the disadvantages of competitive multi-unionism. But, as the problems which have arisen over the EETU–PTU have already amply demonstrated, a purely reactive posture by the trade union movement could lead not only to even more intense inter-union rivalry but to the virtual break-up of the union movement. The fluidity which changes in the labour market and the increasing number of trade union amalgamations is bringing about could provide a positive opportunity for a restructuring of trade unions on more rational lines.

In this process of trade union transformation, the Labour party should adopt the role of 'candid friend'. It is entirely legitimate for party leaders to express their support for the right changes, to offer constructive advice, and to admonish if they believe trade unions are straying too far from the path of reform.

On the issue of strikes, the party needs overtly to adopt a moderating, case-by-case approach. Of course, in a democratic society, strikes must remain as a weapon of last resort. But Labour must always be on the side of conciliation and constructive compromise. On occasions, party leaders and spokesmen will have to condemn particular strikes as being counter-productive and against the best interests of all concerned. (For example, in 1987 I criticized the NUT for its decision to take strike action during the general election as being contrary to the best interests of education.) At other times, it will be best for the party to take a deliberate decision to take a low profile or not to become involved at all.

Labour is not, and cannot be a syndicalist party which is, as a matter of course, on the side of striking workers. Such a stance would not only be electorally disastrous but wrong in principle for a national party which seeks to represent the interests, not just of one group of employees, but a wide range of occupations and interests – including that of the community as a whole.

*   *   *   *   *

STATUTORY EMPLOYEE RIGHTS

In the changed conditions of the 1990s, the Labour party must adopt a less collective approach to industrial relations legislation than in the 1970s; rather, it should give priority to the extension of statutory rights for individuals at work. Though it would clearly be difficult to sell policies which were designed to restore trade union immunities, the reasons for advocating such a shift in emphasis are not primarily electoral. For one thing, Labour's trade union centred approach of the 1970s has proved easily reversible. It would be harder for a future Conservative government to take away individual employee rights than to remove immunities for trade unions. More crucially our workers are now far less protected than their West European counterparts. So the main thrust of Labour's industrial relations strategy for the 1990s must be to give to British employees similar statutory protection to that enjoyed in the rest of Western Europe.

What is needed is the introduction of statutory rights for *all* workers and the establishment of an effective system of enforcement. A British Employment Rights Bill could be based on the European Social Charter of 1965 (which has already been ratified by the British government). Rights in the European Charter include the right to a fair remuneration, the right to just conditions covering hours, holidays and health and safety, the right to equal treatment and opportunities irrespective of sex, race, or national origin, and the right to vocational guidance and training. These basic rights need to be supplemented by additional ones, including full protection against unfair dismissal – and, most important, the right to information and consultation.

The most effective system is likely to be one which is enforced by employees themselves. Employee inspectors in all establishments above a certain size should be established by law. This system should be reinforced by government inspectors and by giving workers rights of appeal to industrial tribunals. The enactment of a comprehensive set of rights for people at work combined with powerful enforcement procedures would go far to protect millions of British workers against unfair and arbitrary treatment.

I have argued above that the monitoring and enforcement of rights at work could provide a new role for trade unions. It is in this context that the Labour party should consider how far the collective rights of unions need to be strengthened. The key question is to what extent the Conservative government's industrial relations legislation, which has curtailed trade union immunities, placed conditions on the establishment and maintenance of closed shops and introduced an extensive system of trade union ballots, should be repealed.

It would clearly not be a credible position simply to say that a Labour government would sweep away all Tory legislation. Statutory ballots for union election and before industrial disputes have proved extremely popular with trade union members and, to some extent, have also improved trade union accountability. With respect to closed shops, it is hard to argue against the holding of ballots before they are established.

On the other hand, the right to free association (including the right for employees to organize, to be properly represented and to be able to withdraw their labour) is a basic democratic right which has been substantially weakened by Conservative legislation. There is therefore a strong case for ensuring that the right to free association, guaranteeing the right to organize, to bargain collectively and to strike, forms part of an Employment Rights Bill.

The debatable area relates to secondary action. One possibility might be that it would be considered lawful if it had passed the test of a ballot. But the real issue is whether or not sympathetic industrial action is necessary to ensure the primary right to strike. I doubt whether that case has yet been made. Until it has been demonstrated conclusively, it would be unwise to restore collective rights in respect of secondary action.

The argument for employee participation, however, is as powerful today as it has ever been. It is now widely recognized that the deeper the involvement the greater the satisfaction. Indeed, most of the recent initiatives in participative management – group dynamics, direct communication, 'cascade' briefings, quality circles, team briefing and employee councils – are based on the assumption that the more employees are involved the more effective will be their contribution to the well being of the firm.

In the 1970s, industrial democracy became a major political issue. But, partly under the influence of directives from the EC, the main focus was on worker representation at boardroom level.

Led by Jack Jones, the General Secretary of the Transport Workers' Union, the TUC proposed that elected trade union representatives should form 50 per cent of a new supervisory board.[10] In January 1977 the majority report of the Bullock Committee, set up to examine the issue of boardroom represent-ation, broadly supported the TUC position, including the right to boardroom representation, through trade union machinery, in all companies employing 2000 workers and over.[11] The Bullock report was, however, rejected not only by the CBI but by major trade unions (such as the GMB and the AUEW). These feared that boardroom involvement would compromise trade union independence. The Labour government, which lost its overall majority in March 1977, decided not to support the Bullock proposals.

In the very different conditions of the late 1980s and 1990s, the emphasis must be on individual rights rather than collective representation. There must be statutory rights of information and consultation throughout industry. Such a development would not only be in the interests of employees. By increasing involvement, it would help maximize the efficiency of the enterprise, to the benefit of the whole community.

Some mechanism is, however, required to enforce and monitor these rights. In this context we could well borrow from European experience by establishing statutory participation councils on the West German model.[12] Employee representatives would be elected from the whole work force and, though trade unionists are likely to be elected in most establishments, there would be no exclusive right to a single trade union channel of representation. In this way, the argument for widening industrial democracy would escape the charge of 'trade union take-over' which was levelled at the TUC and Bullock Committee proposals.

*   *   *   *   *

THE UNION–LABOUR PARTY RELATIONSHIP

Both the trade unions and the Labour party ought now to reexamine the nature and shape of their relationship to see whether it is still appropriate to the world of the 1990s.

The British Labour party's organic link with the trade unions is a product of its history. While the formation of other West

European Socialist parties preceded the birth of the trade union movements, the Labour party, in Ernest Bevin's graphic words, grew out of the bowels of the British trade union movement. As the Labour Representation Committee, it was set up to ensure that trade union interests were no longer ignored in British politics. When in 1918 Labour became for the first time a party open to individual members, the powerful trade union role was organizationally preserved by the ability of trade unions to affiliate at both national and local level, and by the control of 90 per cent of the votes cast at annual conference and by a strong union presence on the national executive. In 1981, the issue of trade union dominance of the party was raised in a new and more acute form when the trade unions were given a major say in electing the leader of the Labour party. Under the procedure then adopted, the trade unions were allocated a 40 per cent share of the electoral college vote.

Most parties of the left in European politics have some kind of relationship with the trade unions. It is also significant that the most successful Socialist or Social Democratic parties are those which, like the Austrians, Swedish and West German parties, have at least informal ties with their trade union movement. But, in contrast to Labour's trade union dominated federal structure, the continental Socialist parties are individual membership parties in which (with the exceptions of the special place of the Socialist trade union fraction at the Austrian Socialist party conference and local trade union affiliation to the Swedish Social Democrat party) the trade unions have no formal position.

Clearly, the Labour party and the trade unions both have an interest in preserving a relationship with each other. Trade unions have always had – and are likely to continue to have – social and political concerns wider than 'bread and butter' issues. Indeed the successful ballots following the 1984 Trade Union Act have given the unions' political activities a new political legitimacy. With respect to the Labour party, trade union members still provide a substantial electoral base which, if the unions are more popular and successful in the 1990s, could well expand. So the question is not whether there should be a relationship but what kind of relationship it should be.

In the early 1970s, Anthony Crosland pointed out: 'We must remember that the unions and the party have their own distinct fields of responsibility, and their own distinct duties and obligations to their members and electors; neither is, nor should be, the creature of the other'.[13] Whatever its origins, Labour must be far more than just a trade union party. It should be a broad based national party, designed to seek and retain national power and concerned with national solutions for national problems. Although the party will respect trade union views, it can never allow itself to be dominated by an interest group, however influential and powerful it may be.

For their part, the trade unions cannot afford to allow themselves to be portrayed as primarily political organizations. After all, members do not join unions in order to be involved in Labour party affairs and they do not expect to see their leaders behaving like Labour party politicians or trying to dictate terms to the Labour party. The political relationship between a Labour government and trade unions should be a consultative one. Clearly trade unions will have more influence with Labour than with a Thatcher administration. But the 1970s 'social contract' model which gave the unions almost equal status with government in the shaping of economic and social policy is no longer applicable to the world of the 1990s. The decisions must be made – and be seen to be made – by a democratically elected government.

The critics can, of course, still point to the formal arrangements whereby the trade unions, as well as being the paymasters, have a dominant say in the election of the leader and an overwhelming preponderance of voters at party conference, as evidence that the Labour party will remain at the unions' beck and call. It is certainly the case that, if a brand new Labour party was being created today, it would be unlikely to adopt the structure and organization which it now has. However, that is not the position in which Labour finds itself. The task is to find practical ways of modernizing the existing relationship.

Three reforms would do much to rebut the charge of trade union domination. The first would be to abolish the electoral college for leader and deputy leader with its special position for trade unions and replace it with a 'one member, one vote' system. As the 1981 deputy leadership and 1988 leadership elections have only too graphically demonstrated, the union vote in the electoral college is a source of acute embarrassment both for the party and the unions. It would be both more democratic and better electorally for the party if the membership chose the leader by a process of one member, one vote.

At the same time, party membership, low by continental standards, must be increased considerably. At the 1988 conference, it was agreed to offer a reduced membership fee to the five million trade unionists paying the political levy, in the expectation that this would lead to greatly increased individual trade union membership. Greater involvement by individual trade unionists would not only ensure that local parties were more representative of the mass of Labour voters but make it more practical for Labour to become a membership rather than a trade union based party.

Another change which needs serious consideration would be to diminish by stages the trade union vote at conference. An initial step might be to reduce it to no more than 50 per cent. Those who argue that this would make the party conference more difficult to control have to face the fact that it is the unpredictability of the largest union, the T & GW (controlling over 12 per cent of the vote) which has been the main reason for conference becoming more volatile over the last decade. Increased local party membership, combined with selection of the delegates by all constituency members, would help ensure that constituency delegates to conference were more at one with mainstream Labour opinion.

The question of party finance remains. A big increase in party membership would go some way to reduce reliance on the trade unions. In the longer term, however, state funding of political parties, on the West German model, will be necessary. State support should be related not only to votes at general elections but also to size of membership. The party should start to campaign now for its introduction. The modern Labour party must become – and be seen to become – less dependent on the unions as institutions. It would also be in the union interest and in accord with the views of union members if the trade union involvement in the party was less overt and more on an individual than on a collective basis.

*   *   *   *   *

SUMMARY

This chapter has argued for a changed role for unions in the competitive conditions of the 1990s. It will be a union priority to promote the joint management–employee interest in profitability, innovation and adaptability. Unions will service members on a more individual basis. Above all, they will monitor and enforce individual rights at work.

In this process of trade union transformation, Labour should adopt the position of 'candid friend'. Over strikes, Labour must always be on the side of conciliation and constructive compromise. The Labour party must also adopt a less collectivist approach to industrial relations and give priority to the extension of statutory employee rights. There must be modifications in the formal trade union links with the party, so as to reduce dependence on the unions, while, at the same time, increasing individual trade union membership.

9 Reforming the Welfare State

The Thatcher governments have subjected the idea of 'welfare' to sustained intellectual attack since 1979. However, despite the Conservative onslaught, the Labour party can have confidence in the underlying strength of the case for the welfare state. Attitudes surveys show that, if anything, public backing for the 'core' welfare services and benefits has grown during the Thatcher years.[1] That is because these provide the most effective means of meeting the needs of the majority of people during different phases of their lives. But continuing popular support does not exclude reforms. On the contrary, the welfare state must respond to new conditions and requirements. In particular, it will need to concentrate on higher standards, value for money, efficient management and giving priority to the consumer, including the establishment of a system of consumer rights. It will also need to make a more effective attack on poverty. This chapter sets out the changes which will be required to equip the welfare system for the 1990s.

*   *   *   *   *

THE CONSERVATIVE OFFENSIVE

The Conservative argument against the welfare state is partly economic. As we have seen, an important strand of monetarism as argued by the Conservatives in 1979 was that the share of public spending in the national economy ought to be reduced. It was argued that, if increased public spending was financed by increased taxes, then it would have a disincentive effect on enterprise, work and savings. An additional argument was that a high level of public spending would 'crowd out' the private sector by preempting finance and resources. Monetarists also maintained that, if public spending was financed by borrowing it led to increases in the money supply and therefore to inflation

The Thatcherite assumption is that a high level of public spending is bad for the economy.

However, behind the economic arguments are older and more basic Tory beliefs. According to many Conservatives, public welfare services are not only inherently inefficient and bureaucratic, but deprive consumers of choice. Hence the arguments for encouraging the growth of private medical and educational facilities as an alternative to state provision. A further Conservative charge is that the provision of social benefits has encouraged a 'dependency' culture in which the incentive to work is being undermined. The Thatcherite prejudice is that welfare is bad for the recipients who are, in any case, largely to blame for their own misfortunes. Hence the argument for restricting the definition of the needy, reducing dependence on state support and cutting back on benefits.

In terms of the overall spending, the Tory approach to social services and benefits has been somewhat more cautious than their rhetoric. Indeed, in some areas, there have been substantial increases in expenditure. For example, although it has not been enough to prevent a public outcry about a deterioration in the service, spending on the National Health Service has actually risen by over 30 per cent in real terms between 1978/79 and 1987/88[2] (though in relation to specifically health service costs the increase was much less). The social security budget has also expanded from 25 per cent to 30 per cent of public expenditure, mainly because of the rise in numbers of pensioners and single parent families and because of the massive growth in unemployment.[3] Expenditure on education has, however, only increased by 7 per cent in real terms over the same period and its share of public spending has fallen (though, because of the fall in the number of pupils, spending per pupil has grown significantly) while public investment in housing has been drastically cut back.

Nonetheless, in policy terms, a number of highly controversial and divisive changes have been introduced. In social security, these include abandoning the link between earnings and pensions and other benefits established by the 1974–9 Labour government; diminishing the real value of child benefit; encouraging people to opt out from the State Earnings Related Pensions Scheme (SERPS) and reducing the benefits it provides; and the reform and rationalization of the main means-tested benefits. This last change, which has aroused considerable opposition, increased benefits (through family credits) to the working poor but only by redistributing resources to them from those out of work. The withdrawal of housing benefit from many pensioners, and reduced levels of support for the under-25s paid for the increased benefits for families on low wages. In addition, the government has abolished the system of single discretionary grants for one-off essential items (such as beds, cookers and clothes) to those on income support and replaced it with the much less generous and primarily loan-based 'Social Fund'. Significantly, the Social Security Advisory Committee, set up by the government in 1980, has concluded that there will be more losers than gainers as a result of these changes to means-related benefits.[4]

In education, the most important reforms introduced by the government have been the introduction of the unified GCSE exam at 16+; the new national curriculum; and the provision under the 1988 Education Act for schools to 'opt out' of local authority control. There are powerful, non-partisan arguments for the first two reforms. The GCSE exam both covers a wider ability group and provides a more effective check on standards than the exams which it replaced, while the case for a common national curriculum is that it will help to ensure that all pupils acquire certain basic skills. The 'opt out' plan is, however, potentially highly damaging. The danger is that, if as Mrs Thatcher clearly hopes, a considerable number of schools opt out, this will create a two-tier school system, with the majority going to inferior schools. Such a development would block progress towards the highly desirable objective of a good quality education for all.

Until Mrs Thatcher's announcement in January 1988 setting up a departmental inquiry, government policy towards the health service appeared to be confined to restraining public spending on health and encouraging cost-saving exercises. The House of Commons Social Services Select Committee (with a built-in Tory majority) estimated that, after allowing for the extra resources needed to take account of demographic and technological change, there had been a cumulative shortfall of £1.8 billion between 1980/81 and 1987/88.[5] In December 1987 a statement from the Presidents of the Royal Colleges of Physicians and Surgeons and Obstetricians highlighted the impact of financial stringency in the most graphic terms: 'Every day we learn of new problems in the NHS – beds are shut, operating rooms are not available, emergency wards are closed, essential services are shut down in order to make financial savings'.

Mrs Thatcher's motive in setting up an inquiry into the health service was not only to stifle the public outcry over the funding of the NHS but to use popular concern as a pretext for introducing far-reaching changes in the service. The Government White Paper, published in January 1989, put forward a number of market-orientated reforms: these included a new scheme to encourage general practitioners with large practices to buy services for their patients from a variety of public and private sources and the establishment of a self governing status within the NHS which would allow hospitals to act more like businesses. Whether these changes will result in profit being put before patients will depend on the strength of the conditions which are imposed on these GPs and hospitals. It is clear, however, that the proposal to give tax incentives on health insurance premiums to retired pensioners was a deliberate attempt to encourage the better off to buy private care and could be the beginning of a two-tier health service. Increasingly, the underlying principles of the welfare system are coming under threat.

*   *   *   *   *

THE CASE FOR WELFARE

The Labour party has, therefore, to reassert the basic case for the welfare state. One crucial notion underpinning the argument for welfare is that of mutual obligation. Citizens pay taxes not only because of the benefits and services which the state provides for them, but because of their civic and moral obligation to ensure that their fellows are similarly provided. But the argument for collective welfare is not simply one of altruism. It is also in the interest of the whole community. It provides the most effective means of meeting the needs of the majority at different periods of their lives. And it strengthens and unites the nation. An economy which is supported by a healthy and well educated labour force will be able to compete more effectively with other advanced economies. A society which gives priority to the welfare of all will not only be a more just society but also more cohesive and therefore more socially and politically stable.

A society concerned with welfare will want to ensure that individuals are provided with a sufficient income to protect them against poverty, whether this arises from sickness, unemployment, disability, low wages, old age or the strains of bringing up a family. And, in order to achieve a genuine measure of equality of opportunity, there must be comprehensive and good quality health and education provision as well as an adequate level of housing for all. Significantly, even Mrs Thatcher accepts the limitations of the market and the need for state intervention in welfare. She has admitted that 'the only way we can ensure that no one is left without sustenance, help or opportunity, is to have laws to provide for health and education, pensions for the elderly, succour for the sick and disabled'.[6]

There is, however, a crucial difference between the Conservative and the Labour positions. Thatcherites seek, as a matter of principle, to limit the scope of state intervention and expand the role of the market. Labour supports state provision of education and health because it is the most effective way to provide good quality health care and education for all.

If health and education is left solely to the market, the needs of the less well off are simply not met. Significantly in the United States where health care is largely provided through private insurance, more than 30 million Americans have no health insurance at all and in serious illness are dependent on charity.[7] All the advanced countries have decided that education is so important for the future of their societies that the state has to be responsible for schooling. In Britain, two-thirds own their own homes, but even in this more obviously market orientated sector Conservatives have accepted that state intervention in the form of mortgage relief is needed to help buyers enter the market and that there has to be some form of collective support for those who cannot either afford to buy or rent accommodation.

Conservatives argue that expanding private health care (a comparatively low proportion of British GDP is devoted to private health care spending) and private education (10 per cent of pupils are currently educated at private schools) would extend choice and channel more resources into health and education. It would certainly be unacceptably anti-libertarian to seek to abolish private health and education. But the danger of a major expansion of private health and education is that, so far from expanding total resources, it would, in practice, divert resources and manpower away from the state system. And, because only the better off could afford the cost, it would not, in any meaningful sense, extend choice. Instead, the result could be to reduce state education and the NHS to 'second class' services, which only the less well off would use, when the real objective should be to ensure good education and health care for every citizen.

But if it is right to be sceptical about the relevance of the market model in education and health, Labour has to demonstrate clearly and conclusively that it is the party of value for money, efficient use of resources, quality control and as much choice as is compatible with high standards for all. Increasingly, consumers want a higher quality of service. The main argument for public education and health must be that it is the best solution for the majority of consumers; and the overwhelming concern should be to ensure that these services are run in the interests of consumers and that any injection of public resources results in a commensurate improvement in the service to the customer. Labour must become the champion both of good management and of consumer rights in public services.

* * * * *

FUNDING SOCIAL EXPENDITURE

If the objective is quality education and quality health for all, then there is no alternative to proper funding of these services from tax revenue. There is extensive evidence that the National Health Service, far from being, as is sometimes alleged, an open-ended commitment on national resources, in fact provides a comparatively high standard of health care at relatively low cost.[8] The health of British babies and mothers, for example, stands reasonably well in comparison with other developed countries and better than some which spend a good deal more on health care. The United States spends over twice as much on health care per head of population as the United Kingdom; yet its state of health is not significantly better. It fails to provide adequate health care to some of the most needy people in US society, although it is arguably over-provided with hospitals and has levels of medical staffing and sophistication in medical equipment which far outreach those in the UK. Although expenditure per head of population tends to increase in line with GDP growth, the King's Fund Institute has estimated that *per capita* expenditure in the UK is nearly 30 per cent below the level that would be expected in terms of the UK's GDP.[9] This suggests both that the National Health Service is an effective means of controlling health costs and is also substantially underfunded. In short, judicious expenditure of public funds in key areas of health care, particularly in relation to the hospital and community services, is likely to be a good investment of taxpayer's money.

Under the Conservatives, expenditure on education generally has been tightly constrained; to the government's lasting disgrace the United Kingdom is also the only major Western European country which has cut resources going to higher education. However, in contrast to health care, British educational standards and opportunities are behind most of our main competitors. For example, research conducted by the National Institute for Economic and Social Research indicates that German school leavers reach a higher level of attainment in a broader range of subjects than do school leavers in Britain. They also achieve significantly higher standards in mathematics throughout the ability range.[10] As has been noted previously, authoritative studies for the Manpower Services Commission and the National Economic Development Office have shown that we are less well educated and less well trained than many of our main competitors. Only half of the workforce in this country hold recognized qualifications (equivalent to O levels or GCSE), compared with two thirds in West Germany and Japan and almost 80 per cent in the United States. Britain is also well down the league in providing education and training opportunities for the post-16 age group, and a much smaller proportion of the relevant age group has qualifications at degree level compared to the United States and Japan.

Yet the role of education is crucial. As Britain, like other advanced countries, moves towards a knowledge based economy, our future will increasingly depend on human capital

– on the intelligence and creativity of our people. In order to close the 'education gap' between the United Kingdom and our main competitors and to ensure opportunities for good quality education, we will need to invest extra public funds in education, particularly to raise standards at school and to expand higher and further education and training.

It may be desirable to increase funding in health and education, but the question remains 'Is it affordable?'. Joel Barnett, Chief Secretary to the Treasury in the 1970s, has warned the Labour party against increases in public spending unmatched by growth. He wrote that the last Labour government 'planned far too high a level of public expenditure in the expectations of levels of growth that, in the event, never materialised'.[11] On occasions, as with the Japanese budgets of 1987 and 1988 (see Chapter 7), there will be a strong case for counter-cyclical public spending to bring the level of demand up to productive potential. But, in the medium term, Joel Barnett's advice is sound. If public spending grows faster than national output, the economy becomes out of balance. Either levels of taxation have to be raised or public borrowing has to be increased. There is also a danger of the 'crowding out' of private investment. As a general rule, public spending should rise only in line with growth in output.

However, if there are strong arguments against public spending increases above the growth in output, the Conservative strategy of continuing to keep increases in public spending below the growth rate as a matter of principle is also misconceived. Already the share of public spending as a proportion of GDP is lower in the United Kingdom than in many European countries.[12] The result is that vital public services, such as health and education, are being unnecessarily deprived of badly needed investment. As we have seen in Chapter 7, the productive potential of the British economy has increased so that it is now possible for the British economy to grow at the same pace as our rivals. It makes good sense to invest a substantial proportion of this growth (sufficient to maintain public spending's share of GDP) in vital public services. If an economy is running a balance of payments deficit, investing in public services (with their below average import content) can also be a more prudent economic option than tax cuts.

Thatcherites argue that the policy of reducing public spending as a proportion of GDP is necessary in order to make room for tax cuts. But has taxation been reduced for the majority since the Tories have been in power? While it is certainly true that income tax has been cut, for the majority the reduction has been more than wiped out by increases in national insurance, VAT and other taxes. Under Mrs Thatcher, it is only the rich who have received substantial tax reductions. For example, as a consequence of the reduction in the top rate from 60 to 40 per cent and other changes in the 1988 budget, the richest 280 000 taxpayers received tax cuts averaging £22 000 (a sum greater than the income of any taxpayer in the bottom 95 per cent of the income distribution).

I have already argued that those who have gained most from society ought to contribute most and that a fair tax system has to reflect ability to pay. This implies increases in top rates (already the lowest except for Switzerland), as well as taxes on capital gains and inherited wealth. But there is a strong case for investigating whether further reductions in the standard rate can be financed by the scaling down, if not the abolition, of the £10 billion going in personal tax allowances on pensions and mortgages. In this way, it may be possible to combine increases in public spending with substantial reductions in taxation for the majority.

*   *   *   *   *

RAISING STANDARDS

It is, of course, true that spending money does not by itself solve problems. There have to be mechanisms to ensure that the increased expenditure is effectively used. Many Conservatives believe that health and education would operate more efficiently if there was more competition or some form of internal market within the state system. But neither the education nor the health services can be easily adapted to market mechanisms.

In the early 1980s, the then Secretary of State for Education, Keith Joseph, though a noted market enthusiast, was eventually forced to admit that 'voucher' schemes (through which individuals would be able to buy education for their children) were impractical and that the Kent 'open enrolment' system (which allowed parents to choose any school for their children) had proved a chaotic failure. The 'opt out' provision of the 1988 Education Reform Act (which, as we have seen, allows schools to opt out of local authority control) is a much watered down version of their earlier plans to introduce market mechanisms into the education service.

The problem with all these market proposals is that they cannot guarantee that every child gets the chance of a good education. Indeed, so far from widening choice, they would effectively deprive many parents of the opportunity to send their children to a good school. Only a minority of children would get places in the 'popular' schools. The majority would have to go to the 'unpopular' schools which, trapped in a vicious circle of low esteem and poor morale, would have little encouragement to improve.

In health care, there are similar calls for 'health' vouchers, American-style health maintenance organizations (businesses to which individuals pay fees in order to subscribe to a package of health care) and for competition for services between health districts (a proposal put foward in the 1989 white paper). A NHS voucher scheme has been introduced for spectacles but this is a relatively straightforward market. A major problem with health care is the very large variation between different groups in their demand on the service. Another is that it is the doctor (a provider of services) as much as patient (as consumer) who makes demands for services.

The National Association of Health Authorities have rejected both health vouchers and health maintenance organizations as inappropriate.[13] It has, however, welcomed the proposal for a regional experiment in competition for services between districts, while expressing considerable concern about whether or not increased efficiency may be achieved at the cost of more unequal access. The Social Services Select Committee of the House of Commons, which has also recommended limited experiments with internal markets, commented: 'If the concept of the internal market is to be taken further, it will require to be very carefully planned, monitored and assessed to ensure that too high a price is not paid for its benefits. It should not be introduced nationally before a thorough piloting has been done'.[14] Unwisely, the goverment, in proposing a number of national schemes in its white paper, has ignored this advice.

However, if there are considerable problems with internal market schemes, there are overwhelming arguments for reforms in both the health and education services which improve efficiency and raise standards, including more effective management, rigorous quality control, and an enforceable system of consumer rights. The Labour party should strongly support such changes.

When I was Labour's Education spokesman, I argued that Socialists must make the 'standards' issue their own.[15] For many years, educational progressives have been reluctant to use the word 'standards' as part of their vocabulary. They have been rightly concerned to emphasize the need to widen access and opportunity through the ending of selective secondary education and the expansion of post-school education and they have been understandably wary about the association between standards and learning by rote, excessive emphasis on examination results and a narrowly 'academic' view of education achievement. But the consequence of this reluctance has been to allow 'standards' to become the watchword of the Right. Yet most parents rightly consider that 'raising standards' is the key to good education. It reflects their insistence that their children are taught in effective, well-ordered schools. It demonstrates their desire that their children's progress is monitored, assessed and acknowledged. Above all, it expresses their passionate concern that their children should develop, learn and achieve at school.

It was because I believed so firmly in the importance of raising standards that, on behalf of the Labour party, I warmly welcomed the introduction of the new 16+ exam, gave firm support to the appraisal of teachers, consistently advocated the establishment of a common national curriculum in secondary schools and backed increased parental representatives on school governing bodies. I also argued for a charter of parents' rights which would give all parents the opportunity to become involved in their children's education, would strengthen home–school links and would also assist in the improvement of educational standards.[16]

The Labour party has sensibly proposed a home–school contract which outlines rights and responsibility for both parents and school. Such contracts would cover information about the school and the child's progress, involvement in the child's learning process, open access to the school and teaching staff, a procedure for dealing with complaints and settling disputes and support for strengthening the link of the school with the local community.[17] Information rights would include a parents' prospectus, regular school reports, an annual statement of learning needs, and pupil profiles at 16. Parents ought to participate in home reading schemes and plan a key role in home work. They should have interviews with teachers regularly. They should have a named contact in the school, and be able to attend properly organized class–parents' evenings. Each local authority should set up an education ombudsman to deal with parents' complaints and draw up plans to strengthen links between schools and their local communities. Finally, parents would have the right to expect adequate resources for their children's education, including maximum class size, minimum spending levels on textbooks and equipment, and buildings maintained to standards deemed adequate by Her Majesty's Inspectorate. The argument for making such a contract enforceable in law is that it would act as a guarantee of parents' rights and as a spur to improved educational performance.

The 1988 Education Reform Act has devolved a considerable degree of financial accountability to school heads. As things stand, however, the educational benefits of this reform are at best ambiguous. What is badly needed is the development of procedures to measure the educational effectiveness of schools. The first requirement is accurate performance indicators. These will need to go beyond exam results and try to assess, by taking into account different economic and social backgrounds, the 'value added' by schools. With the help of such indicators, local educational authorities and governing bodies will be in a stronger position to call heads and their staff to account. The valuable work of Her Majesty's Inspectorate (HMI) in individual schools would also be reinforced and strengthened.

Given the wide degree of variation in provision, there is also a case for a contract between the Secretary of State and local education authorities on minimum standards, including class size, spending on books and equipment, and the state of buildings. The HMI should also be obliged to publish an annual report not just on levels of spending but also on the effectiveness of individual authorities. The Secretary of State should be empowered to follow up these reports by obliging local authorities to say publicly what they are doing to improve their performance.

Health service standards should be improved in three main ways – by strengthening patients' rights, by introducing mechanisms for improving managerial performance and by introducing a comprehensive system of inspection. In its evidence to the Prime Minister's inquiry on the health service, the National Association of Health Authorities (NAHA) have proposed a contract between patients and health district.[18] A health care contract would specify the level of service that could be expected and lay down the maximum periods which patients might have to wait for a treatment for a particular condition. In addition, doctors and hospital staff would be obliged to share information with patients and a more effective complaints procedure would be set up. The NAHA are attracted by suggestions that 'if a health service fails to deliver on such a contract, patients would themselves have the right to shop around for a specified treatment and expect their local authority to pick up the bill'. It warns of the costs of such a system, but it is hardly credible that the costs could outweigh the advantages to the patient. As with education, there is a strong case for such a contract being legally enforceable.

It is essential to improve the management of the health service. Gordon Best, Director of the King's Fund Institute, has argued that already the NHS has been transformed from 'a classic example of an administered public sector bureaucracy into one that increasingly is exhibiting the qualities that reflect positive, purposeful management'.[19] However, despite the progress, there is a long way to go. In an influential report, the Social Services Select Committee of the House of Commons has pointed to the lack of a clear statement of aims or corporate plan for the NHS, the inadequacy of information by which to judge the service's performance, and the overall failure to involve doctors in the management of resources.[20]

As with the education service, the first essential is to develop performance indicators which measure not only the efficiency of resource use (activity levels, costs, length of stay) but also its effectiveness (outcome of treatments). This in turn should make it more feasible to involve doctors, decentralise decision-making down to the health districts and reward good practice. Accountability would be provided by contracts between districts and regional authorities and by the overall framework of objectives set by a National Management Board (as proposed in the Social Services Select Committee report).

Finally, inspection procedures in the National Health service need to be dramatically improved. Astonishingly there is no comprehensive inspection procedure. There is a strong case for an inspection agency, similar to Her Majesty's Inspectorate of Schools, to monitor the performance of district health authorities and hospitals and to report to the National Management Board and the Secretary of State.

*   *   *   *   *

ATTACK ON POVERTY

As well as the delivery of high quality services, the other main function of the welfare state is to provide an adequate minimum income to ensure security at different stages of the life cycle such as in child rearing and old age; to cover contingencies such as unemployment, sickness and disability; to meet vital needs such as housing, and generally to protect people against poverty both in and out of work. In an increasingly prosperous Britain, poverty ought to be on the decline rather than on the increase. But, under Mrs Thatcher, the numbers of those with incomes on or below the official poverty level has gone up from six million to well over eight million. This situation should be totally unacceptable in a civilised and affluent society. A major attack on poverty must, therefore, be a top priority for a Labour government in the 1990s.

There are four main reasons for the increase in poverty which has occurred during Conservative rule; the growth in unemployment, low wages, increased housing costs and inadequate levels of benefit. Even though unemployment has started to fall, it will still be not much below 2 million by the time of the next election. Unemployment has not only reduced the living standards of the unemployed. It has also, in combination with loss of employment rights, depressed the wages of the low paid in work to their lowest recorded level relative to average pay. After the virtual elimination of subsidies on local authority housing expenditure, council rents have spiralled, while every household has had to pay more in rates to make good the dramatic cuts in rate support grant. Since 1979, social security rates have fallen by a seventh in relation to average earnings.

These varied causes of the rises in poverty suggest that a package of remedial policies will be required. As unemployment is the single most important factor in the growth of poverty, a major new initiative, including a combination of macro-economic, regional and labour market measures (as proposed in Chapter 7), will be required to bring more of the unemployed back into work. Reequipping the long-term unemployed with new skills is not only good for the economy: by assisting the unemployed to find jobs it could have a significant impact on the extent of poverty.

Low pay is the second major cause of poverty among those of working age. 750 000 families are forced to rely on means-tested benefits to top up low wages. In a number of other countries, statutory minimum legislation sets standards for decent wages. In the past, I have argued for the introduction of similar legislation in this country. However, in the conditions of the 1990s, it would be wrong to ignore the possible consequences for employment (and inflation as well). Initially, it may be wise to rely on reinforcing and extending wages councils, strengthening individual rights at work, expanding retraining, and increasing child benefits to help lift some of the low paid out of poverty.

With respect to housing costs, it is glaringly unjust that the wealthier home owners should continue to be subsidised through mortgage relief while, because of the cuts in housing subsidy and rate support grant, tenants have had to pay greatly increased rents and rates. A fairer and more balanced system of housing finance would help to reduce the burden on the poor.

It is obvious, however, that alongside improvements in employment, pay and housing, major reforms will also be needed in the social security system. The Beveridge report, based on the principle of 'social insurance', assumed that only a small minority would have to rely on means-tested supplementary benefits. Universal benefits, designed to cover the main contingencies and life-cycle stages (such as sickness, unemployment, child rearing, old age, etc.) would lift the vast majority out of poverty. But the universal benefits have never been set at a level deemed sufficient to cover the needs of all households. As a consequence, even under Labour governments, the so-called supplementary provisions have helped provide the normal means of support for millions.

At the same time, the insurance principle, which Beveridge held so dear, has been substantially undermined: 'National insurance contributions began as a payment related to one's own prospective benefits. They became a levy based on the current benefits to others. The level of national insurance contribution, like any other tax, is now set by the overall revenue needs of the government'.[21] In addition, because social insurance has proved an inflexible mechanism for dealing with changing social and economic conditions, a whole range of *ad hoc* benefits, financed by general taxation, have been introduced, including Family Income Supplement (now Family Credits), housing benefit, child benefit, one parent family supplement and disability benefit.

In the short term, a poverty relief programme which includes increases in the levels of social benefits, especially pensions and child benefits, will be necessary. One possible means of financing these increases might be through the reform and extension of national insurance, particularly on the higher paid. In the medium term, however, a more far reaching solution will be necessary.

The arguments for a closer integration of tax and social benefits, bringing together benefits and tax into a single framework for assessment and payment as part of the income tax system, are increasingly persuasive.[22] The most obvious advantage is administrative. The tax and benefits systems have become increasingly more like each other in the information which they require, in the ways which they use it and in the clientele with which they deal. It would be administratively more efficient to combine contingent and income-related information together. Secondly integration could provide a more effective means than the present system of targeting resources at those that need them. Significantly, the take up rates of the main means-tested benefits vary from 74 per cent in the case of supplementary benefit (now income support), 70 per cent for housing benefit, and scarcely 50 per cent for Family Income Supplement (now Family Credits). The proponents of integration argue that the practical and psychological disadvantages of means testing will largely disappear because the new integrated system will be able to make use of information which is, or could be, collected through the tax system. Under integration, it is claimed, targeting will be both more effective, more flexible and more humane. Thirdly – and perhaps most important of all – by providing an effective and reasonable minimum increase to those in need, it could make a major impact on poverty.

However, there are counter-arguments which have to be taken into account.[23] The first is that it would increase means testing. But this would be the case only if means testing was extended beyond existing means-tested benefits (income support, housing benefit and family credits). It would be quite possible to confine the new minimum benefit to those entitled to existing means-tested benefits, while keeping universal contingency benefits such as pensions and child benefit (though the latter could effectively be related to means through the tax system). Another argument is that, because benefits are rapidly cut back when recipients improve their positions, integration would sustain rather than reduce the poverty or unemployment traps. This may be a valid point, but it assumes that those in poverty prefer to remain dependent on state benefits. It has also been suggested that a system of social security which so obviously benefited the poor might not have the support of the better off. The trouble is, however, that the better off have never been prepared to pay the level of taxes to sustain universal benefits at a high enough level to lift all households out of poverty. The last counter-argument is perhaps the most powerful of all. The critics point to the undoubted administrative difficulties and to the fact that no other country has yet achieved an effective integration between tax and social security systems.

As this fierce debate on the merits of integration demonstrates, there is clearly a profound disagreement on methods between experts who agree on the objective of tackling poverty. In these circumstances, a Labour government should establish a fundamental review of the effectiveness of the British social security system and of proposals for reform. The Conservative government's inquiry was scrappy, *ad hoc* and piecemeal, concerned above all to control costs, and glaringly failed to provide long-term solutions. There should be an authoritative and wide ranging Royal Commission whose recommendations, particularly on the integration of tax and benefits, could provide the basis for a new consensus on the reform of social security and for an effective attack on poverty.

*   *   *   *   *

SUMMARY

The case for a strong welfare state will be as powerful in the 1990s as in the past. Investment of the fruits of growth in vital public services such as health and education will be both necessary and affordable. But services must be run in the interests of the consumer and injections of public resources must result in an improvement in quality. In this context, market solutions have, at the most, only a limited application. Hence the argument for legally enforceable rights for parents and patients, for more efficient and accountable management, and a stronger system of inspection. There will also need to be a major attack on poverty, through a package of remedial measures, including action on employment, pay and housing, as well as increased social benefits. In the longer term, the integration of tax and benefits should be seriously considered. An effective and modern welfare system must reflect changing needs and conditions.

10 The Democratic Agenda

Under Mrs Thatcher, British democracy may not yet be in mortal danger but is beginning to look distinctly frayed at the edges. Rights have been diminished; independent bodies, such as local government, the trade unions and the BBC, have been under persistent attack; and the government has not only become intolerant of criticism and insensitive to vital democratic conventions but behaves in an increasingly authoritarian and centralising manner. The Labour party has been presented with both an opportunity and responsibility to set out a new democratic agenda. At the next election, it must put forward a comprehensive programme of reforms which will protect and extend individual rights, increase accountability, strengthen parliamentary institutions and decentralise power.

* * * * *

THE AUTHORITARIAN TENDENCY

Rhetorically, Mrs Thatcher has assumed the role of the champion of freedom and democracy, especially on trips to Eastern European countries. But an examination of the Conservative record on democracy reveals that her grandiose pretensions cannot be sustained. As we have seen, Thatcherites argue that the introduction of the council tenants' 'right to buy', the increased rights of trade union members in voting on industrial disputes and in leadership elections and the establishment of employee rights to shares in privatized industries amount to a major extension of freedom. But, in a number of crucial areas, the Conservative government has shown a lack of respect for individual rights. It has increased the powers of the police over the citizen (for example, by introducing new powers of 'stop and search') and narrowed the rights of accused persons (by curtailing the right to silence and by removing the unconditional right to challenge juries). Most glaring of all has been the government's attempt, in the name of national security, to limit freedom of speech. It imposed a three line whip on a Conservative backbencher's Bill to reform the almost universally condemned Section 2 of the Official Secrets Act and introduced restricting and unsatisfactory legislation of its own. It used Section 2 to prosecute Sarah Tisdall and Clive Ponting for leaking 'official secrets'. Over the '*Spycatcher* affair' and other issues, it tried to persuade the courts to curtail press freedom. Significantly, there have been 17 judgements against the UK in the European Court of Human Rights since the Conservatives came to power – more than for any other county.[1]

One of the most disturbing aspects of Mrs Thatcher's rule has been the way in which the government has acted against independent sources of power. It abolished the Greater London Council, the Inner London Education Authority, and the Metropolitan County Councils, all Labour controlled. It restricted the power of local authorities through curbs on spending and by rate capping and by attempting to reduce the role and responsibility of local government – particularly over housing and education. The introduction of the poll tax and the uniform business rate will further increase central control. Labour legislation severely curtailed trade union freedom of action, while in 1984 the government banned union membership at the Government Communication Headquarters (GCHQ).

The Conservatives have also put pressure on the broadcasting authorities to an extent which under previous governments would have been considered unacceptable. In 1985, the Home Secretary, Leon Brittan, succeeded in getting the transmission of a BBC programme on the IRA delayed. In October 1986, the Chairman of the Tory party, Norman Tebbit, fiercely attacked the BBC for alleged bias over television coverage of the US bombing of Libya in April 1986. In January 1987, the Director General of the BBC, Alisdair Milne, was forced to resign – in part, it was alleged, because of the BBC's rows with the Conservative party. In the same month, the Special Branch police officers raided BBC offices in Scotland, after the government had obtained an injunction over a planned programme on the Ministry of Defence's 'Zircon' spy satellite project. In June 1988, the government attempted to stop an ITV programme on he shooting of IRA gunmen by British agents in Gibraltar. In

October 1988, the Home Secretary, Douglas Hurd, banned appearances on the broadcasting media by representatives of proscribed paramilitary organizations in Northern Ireland and their political wings (including elected councillors and MPs).

The government has also been in conflict with the Church of England, some of whose senior figures have questioned the morality behind government policy. In February 1988 the Home Secretary, Douglas Hurd, went so far as to advise the Church to confine its comments to private ethics and keep off social questions. Even Prince Charles, who has expressed commendably progressive views on issues such as housing and the inner cities, has been roundly criticized by prominent Conservatives like Norman Tebbit.

A key feature of a healthy democracy is the respect with which a government treats its political opponents. The former Conservative Prime Minister, Harold Macmillan, for example, always recognized the legitimacy of the Labour party and its ideas and values, even though he disagreed with them. He even appointed leading Labour figures as chairman of the National Coal Board and as High Commissioner to Kenya. In contrast to most of her Conservative predecessors, Mrs Thatcher does not trouble to conceal her contempt for the Labour party. Her conviction of her own rectitude, her disregard for the views of those that disagree with her (including critics within her own party) and her messianic mission to kill off Socialism[2] have combined to induce a dangerous and unhealthy frame of mind in which the very function of opposition is called into question. Indeed, the Prime Minister's intolerance of criticism sometimes smacks more of an unreformed East European regime than of a democratic West European government.

* * * * *

LABOUR AND DEMOCRACY

With individual rights, independent centres of power and democratic conventions all under pressure from an increasingly authoritarian government, Labour has a duty to give a higher priority to democracy than in recent years. In the past, the Labour party has made a major contribution to British democra tic institutions. The rise of Labour gave working people for the first time their own voice in parliament. In 1940, the Labour party agreed to join a coalition under Winston Churchill for the duration of the war expressly to defend British democracy against Hitler. After the war, the 1945 Labour government created the basis for a more cohesive democratic life by introducing the National Health Service and by establishing a comprehensive system of social security. The Wilson administrations of the 1960s and 1970s set up the parliamentary ombudsman and extended rights, particularly those relating to sexual and racial discrimination.

But, in opposition, Labour's commitment to democratic advance has lost momentum. Indeed, the party has sometimes seemed strangely uncertain about its position on democracy. In the early 1980s, Mrs Thatcher's authoritarian disrespect for previously accepted democratic norms provoked a counter-reaction from some Labour activists. In Liverpool and London, the rhetoric, if not always the practice, of the new wave of leftist councillors was to reject so-called 'Tory' laws and to argue for extra-parliamentary action. The hostility to parliamentary orthodoxies and to the rule of law expressed by many party activists was met with a defensive response by Labour's parliamentary leadership. At a time when Labour's commitment to parliamentary democracy was being questioned, especially by its political opponents, it was not considered opportune to prepare a new democratic programme.

There was also a tacit agreement that democratic reform was often more trouble than it was worth. The centralist tradition in the Labour party had always emphasized state ownership and central government initiative to promote greater equality and efficiency. Extensions of democracy and decentralization could, it was felt, hold up Labour's industrial and social programmes. Pragmatists could point to the unhappy experience of the Callaghan government over the long drawn out and fiercely disputed devolution legislation in the 1970s which ultimately brought the Labour administration down.

Underlying these considerations was the 'gut' feeling that perhaps democratic reform was not really Labour's issue. In part, this relative indifference was a product of history. In contrast to the experience of many continental Socialist parties, Labour inherited a largely complete parliamentary system. The principle of universal suffrage had already been won and the main contours of the parliamentary system had emerged before the advent of Labour as a serious political force. In recent years, it has been the Liberal party which has tended to make the running on the constitutional issues, such as support for electoral reform and a Bill of Rights. Labour has dismissed the first proposal as third party special pleading, and the second as a 'sell out' to the judges. Neither has been properly considered on its merits.

Yet it has long been recognized by Socialists that democracy and Socialism must go hand in hand. In 1899, the great German revisionist, Eduard Bernstein, wrote: 'Democracy is at the same times means and ends. It is the means for the struggle for Socialism and it is the form Socialism will take once it has been realized'.[3] He strongly emphasized the educative role of democracy: 'The right to vote in a democracy makes its members virtual partners in the community and this virtual partnership must in the end lead to real partnership'.[4] He also underlined the importance of rights: 'The idea of democracy includes . . . a notion of justice – an equality of rights for all members of the community, and in that principle the rule of the majority, to which in every concrete case the rule of the people extends, finds its limits'.[5]

Bernstein's agenda is astonishingly relevant today; the emphasis on the extension of rights, the need for checks on arbitrary rule and for democratic accountability, the necessity for the constitutional and peaceful change of government, the case for the dispersal and decentralization of power, the argument for citizen participation and the insistence on the overriding importance of democracy. Socialists have to be democrats above all, concerned to defend and extend individual rights, to protect and strengthen democratic institutions and to disperse and decentralize power.

Labour should start by itself setting a good example. I have already argued that the present electoral college system for electing the leader and deputy leader ought to be replaced by 'one member, one vote'.[6] The principle of one member, one vote ought also to be extended to the selection and reselection of members of parliament and parliamentary candidates (in place of the cumbersome 'mixed' electoral college introduced at the 1987 conference) and to the choosing of conference delegates

Labour must become a genuinely democratic party, based on individual members.

There is also a strong case for involving party members more directly in the development of policy. The Labour party could well heed the example of the Swedish Social Democratic party (SAP) in the way in which it consults its members on policy statements and new party programmes as a matter of course. Each member is given a booklet that explains an issue and sets out policy options. These are then discussed at local party meetings. This consultative process ensures not only that party members come to grips with issues but also that policies are carefully thought through before being finally adopted at the three year party congresses. The words of Bo Toresson, General Secretary of SAP, have relevance for the British Labour party: 'Our party must serve as a model for the society we wish to create'.[7] The consultation of local parties as part of Labour's policy review is a promising sign for the future.

Labour's behaviour in local government should also be above reproach. Labour councils and councillors should abide by the rules; there should be no procedural 'short cuts'; and democratic conventions should be respected. Jeremy Beecham, leader of Newcastle City Council, has stressed that councillors are elected to represent the whole community: 'The politics of gesture, bluff and illegality have done much damage over the years and the shift of power from elected representatives publicly accountable to their communities to local government committees and district and country parties have in some places accelerated this trend ... There is, and ought always to be, an obligation on elected representatives to consult with local parties. But to subordinate them to local parties ... is not healthy, especially when the whole basis of Labour's campaign is to stress the need for independent, accountable, democratic government'.[8] Undemocratic behaviour at local level is not only wrong in principle. It is also a certain vote loser.

What is more, it undermines Labour's credibility as a party seeking to introduce democratic reform at national level. For Labour must go into the next election, committed to a comprehensive programme of democratic change which will extend rights, strengthen democratic institutions and, where appropriate, decentralize and devolve power.

*   *   *   *   *

A BILL OF RIGHTS

The first priority should be to safeguard and expand individual rights. The crucial question here is whether, despite the party's scepticism, Labour should now back the idea of a Bill of Rights. I am convinced that there is a powerful case for such a Bill. The key argument for a Bill of Rights is that it gives the individual the capacity to challenge government action in the courts under a number of basic tests of principle.[9] It can therefore provide both a remedy for grievance and a protection for minorities. As such, it represents a transfer of power to the citizen and a restraint on the misuse and abuse of power by government.

According to the conventional wisdom, the combination of the rule of law, parliamentary sovereignty and ministerial responsibility provides a more effective guarantee of individual rights than would a Bill of Rights. Dicey's famous dictum that, although the Habeas Corpus Acts 'declare no principle and define no rights, they are for practical purposes worth a hundred constitutional articles guaranteeing individual liberty'[10] sums up the traditional case. It is certainly true that, if judicial decisions and statutes in the areas which are covered by Bills of Rights were collected and codified, it would be found that Britain already has in embryo a system for the protection of human rights. But our legal framework has crucial disadvantages. Our common law is more a system of remedies than of positive rights. It is also restricted by precedent, statute and statutory instrument. So it lacks the capacity for growth that is inherent in general statements of principle.[11] Statutory law suffers from the defect that it does not necessarily cover all the fundamental rights; in any case, given the doctrine of parliamentary sovereignty, laws can be changed.

For, according to British constitutional theory, parliament has the right to make and remake law. There are no legal rights which are fundamental in the sense that they enjoy special constitutional protection or have a higher status than other legislation. In this sense, safeguards against the abuse of power rest not on law but on conventions and understandings. There is therefore, nothing to stop a government with a majority in parliament legislating to remove basic human rights. For Labour supporters, the lesson of the Thatcher years must surely be that the doctrine of parliamentary sovereignty is an incomplete mechanism for safeguarding rights.

Ministerial responsibility, in the sense of being accountable to Members for grievances, also provides an inadequate protection. Members of parliament have a number of weapons at their disposal – letters, parliamentary questions, adjournment debates, select committee investigations and so on. But Ministers, backed by a majority in the Commons, are normally in a strong position to resist scrutiny. In any case, the business of a government department is often so extensive that key decisions are taken by civil servants who, according to constitutional theory, are not accountable to parliament. The government's plan to devolve much government business by setting up a whole host of agencies, able to operate with a considerable degree of independence, is likely to weaken ministerial accountability even further.[12]

It was the weakness of parliament as a means of redressing grievances that persuaded the Wilson government to set up in 1967 a Parliamentary Commissioner or Ombudsman to investigate complaints of maladministration referred by MPs. In 1973 the powers of the Commissioner were extended to the Health Service while, in 1974, Commissioners for Local Government were also established. The Parliamentary and Local Government Commissioners have certainly justified their existence. But a crucial limitation of the institution of Ombudsman is that it cannot enforce recommendations nor bring legal proceedings. And it can cover only maladministration. It cannot deal with unreasonable, unjust or oppressive acts – very much the territory of the Bill of Rights.

Britain is now one of only three democratic countries (the others are Israel and New Zealand) without a Bill of Rights. One authority has pointed out that 'what passes for wisdom in the United Kingdom is an ever more isolated view among the modern democracies . . . and it has become a barely tenable position for the United Kingdom to maintain as a full party to the European Convention on Human Rights and as a member of the European Community'.[13] Ironically, Britain played a major role in drafting the European Convention and was the first state to ratify it. British governments then proceeded to export the rights and freedoms of that Convention to twenty five newly independent Commonwealth countries, while continuing to resist the introduction of a Bill of Rights in this country.

The European Convention on Human Rights, which came into force in September 1953, covers such 'classical' freedoms as protection against torture or 'inhuman or degrading treatment or punishment' (Article 3) and against slavery or forced labour (Article 4); the right to liberty and security of person (Article 5) and to a fair trial (Article 6); and freedom of 'thought, conscience and religion', of expression and information and of peaceful assembly and association (Articles 9–11). Other rights include the right to life (Article 1) and the right to respect for private and family life (Article 8). The scope of the Convention has been increased by the addition of protocols which protect property ('except in the public interest'), ensure the right to education and provide for free elections and liberty of movement.

Significantly there have been 21 judgements (including 17 since the Conservatives came to power) against the United Kingdom in the European Court of Human Rights, the largest number for any signatory nation. It has been rightly said that the list of British cases is 'long, controversial and far reaching'.[14] It includes the inhuman treatment of suspected terrorists in Northern Ireland; inadequate safeguards of personal privacy against telephone tapping by the police; unfair discrimination against the British wives of foreign husbands under the Immigration Rules; inhuman prison conditions in cases of solitary confinement and segregation; unjust restrictions upon prisoners' correspondence and visits; judicial birching in the Isle of Man; corporal punishment in Scottish schools; criminal sanctions against private homosexual conduct in Northern Ireland; ineffective judicial protection for detained mental patients and would-be immigrants; inadequate safeguards for parents refused access to children in care; the dismissal of workers because of the arbitrary operation of the closed shop; the nationalization of aircraft and shipbuilding companies without adequate compensation; the denial of equal citizenship rights to British passport holders from East Africa; and interference with free expression by the Law Lords in extending the common law offence of contempt of court. The reasons for Britain's relatively poor record on human rights must surely be the inadequacy of our existing system and the failure by successive governments to incorporate the provisions of the Convention into United Kingdom domestic law.

The case for incorporating the European Convention into United Kingdom law is that it would become in effect a national Bill of Rights whose articles and protocols have already been internationally ratified by this country. Hopefully, incorporation would make a major contribution to the protection of human rights – 'a rallying point in the state for all who care deeply for the ideals of freedom'.[15] In its 1978 report, the House of Lords Select Committee concluded that the European Convention 'seems likely to have far more practical effect on legislators, administrators, the executive, citizens as well as legislators, if it ceases to become an international treaty obligation and becomes an integral party of the United Kingdom law'.[16]

Incorporation does not imply entrenchment. Because of the constitutional convention that our parliament cannot bind its successors, it would always be possible for parliament to amend or even repeal a Bill of Rights. But it would be desirable for the Bill of Rights to contain a clause which required any amending or repealing legislation to state so expressly. This would give a Bill of Rights statute a higher status than ordinary legislation and, therefore, make it more difficult to change, though it would not prevent the explicit will of parliament from prevailing in the end.

The critics' main concern is that a Bill of Rights would give too much power to judges. They believe that our judges are likely to be biased against minorities and governments of the left and are too executive or establishment-minded to be entrusted with a Bill of Rights.

But judges do not exercise excessive powers in other advanced democratic countries like France, Germany, India, Canada and the United States (all with Bills of Rights). What happens in those countries is that important public problems are shared more widely across the three branches of government – executive, legislature and judiciary. In Britain the judiciary is increasingly becoming involved in solving those problems because litigants are increasingly seeking administrative justice from the courts rather than from parliament or the executive. However, in the absence of a modern code of principles of good administration (enforceable by law) and in the absence of a Bill of Rights, the courts have to decide questions involving competing public interests, without the benefit of any statutory framework. It is this confused situation which, arguably, gives more power to judges than they should enjoy and it certainly creates great uncertainty.

Clearly, the track record of the British judiciary, particularly on industrial relations issues, leaves something to be desired. It is also obvious that, if judges consistently take a biased or restricted view, they will make a Bill of Rights ineffective. But the critics may be taking too pessimistic a view. The judges have already shown themselves skilled at interpreting European community law in regard to equal pay and sex discrimination: 'Those sceptics who doubt the ability of British judges to protect the fundamental rights of the Convention should consider their impressive record in translating the fundamental rights of community law into practical reality'.[17] This encouraging evidence of judicial integrity not only suggests that a Bill of Rights could act as an educative force on legislators and administrators but could also become a means of educating the judges to the values implicit in a more 'civil liberties' orientated approach to the law, to the benefit of the whole community. In any case, citizens will still be able to appeal to Strasbourg. There will, therefore, be a safeguard of last resort against poor legal decisions. This is not to argue that by itself a Bill of Rights will provide a solution to all issues of individual rights. It will clearly need to be supplemented and fleshed out in a number of crucial areas, especially freedom of information and administrative law.

It is widely accepted that the operations of British government and administration are excessively secretive. One authority has commented that the British government's monopoly over official information 'makes the doctrine of ministerial responsibility difficult to operate, and undermines the effectiveness of public participation in decision-making'.[18] There is now an overwhelming case for Britain to emulate Sweden, the United States, Canada, Australia, New Zealand, Austria, Netherlands, Norway, Denmark and France and introduce freedom of information legislation.

A Freedom of Information Act would create legally enforceable rights of public access to all official information, with the exception of specifically exempt categories. In those countries already operating freedom of information legislation, the exempt categories cover defence and national security, the detection and prevention of crime and the protection of third parties from breach of confidence. In other words, contrary to conventional orthodoxy, it has proved quite possible to secure government's legitimate interests, while at the same time opening up its activities to public scrutiny.

It would also be easier for citizens to hold government departments to account if there was a proper system of administrative justice. Over the last fifty years, a considerable number of administrative tribunals have been set up, separate from the courts, to decide on disputes between individuals and the administration. But their constitutions, their manner of appointment and procedures, including the right of appeal, have varied widely. It has been suggested that there is now a strong case for a more uniform set of rules for administrative justice, including the promulgation of a statutory administrative code, enforceable by judicial review.[19] This code could require that reasons should be given for administrative decisions; stipulate that such decisions must be taken within a reasonable period; and proscribe the taking of decisions with retrospective effect.

It is also essential to ensure that citizens are in a position to secure justice. Under the Conservatives, legal aid has already been dangerously cut back and, compared with 1979, nearly 30 per cent fewer people are entitled to legal aid. In a number of crucial areas (such as industrial, immigration and social security tribunals) there is either inadequate or virtually no representation at all. If the Bill of Rights and a reformed system of administrative justice is to operate effectively, then there will have to be a major extension of legal aid.

*   *   *   *   *

RECONSIDERING PR

A fair electoral system is essential to the effective working of a healthy democracy. Since it became one of the governing parties, Labour has always supported the existing 'first past the post' arrangements and opposed proportional representation (PR). In my view, Labour should now reconsider its position on PR.

In the past, the arguments against the introduction of PR have always seemed decisive. Throughout the 1950s and 1960s, the British 'first past the post' electoral system was effective enough in translating votes into seats. It ranged from a difference between the two main parties' share of the votes and their share of seats of 11 per cent in 1964 to a mere 1 per cent in 1951; the average gap was only 6 per cent. In addition, the 'first past the post' system ensured governments with stable parliamentary majorities *and* a regular change of government.

It is only in the 1970s and 1980s, with the growth of a 'third' party, that the case for PR has become more compelling. In the five elections of the 1970s and 1980s, the average gap between the two largest parties' share of votes and share of seats was 19 per cent.

In 1983, the gap rose to a staggering 23 per cent. The other side of the coin has been the glaring disparity between the share of votes won by the third party and its seats in parliament. In 1983, the Alliance won 25 per cent of the vote and only 4 per cent of the seats: in 1987, it won 23 per cent of the vote and under 4 per cent of the seats. In 1983, the Alliance returned 23 MPs. Had their strength in parliament been proportional to their vote, they would have been entitled to 164 MPs. In 1987, when the Alliance returned only 22 MPs, they would have been entitled to 147 MPs.

In the south of England, the Labour party is very much in the same position as the centre parties nationally. Like the Alliance voters in 1983 and 1987, Labour's southern voters return very few MPs. Yet, under a PR system, the unlikely shires of Dorset, Devon, Somerset and Wiltshire would have elected at least one Labour MP, between two and four in Avon and two in Gloucestershire.[20] It seems clear that, over the last five elections at least, the 'first past the post' system has become disturbingly ineffective at translating votes into seats.

The existing electoral system has been better at ensuring that governments have stable majorities. Mrs Thatcher's three administrations have all been elected with big parliamentary majorities. However, the Conservatives' parliamentary dominance has greatly exceeded their electoral performance. As has already been noted, despite Mrs Thatcher's triumphalism, the Conservative share of the vote in 1979, 1983 and 1987 was only marginally greater than their share in 1966, when Edward Heath was so decisively defeated by Harold Wilson. But in the 1970s and 1980s, the combination of a divided opposition and a 'first past the post' electoral system gave the Tories massive election victories. Under PR, the Conservatives would either have had to share power or, more probably, would have been in opposition.

In today's political conditions, the 'first past the post' political system makes Conservative governments more likely. A leading political commentator has pointed out that 'Labour has been too weak to defeat the Tories on its own, while the electoral system has prevented the combined non-Conservative parties from constructing an anti-Thatcher majority in parliament'.[21] Furthermore, because of the increased geographical concentration of votes, it has become harder to translate a swing in votes into a gain of seats. Whereas in the 1950s and 1960s a 1 per cent swing in votes led to 18 seats changing hands, in the 1970s and 1980s a 1 per cent swing led to only 10 seats changing hands. The 'first past the post' system suited the 1950s and 1960s when there were two large roughly equally balanced parties slogging it out. It has been less than adequate in the 1970s and 1980s when a divided opposition has ensured Conservative dominance.

The most powerful argument against PR is that it would put a disproportionate amount of power in the hands of the third party. Under PR, coalitions would be the normal mode of government (though, as in Sweden, parties can still win overall majorities); and, like the FDP in West Germany, the smaller third party would, by changing coalition partners, be able to make or unmake governments. There is clearly some force in the contention that third parties would be in a pivotal position. However, third parties cannot afford to ignore public opinion; otherwise, they pay an electoral penalty. So critics of PR may exaggerate the room for manoeuvre which pivotal parties enjoy.

After considering the arguments for and against, my conclusion is that, in the conditions which are likely to prevail in the 1990s, PR would not only provide a fairer electoral system but would also be likely to work in Labour's favour. I accept, however, that the issue of PR is exceptionally difficult for the Labour party to decide now. On the one hand, because of the combination of the electoral system and the split in the opposition vote, the Tories have won the last three elections and are in a strong position to win the elections of the 1990s. On the other hand, a decisive shift in political fortune might still enable Labour to gain power by itself winning enough seats to enjoy the fruits of 'first past the post'. A decision to back PR now would be considered as a tacit acceptance by Labour that it no longer believes that, in the near future, it is likely to win power on its own. It would, in effect, be saying to the world that it can gain power only by sharing it.

Such a dramatic admission of relative weakness is unlikely to occur and certainly should not be expected before the next election. It would, however, be foolish for the party to continue to refuse to discuss the electoral system. The truth is that, whether it likes it or not, PR is now on the political agenda. Sooner rather than later, Labour is going to have to come to terms with it and decide which system of PR is likely to suit its interests. The Labour party would certainly be well-advised to start thinking about PR now rather than be suddenly confronted with the issue as a result of a 'hung' parliament in the 1990s.

*   *   *   *   *

PARLIAMENTARY REFORM

There is also a strong case for parliamentary reforms. It is, of course, entirely unrealistic to expect parliament to play the part which it used to play in the nineteenth century before the growth of party and the increase in the power of government. The British parliament can never be as strong as in a system in which, like the United States, there is a separation of powers and the legislature has a key initiating role. Governments with large majorities can almost always dominate the House of Commons. This dominance is even more assured when the opposition is divided, as in the 1983 and 1987 parliaments. But a healthy democracy needs a more effective parliament than we have at present.

The two most promising reforms in recent years have been the decision (taken in 1988) to televise the House of Commons and the setting up (in 1979) of departmental select committees. It is too early to predict with any confidence the impact of TV on the House of Commons. However, its supporters believe (rightly in my view) that televising the proceedings of the Commons will strengthen its position as 'the forum of the nation', as the vital link of communication between the executive and the electors, and as the main cockpit of the party battle. In so doing, it would bring much needed life back to the Chamber which, after question time and statements and perhaps the two main introductory speeches to a debate, often becomes a desolate and deserted place.

The system of departmental committees was established, following the report of the 1977–8 Select Committee[22] (of which I was a member), by the newly elected Conservative government in 1979. Opening the debate on procedure the then leader of the House, Norman St John Stevas, said that this change was 'the most important parliamentary reform of the century', intended to 'redress the balance of power to enable the House of Commons to do more effectively the job it has been elected to do'.[23]

This extravagant claim has not been fulfilled. Indeed, it could never have been fulfilled, given the existing constitutional framework of collective and individual ministerial responsibility and a government backed by a large and disciplined party majority in parliament. But, over the last decade, the departmental select committees, despite varying performance, have firmly established themselves. Their activities are reported frequently in the 'quality' press and on radio and TV. Backbenchers are eager to serve on them. Most important of all, Ministers and civil servants are now expected on a regular basis to justify themselves and the work and policies of their departments in response to detailed and often sustained questioning by committee members. A balanced assessment of the record of departmental committees is that they are now 'widely accepted as a legitimate and valued extension of the armoury of back bench scrutiny'.[24]

There is, therefore, a powerful case for strengthening the role of these investigatory committees. First, a departmental select committee ought to have full powers 'to send for persons, papers and records'. As was shown over the invasion of Cyprus and the Chrysler crisis in the 1970s and the Westland affair in the 1980s, the government can still resist a committee's demands. Their power should be unconditional and should incorporate the right to question civil servants, including the chief executives of the new agencies which are being set up to devolve government business. Secondly, as the Procedure Committee proposed, at least eight days should be set aside for debating Committee reports on the floor of the House and governments should be forced to reply promptly to reports.

Committee hearings are already broadcast on radio. They should also be frequently televised. As the experience of the United States demonstrates, Committee hearings, with their investigative format, lend themselves exceptionally well to television. There is also a case for an extra research allowance for select committee members and, as the Procedure Committee proposed, for paying Departmental and main Select Committee Chairmen 'a modest additional salary'. This would serve both to underline the prestige of investigatory committees and encourage able MPs to look on membership of these committees as an alternative career path to that of government Minister.

If parliament now has a potentially powerful means of checking the executive in the developing system of investigatory committees, the way forward in improving the scrutiny of legislation is less clear. Although standing committees conscientiously examine Bills clause by clause and line by line, in practice the Committee Stage usually reflects the party battle on the floor of the House. The consequence is that, unless there is a rebellion by government backbenchers, there are unlikely to be major amendments, even if there are obvious flaws in the legislation.

Paradoxically, it is the unelected (and, in many ways, archaic) House of Lords which has in recent years taken on the role of revising legislation. I used to favour abolition of the House of Lords. But, until the House of Commons can devise a means of improving its own scrutiny of legislation, it would be unwise to do away with a second chamber altogether. Reform, however, will be required. If, as I propose below, the United Kingdom develops, over the next decade, a system of regional assemblies, the House of Lords could become a chamber which combines regional representation with notables drawn from major organizations and pressure groups. In the meantime, the voting power of hereditary peers should be removed. It is entirely anachronistic that, as over the government's poll tax legislation, they should influence national decisions.

*　　*　　*　　*　　*

THE DEVOLUTION OF POWER AND A WRITTEN CONSTITUTION

As well as the reform of parliament, power should be dispersed and devolved downwards. The insistence on a pluralistic, decentralized approach which sees the role of the state not as a centralizing force but as an enabling instrument should be at the core of Labour's plan for democracy. Even before Mrs Thatcher came to power, Britain was a remarkably centralized country. Since 1945, local government had lost responsibility for hospitals, gas, electricity, trunk roads, water and sewerage. In England and Wales, there was no regional tier of any sort; in Scotland, though there was considerable administrative devolution, there was no democratic control. Northern Ireland had been under direct rule from the centre since 1974. The failure in the 1970s of attempts by Labour governments to introduce devolution in Scotland and Wales was yet another victory for the centralizing tradition in British politics.

Since 1979, Mrs Thatcher's sustained attack on local government has further weakened local democracy and strengthened central government. As noted earlier, the Conservative government has undermined the power of local authorities by restricting their ability to raise and spend money and by attempting to reduce the services which they provide. It has abolished the local authorities which most fiercely opposed the government. The Conservative government has also resolutely opposed the idea of devolution in Scotland or Wales or of regional assemblies in England. Yet, there are still overwhelming arguments for a strong system of local government, for elected assemblies in Scotland and Wales and for regional government in England.

Local government is essential to a flourishing democracy mainly because it is local. In contrast to central government, it can respond to local needs and issues. It can involve local people in decision-making. It can test out at local level different ways of solving problems and delivering services. It can serve as a check on an over-mighty central government. However, in the changing conditions of the 1990s, it will not be enough for a Labour government merely to restore local government to the pre-1979 position. Two Fabian authors have convincingly argued that local authorities have, in most cases, become agencies for the administration of a nationally determined pattern of services, often unresponsive to local needs, and that what is now required is a wider conception of the function of local authorities.[25] A local authority should play a strategic role, expressing the concern of the community with the needs and problems facing its area. The provision of responsive services would be one way of meeting those needs, but the local authority would also be an enabling authority working with other agencies and organizations. It would also be more accountable to the community.

It follows from this analysis of the role of local government that the key question is not so much about structure or even about finance, important though these are, but about giving British local authorities, as in most other countries in Western Europe, wider powers of competence. The draft European Charter for Local Self-Government, which the Conservative government has refused to sign, states: 'Local authorities shall within the limits of the law have full discretion to exercise their initiative with regard to any matter which is not excluded from their competence nor assigned to any other authority'. Giving these authorities such a general competence would enable them to assume a strategic role in the community and develop structures and procedures to sustain that role.

At the same time, local authorities will need to become both more responsive and more accountable to their communities. As with health and education, the accent must be on the delivery of a high standard of service to the public, on efficient management and on quality control. In the development of greater account-ability, an important issue is the domination of too many areas by one party. David Blunkett and Keith Jackson have pointed out: 'Long-guaranteed party majorities – whether of the Right or Left – have often led to the emergence of party cliques or bosses who take little account of the needs of the community'.[26] There is, therefore, a case for the introduction of proportional represen-tation at local level to provide a broader form of representation.

It will also be necessary to secure an adequate basis of finance. The Labour party is right to insist on the abolition of the grossly unfair Conservative poll tax which is to a great extent unrelated to ability to pay. Labour's proposal for a broader system of local taxation, based on a tax on domestic property (assessed by capital valuation) and supplemented by a local income tax, has much to recommend it. There will also be a strong case for reforming the confused structure of local government, in order to create a more rational system, centred on multi-purpose district authorities.[27]

The argument for regional devolution is much the same as for local government but with an extra dimension added. Already there is substantial administrative devolution by central government, not only in Scotland and Wales but in the English regions as well. In addition, there are other vital regional functions, such as health and water, for which there is no existing democratic accountability. Launching the 1987 Scotland Bill, Donald Dewar, Labour's Scottish Spokesman, pointed out that devolution for Scotland 'would place the massive administration which already exists in the Scottish Office under democratic control'.[28] Regional devolution is necessary to help provide a more stable and enduring constitutional settlement between the centre and the localities. As we have seen, local government has not been effective in the past in resisting the encroachment of central government. A system of democratically accountable regional government would establish stronger countervailing power. Perhaps most important of all, devolution is required to give focus to the powerful sense of nationhood which exists in the United Kingdom. The revival of Scottish nationalism in the late 1980s demonstrates the persistence of the challenge to the idea of a centralized United Kingdom. Apart from Scotland and Wales, there is also a strong sense of regional identity in parts of England, especially the North, which has to be taken into account.

One of the main weaknesses of Labour's devolution proposals in the 1970s was that it was assumed that it was possible to introduce devolution for Scotland and Wales in isolation from the rest of the United Kingdom. The next move forward has to be more carefully and comprehensively planned. Very sensibly, the 1987 Labour party consultative document argued for the establishment of a tier of regional authorities in England alongside a Scottish assembly and an elected body for Wales. Significantly, it was accepted that the same size or pattern of regional authorities need not apply throughout the whole country. In areas with a strong regional identity, such as the North of England, there is likely to be support for a region-wide assembly. In the South, however, a traditional regional solution is more difficult. Most of the South East, for example, looks to London.

Here, it may be sensible to consider the West German model in which several of the *Länder* are based on cities. However, whatever their precise size, functions or financial base, there must be a comprehensive pattern of elected regional authorities, covering England as well as Scotland and Wales.

Constitutional reform on the scale described above will need backing from a wide consensus of opinion if it is to be firmly based. The experience of the 1980s in which a determined Conservative government was able to change and even do away with part of local government also raises the question of whether Britain in the 1990s requires a more formal, written constitution in which the role, rights and duties of the centre, regions and locality are clearly defined and guaranteed. There is therefore, a case for establishing a Royal Commission on the Constitution not only to put forward detailed solutions on regional devolution but also to examine the case for a more effective statutory mechanism of constitutional protection.

*   *   *   *   *

SUMMARY

Mrs Thatcher's authoritarian style of government has diminished our democracy. Labour must, therefore, put forward a programme of democratic reforms which will extend rights, increase accountability, strengthen parliamentary institutions, and decentralize power. There is a strong case for establishing a Bill of Rights, based on the European Convention of Human Rights, introducing a Freedom of Information Act, reforming administrative law, strengthening the role of parliament's investigative committees, revitalizing local government and setting up elected assemblies, not only in Scotland and Wales but also in the English regions. Labour must also reconsider its position on electoral reform and set up a Royal Commission on a Written Constitution.

11 Internationalism without Illusions

It is relatively easy to set out Labour's external objectives. Denis Healey has argued that 'our main task as Socialists is to establish some collective democratic control over the international anarchy on the basis of greater economic and political equality between the richer and poorer countries'.[1] Looked at in British terms, our aims are to work for those international conditions which best promote our domestic prosperity and security, to act as a good neighbour, and to assist in preserving world peace. But the extent to which a medium-sized power like Britain is able to act independently is inevitably circumscribed by geostrategic, political, demographic and economic conditions. So the formulation of a Labour foreign and defence policy appropriate to the 1990s has to be firmly based on a realistic appreciation of Britain's position in the world.

* * * * *

MEDIUM-SIZED EUROPEAN POWER

The United Kingdom still has international concerns but is clearly no longer in any meaningful sense a world power. In 1964, still reflecting the immediate post-war situation, Labour's new Prime Minister, Harold Wilson, proudly proclaimed: 'We are a world power, and a world influence, or we are nothing'.[2] Yet, even in 1964, Britain's power was being rapidly eroded. In 1967, following devaluation, the Labour government was forced to announce that the 'East of Suez' role was to end. By the early 1970s, the United Kingdom had abandoned most of its global commitments.

The British decline reflected economic realities. Japan, West Germany and France had already overtaken Britain economically. In 1973, Britain's entry into the EC confirmed her diminished global status and that she was now primarily a European power. But British politicians, particularly Conservatives, have continued to overestimate and overstate Britain's position in the world. The message of Conservative election posters in 1987 was that 'Britain is great again', while Mrs Thatcher deliberately appealed to nationalistic sentiment with her claim that Britain was 'no ordinary country'. The apogee of the Thatcherite attempt to relaunch Britain on the world stage was the Falklands expedition in 1982 and the subsequent espousal of a 'Fortress Falklands' policy – the building up of the long-term defences of an island eight thousand miles away in the South Atlantic.

Yet the idea that Britain can again be a world power is, of course, an illusion. It should be remembered that the success of British forces in the South Atlantic owed a great deal to American logistic and intelligence support. It is also instructive that, faced with a more formidable potential opponent and without American assistance, the Conservative government had to come to terms with Communist China over the future of Hong Kong. Similarly, the realities of power forced Mrs Thatcher, against her instincts, to agree to a Rhodesian settlement which guaranteed black majority rule.

There is another illusion which has bedevilled our foreign policy in the 1980s – and that is the so-called 'special relationship' with the United States. It is true that in the 1940s and 1950s the old wartime alliance between the United States and Britain was successfully transformed into a new arrangement between a senior and junior partner. This led to the establishment of the Marshall Plan and the setting up of NATO. But, in the 1970s and 1980s, as British power declined and the American focus of interest shifted, the emphasis on a 'special relationship' became not only anachronistic but a hindrance to the development of a new British role. The United States is increasingly as much concerned with what happens in the Pacific basin and in Central and Latin America as in Europe. And, in Europe, the United States looks not to Britain but to the EC countries as a whole, and particularly to the more powerful West Germany. A Britain which still assumes that it enjoys a privileged position as a transatlantic intermediary between the United States and Europe risks falling between two stools, 'an increasingly irrelevant, if well loved, poor relation in Washington, and a "bad

European" in a continent increasingly dominated by the Franco–German axis'.[3]

It is also an illusion that Britain is specially qualified to play a mediating role between East and West. Harold Macmillan's fur hatted expedition to Moscow in 1959 has encouraged similar visits by British Prime Ministers, including the highly publicized pre-election trip by Mrs Thatcher in 1987. But the idea that British leaders can significantly influence superpower relations is strictly for domestic consumption. When the two superpowers wish to get close together, they are perfectly capable of doing so without the help of lesser intermediaries – as the INF treaty clearly demonstrated.

The Labour party, too, has had its illusions about British power and influence. The party's prolonged opposition to membership of the EC was in part based on an overestimation of Britain's ability to stand outside. Labour Prime Ministers, such as Harold Wilson and James Callaghan, also placed considerable emphasis on the 'special relationship' with the United States. On the left of the party, there has been a tendency to believe that a Socialist Britain can act as a moral force throughout the world. Indeed, one of the underlying arguments for unilateral disarmament has always been that it would persuade others to follow the British example.

The time has come for a Labour foreign and defence policy without illusions. As we go into the last decade of the twentieth century, the reality is that Britain is a medium-sized European power in a world which is increasingly economically interdependent but is still, to a considerable extent, dominated by superpower rivalry. Given our limited size and power, British influence is most effectively exerted through regional and international groupings such as the EC, NATO, the Group of Seven, OECD, IMF, GATT, the Commonwealth and the UN. Of course, these institutions serve different functions. The Commonwealth and the UN (Britain remains a permanent member of the Security Council) are primarily international forums in which such key issues as economic development, disarmament, South Africa and the Middle East can be discussed with countries outside Europe. The Group of Seven, OECD, the IMF, the World Bank and GATT are important economic institutions to which a medium-sized industrial country must belong to if it seeks more coordinated world economic order. NATO is the regional defensive organization of which Britain is a founder member. And the EC is the regional trade, economic and political institution which Britain joined belatedly sixteen years after its inception. It is the British contribution to the EC and NATO which is discussed below. Not only are these two organizations the most vital to our national interests. It is also mainly by the quality and strength of our commitment to these two bodies that our international role and our reputation as good partners and neighbours will be increasingly judged.

*   *   *   *   *

A CONSTRUCTIVE EC ROLE

Since British entry in 1973, Britain's relationship with the European Community has been marred by bad tempered wrangling, mutual misunderstanding and dashed hopes. It is essential both for British interests and for the future of Europe that the United Kingdom plays a more constructive European role. The British Labour party, which has for so long opposed British membership, is now very well placed to develop, in conjunction with its sister European parties, policies for the European Community appropriate to the 1990s.

The basic problem with British membership was that Britain did not join until after the overall stance and institutional framework of the Community had already been established. The original Community was a compromise between the West German desire for a free market in industrial goods and the French need for agricultural protection. The Germans were prepared to pay for the Common Agricultural Policy (CAP), provided the markets of the Six were open to West German industry. The British, however, resented having to become one of the paymasters of the Community, when in terms of *per capita* income Britain was one of the poorest members. Nor could they bring themselves to accept a CAP which underwrote wasteful over-production or a Community budget which allocated two-thirds of its spending to the less than 10 per cent of its labour force employed in agriculture. What was even more galling was that British industry failed to benefit sufficiently from access to a market of 250 million. Although trade with the EC expanded considerably, Britain consistently ran, not a trade surplus, but a deficit with the rest of the Community. In any case, British entry coincided with the first 'oil shock' and the end to the years of European super-growth which had characterized the 1950s and 1960s.

If Britain remained a reluctant member of the Community, the continental members of the European Community were deeply disappointed by the British. They had hoped that the British would bring with them, not only their celebrated pragmatism, but also a new sense of purpose and commitment. They found us carping, unconstructive, and, above all, ambivalent about our role in the Community. Under Mrs Thatcher, the British government blocked the expansion of Community regional and social expenditure (the so-called structural funds), adopted a minimalist position on institutional change, and refused to link sterling to the European Monetary System (EMS). When the EMS was originally set up in 1979, the Labour Prime Minister, James Callaghan, had feared that full membership of the EMS might tie the pound to an unrealistically high exchange rate. He also did not wish to be seen to 'gang up' on the United States. But the problem for Britain was that, in remaining aloof from the EMS, it ran the risk of leaving the leadership of the EC in the hands of the French and the Germans. Despite this danger, Mrs Thatcher continued to oppose sterling's participation in the exchange rate mechanism (ERM) of the European Monetary System primarily because she gave a higher priority to a largely illusory British independence.

During the 1980s, the European Community failed to tackle crucial problems such as sluggish growth, industrial weakness and high unemployment. Instead, a series of bad tempered and inconclusive summits were preoccupied by the linked problems of the CAP, the EC budget, and the British budgetary contribution. Gradually, however, a consensus was reached on these issues. A compromise was hammered out which put a ceiling on Britain's payments. At the February 1988 Brussels summit, it was also agreed in principle to curb farm spending and to increase spending substantially on the structural funds – the regional, social and agricultural funds. The way was cleared for a new move forward for the EC.

The British Conservatives are patently ill-equipped to make a constructive contribution to the debate on Europe's future. As

Mrs Thatcher's speech at Bruges in September 1988 demonstrated, she is at heart a British nationalist who is antipathetic to the idea of an increasing number of decisions being taken at a European level. Ideologically, because of her unconditional commitment to market forces, she cannot understand the need for the European Single Market to be complemented by European social, regional, environmental and industrial policies. Mrs Thatcher's European strategy is also based on a gross overestimate of British power. Despite all the evidence to the contrary, she still believes that Britain can play the lead role in Europe. At the same time, she has continued to put considerable emphasis on the so-called 'special relationship' with the United States, thus once again calling into question Britain's commitment to Europe.

The Conservative posture on Europe has presented the Labour party with a great opportunity. In the past, the root and branch opposition to the European Community has meant that it has confined its activities to criticizing ineffectively from the sidelines. Over the last two years, however, Labour has taken significant steps forward. The 1987 election manifesto made no mention of the party's policy of 'withdrawal'. In March 1988 the party leader, Neil Kinnock made it clear that any talk of withdrawal was both 'politically romantic and economically self-defeating'[4] and, in his speech to the 1988 Labour party conference, he called for the creation of a 'Social Europe'. For the first time, Labour agreed to fight the 1989 European elections on a joint manifesto with other European Socialist parties.

What is now required is for the Labour party to commit itself wholeheartedly to the European Community. The reality is that Britain's future now lies in Europe. It is not a question, as Mrs Thatcher wrongly believes, of Britain assuming a leadership role within the Community. That may have been on offer at an earlier stage. But in the 1990s Britain is no longer a world power nor even the most powerful country in Europe. The United Kingdom is, however, a medium-sized European power which, in cooperation with other countries, has an important part to play in the development of the European community. Even in opposition, the Labour party, in conjunction with our sister parties (some of whom, like the French and Spanish Socialists, are in government) can influence the European agenda for the 1990s.

In his notable speech to the 1988 TUC Conference, the President of the European Commission, Jacques Delors, proclaimed that 1992 represented much more than the creation of an internal market. He stressed that the single market involved cooperation and solidarity as well as competition, and emphasised the need for a 'social dimension' to the new Europe. Indeed, it is increasingly clear that, unless there are complementary countervailing strategies, the benefits of a genuine internal market will be confined to the already successful groups and regions. It is essential that the Labour party plays a prominent part in helping devise these complementary strategies and in drawing up European economic, industrial, social and political policies appropriate for the 1990s.

The case for coordinated economic action on an international scale has already been made in Chapter 7.[5] Such action has to include the two biggest economies – the United States and Japan. But the combined weight of the European economies means that what happens in the largest international trading bloc is vital not only to the world as a whole but also to individual European nations. As the Cecchini report on the single market pointed out, if the twelve members of the EC could agree to expand their economies up to their productive potential, they would generate more jobs, more investment, more consumption and more government revenue.

In the 1990s there is also likely to be greater monetary coordination at the European level. I have already argued for British membership of the exchange rate mechanism of the European Monetary System, on the grounds that it would lead to greater exchange rate stability, a lower level of interest rates, and to a useful counter-inflationary discipline. Politically, it is also important that the United Kingdom is included in any discussions on monetary integration (including the eventual setting up of a European bank). The danger for the United Kingdom is that, as over the formation of the Common Market in the 1950s and 1960s, this country could be left out of key decisions which will shape Europe's future. Joining the EMS as a full member would, at the very least, ensure that British views were not ignored.

Just as an industrial policy is essential at national level, so the completion of the internal market must be accompanied by the establishment of a European industrial and research and development policy. The former Conservative Cabinet Minister, Michael Heseltine, has rightly pointed out that each of the twelve countries 'attempting to reinvent the wheel with its taxpayers' research budgets, holds the totality of Europe back by wasteful overlap, and each suffers for it'.[6] The consequence of the relative failure to cooperate in advanced industrial projects and in research and development is graphically illustrated by Europe's backwardness in electronics and information technology (IT). Japan, with a population about one-third that of Europe, produces around 70 per cent more IT goods and services than Europe. Without more effective cooperation, Europe is likely to drop further behind in the technologically advanced sectors.

Another area in which there will have to be a major European initiative is regional policy. The European Commission White Paper on completing the internal market made it clear that the objective is to ensure that 'the market is flexible, so that resources, both of people and materials and of capital and investment, flow into areas of greatest economic activity'.[7] It recognizes, however, that this could exacerbate existing discrepancies between regions and thus jeopardize the goal of economic convergence. Hence the argument for greatly increased European regional and structural funds. At the 1988 Brussels summit it was agreed to increase these funds by 80 per cent by 1992. This was a useful start, but ever so much more will be required if the disruptive efforts of the internal market are to be avoided. The structural funds still amount to less than a third of the Community budget.

The idea of social 'harmonisation' or the levelling up of social provision was an integral part of the Treaty of Rome. With the completion of the internal market, it will become even more necessary. It is essential that the Labour party gives strong backing to Jacques Delors's proposals for a European-wide 'floor' of guaranteed social rights, the participation of employees in the decision-making process of European companies, and the extension of continuing education to all workers. As the UK's social provision under Conservative governments drops behind the rest of the EC, the Labour party has a special interest in joining with other European Socialist parties in insisting on the creation of a 'Social Europe'.

One of the features of recent years has been the development of European Political Cooperation (EPC) in international affairs. Title IV of the Single European Act provides a legal basis for the first time for members to act jointly on foreign affairs. In addition, the Community's role in international trading relations, and, through the Lomé convention and other agreements, in development policy means that the EC is becoming increasingly important in decision-making on international issues. The Labour party, concerned to build up a more influential British position on detente, human rights and Third World and development matters, should support, wherever possible, the channelling of external initiatives through the Community. In the 1990s, British influence will be most effectively exerted there.

A European Community which has been strengthened in the ways described above will also need to be made more accountable. A report prepared by the Institutional Committee of the European Parliament has referred to 'the democratic deficit'. With the completion of the internal market and with the establishment of other Community programmes, there will, as Jacques Delors has warned, have been a major transfer of power from the national to the Community level without a corresponding increase in democratic control.

Labour must make a positive contribution to the debate on democratic reform. The agenda should include not only giving national parliaments a greater role in debating Community issues but also strengthening the European parliament. In the past, the great weakness of the European Assembly has been its lack of influence over Community legislation. However, under the Single European Act, the Assembly has been given a new involvement in certain areas (including the internal market) under the formula of 'cooperation with the European parliament'. There is a strong case for extending this 'cooperative' procedure (which gives the Assembly the power to propose amendments to the Council of Ministers' proposals) to all Community legislation. In addition, the European parliament's powers over the Commission (it can dismiss the Commission by a two-thirds majority) should arguably be increased to include a consultative role in the appointment of Commissioners. A stronger European Community has to be balanced by a stronger European parliament.

*   *   *   *   *

MAKING SENSE OF DEFENCE

Like foreign policy, Labour's defence policy for the 1990s has to be based on a hard-headed appreciation of realities, including the decisive rejection of the party's defence plans at the 1983 and 1987 elections. It has also to take account of developments in superpower relations and the improved prospects for detente and disarmament. Above all, it has to provide for Britain's security and assist in the preservation of peace.

All the poll evidence suggests that at the 1987 election, as in 1983, the defence issue was a considerable handicap to Labour and a big advantage for the Conservatives. At least a quarter of the voters mentioned defence as one of the most important election issues and the Conservatives enjoyed a bigger lead on that issue than on any other.[8] Even more significant was the large number of voters (amounting to at least one million) who said that they were put off Labour by its defence policy. If it could be convincingly argued that its policies were misunderstood by the electorate and were likely to become more credible in the future, then it might be plausible for the party to continue to ignore its unpopularity on defence. The problem for the Labour party is that there are major flaws at the heart of its 1987 defence strategy.

It is certainly the case that during the 1987 campaign the Conservative party grossly traduced the Labour position. Mrs Thatcher claimed that Labour would leave Britain defenceless and branded Labour's policy as a recipe for defeat and surrender. She conveniently ignored Labour's pledge to use resources freed by the cancellation of the Trident nuclear weapons system to strengthen conventional forces and skated over Conservative plans to cut back conventional spending, despite its promises to NATO. But there were crucial weaknesses in Labour's non-nuclear policy which were mercilessly exposed in the months leading up to the election and in the campaign itself.

The part of the non-nuclear policy on which there was the most potential popular support was the commitment to get rid of American Cruise Missiles from Britain. But Mr Gorbachev's announcement in February 1987 that he was prepared to negotiate on the 'zero option' for Longer Range Intermediate Nuclear Forces separately from the Strategic Defence Initiative (SDI) cut the ground from under Labour's feet. Mrs Thatcher could now argue, with considerable justice, that it was the deployment of Cruise which had forced Mr Gorbachev to the negotiating table. In other words, multilateralism had been seen to work.

Labour's promise not only to send back Cruise but also to close down all other American nuclear bases took insufficient account of the impact of such a decision on the Alliance. To the Americans, the siting of nuclear bases in Britain had a political importance over and above its strategic significance, because it was a symbol of the British commitment to the nuclear umbrella. As even sympathetic Americans pointed out, if Britain took a unilateral decision on the bases, it could destabilize the Alliance. In an unprecedented move during the 1986 Labour party conference at Blackpool, the American Ambassador bluntly stated that the United States would have to think carefully about whether or not it was advantageous to continue to maintain bases in Great Britain at all.

The fact that Labour seemed uncertain whether, despite supporting membership of NATO, it accepted the concept of nuclear deterrence added to the confusion. Denis Healey, the Shadow Foreign Secretary, was prepared to back the American nuclear deterrent, so long as the Soviets continued to possess nuclear weapons. But Neil Kinnock told the Blackpool conference that nuclear retaliation by the United States on Britain's behalf was immoral.

Even more damaging electorally was Labour's commitment to get rid of Britain's own nuclear deterrent unilaterally. Though the cancellation of the Trident system had at times somewhat more support, immediate and unilateral decommissioning of the Polaris fleet never had the backing of more than a third of the electorate. There was profound scepticism about whether the moral example of unilateral disarmament would actually be as infectious as Labour claimed. If Britain got rid of her bombs, would the Russians really be prepared to follow suit? So long as the Soviet Union possessed nuclear weapons, most voters felt that Britain needed to keep her nuclear weapons as an insurance policy. Labour had also to contend with the highly debatable but widely held belief that the possession of nuclear weapons was not only a guarantee of a measure of influence at the top table but also a potent symbol of national will.

If there were major strategic and electoral problems with Labour's 1987 defence policy, it was at least based on an acute awareness of the unimaginable horrors of nuclear war, and of the appalling waste in locking up so great a level of resources in the superpowers' huge nuclear arsenals. Looking to the 1990s, Labour's argument for a reduced NATO reliance on nuclear weapons will continue to be relevant. Above all, the case for giving priority to disarmament over the next decade will be overwhelming.

The prospects for nuclear disarmament are now better than at any time since the end of the Second World War. Both the United States and the Soviet Union have been compelled by a combination of economic and political factors towards the negotiating table. In the United States, the large continuing budget deficit and the approaching end of his presidential term persuaded President Reagan to go all out for arms control agreements with the Soviet Union. His successor, George Bush is likely to follow the same course. At the same time, the new Russian leadership under Gorbachev faces acute domestic economic and political problems. The urgent need for reform (*perestroika*) implies an accommodation with the United States to control the dangerous and costly arms race and provide a stable international environment. Gorbachev has rightly argued that the most important issue in Soviet-American relations is not to chase myths but to see things the way they are: 'We proceed from the fundamental fact that neither the American people nor the Soviet people want self-destruction. Convinced of this, we have embarked upon a path dedicated to better relations with the United States and we expect reciprocity'.[9]

The progress made so far has been impressive. The INF Treaty in December 1987 in which the two superpowers agreed on the elimination of all land-based short and longer range intermediate nuclear missiles (the so-called double-zero) for the first time actually reduced the number of nuclear weapons by about 4 per cent. If the START negotiations are successful, they would lead to a massive 50 per cent reduction in long range strategic missiles, and open the way to further agreements in the future. But the process of negotiated nuclear arms reductions is still fragile. It depends most of all on continued support in the United States and the survival of the Gorbachev leadership in the Soviet Union. But there is also the crucial European dimension. Among some of the political leaders of Western European countries, there is some concern about the consequences of denuclearization. One influential journalist has suggested that for them 'Reykjavik produced not a vision of peace but a nightmare, the nightmare of a Europe made safe for conventional warfare'.[10] Certainly, in the post-INF treaty world, the credibility of the American nuclear guarantee to Western Europe, which deployment of Cruise and Pershing was meant to enhance, has once again been questioned. In the case of attack by Warsaw Pact conventional forces, would the United States really threaten to use its strategic nuclear weapons? Or, to put it at its starkest, would an American President risk Chicago for Hamburg? Hence the suspicion, expressed most forcibly by Mrs Thatcher, that a deal to eliminate battlefield nuclear weapons (the so-called 'third zero') would in practice leave NATO countries at risk from the Warsaw Pact's conventional superiority. Uncertainty could be increased by calls from US political leaders, anxious to bring the US budget deficit under control, for an increased European contribution to conventional defence spending linked to a reduction in American conventional forces committed to Europe.

It is against this background of, on the one hand, new hope for detente and disarmament and, on the other, some Western European ambivalence about what this could mean for the European continent that Labour defence policy has to be considered. Such a policy has both to provide for Britain's security and make a constructive contribution to Europe and North Atlantic defence *and* to assist in the development of detente, the process of arms reduction and disarmament and the preservation of peace.

It needs to be stressed, at the outset, that Labour's objectives are far more likely to be achieved within rather than outside the North Atlantic Alliance (the defence organization which, it should be remembered, a Labour government helped to set up). A neutral Britain would not only, like Sweden, have to keep up a costly defence programme; it would also have far less influence on American or European defence strategy or on disarmament negotiations. What is more, the destabilising impact to NATO of a British withdrawal would make Europe less rather than more secure. The case for Britain remaining a member of the Alliance, with all the opportunities which membership affords to influence key decisions, is likely to be even greater in the 1990s than in the 1980s.

NATO has always been a nuclear alliance, protected by the American nuclear deterrent. The Labour party should accept that, until the Soviet Union gives up its own nuclear weapons, the protection of the American nuclear umbrella will be necessary. What Labour should be advocating inside the Alliance is a reduced dependence on nuclear deterrence, a defensive strategy within Europe, and a persistent emphasis on detente, confidence-building measures and arms reduction and disarmament.

The current strategy of 'flexible response' (whereby NATO can respond to the conventional attack by Warsaw Pact forces with nuclear weapons) should be abandoned in favour of 'no early use' as a step towards a 'no first use' strategy. Such a shift in NATO thinking will not only enhance the prospect for the elimination of short range land based nuclear weapons but also focus attention on the crucial question of securing a balance of conventional forces between NATO and the Warsaw Pact in Europe.

As to the present situation, a number of informed observers, including the International Institute for Strategic Studies, have judged that the imbalance between NATO and Warsaw Pact conventional forces is not as threatening as is sometimes suggested. The numbers favour the Warsaw Pact but the preponderance is not sufficient to guarantee victory. Even in those areas in which the Warsaw Pact has the greatest advantage, such as the numbers of tanks, it has been argued that their superiority is below the level required for successful attack. However, for a secure future, it is clearly necessary that either NATO forces should be strengthened or, preferably, that the imbalance should be tackled as part of the new negotiations on conventional forces in Europe. As we have seen, strong economic and political pressures both within the Soviet Union and the United States are building up for reductions in conventional forces. The principle of asymmetry (or of one side making bigger cuts than the other) has already been accepted by the Soviet leadership in the INF agreement. There is no reason why a Soviet Union which is genuinely concerned to secure stability in Europe should not also make disproportionate cuts in conventional forces. Gorbachev's dramatic speech to the United Nations in December 1988 announcing unilateral cuts by 10 per cent in Soviet forces is a good omen for the future.

In addition to these negotiations, there are a number of other crucial areas of discussion where progress must be made, including chemical weapons (where the Soviet Union also has superiority), short range land based nuclear weapons, and strategic nuclear weapons. Once the START 1 talks on reducing the superpower strategic arsenal by 50 per cent have been concluded, there will begin what Peter Shore has called 'the most serious of all nuclear disarmament talks' – START 2 which will discuss the 12 000 remaining strategic warheads (held in almost equal proportions by the two superpowers).[11] A precondition of success in all these arms control talks will be the establishment of mutual confidence and the improvement of political relationships between East and West.

It is in the context of both maintaining collective security and stability *and* furthering detente and disarmament that decisions about British weapon systems, such as Polaris and Trident, need to be made. A Labour government, coming to power in the 1990s, will want to exert the maximum possible leverage on the process of negotiated nuclear disarmament. It will also need to ensure that British decisions on weapons systems do not weaken European security. As a general principle, Labour is more likely to secure its objectives if it shifts its policy position away from unilateralism to a firm commitment to negotiated disarmament.

By the 1990s, Polaris, though still able to threaten parts of Russia, will be coming to the end of its life. Even so, it would not be sensible for an incoming Labour government to decommission Polaris unilaterally or even to bargain our deterrent away on a bilateral basis with the Soviet Union. There is not much gained for world or European security in reducing the Soviet strategic arsenal by the equivalent to the number of British warheads if there are still many thousands of Soviet warheads left. The best policy is for Labour to announce that, as a nuclear power, Britain would be eager and willing to make its contribution to a general agreement to reduce and, if possible, eliminate all nuclear weapons.

What to do about Polaris's successor system, Trident, presents Labour with a difficult dilemma. In 1987, Labour was correct to argue that the £10 billion cost of Trident would have been better directed to conventional forces. The Trident system is not only extremely costly but, because it can be fitted with over 500 warheads, goes well beyond minimum deterrence. And, unlike the French nuclear deterrent, it is not a truly independent system, because it is bought from and stored and serviced in the United States. However, by the 1990s, much of the money will have been spent or committed. Trident will come into operation in 1994. The question for Labour will be whether to cancel Trident or to complete the programme in order to retain leverage in disarmament negotiations.

The answer on Trident will depend in part on the state of detente and disarmament negotiations. If negotiations are going well, cancellation or at least scaling down could become an important British contribution to their success. Indeed, the superpowers will expect a response from Britain. As to Labour's position if talks have stalled or broken down, then the deterrent should be retained as a bargaining counter in any further disarmament talks. There may also be a case for at least temporary retention if, as some fear, there is some measure of American disengagement from Europe. This is not to argue that the British (or French) deterrent can possibly replace the American nuclear guarantee to Europe. But it could conceivably provide reassurance, as well as a breathing space.

The idea of a strengthened European position on defence ought to receive enthusiastic Labour support. As a recent study of British foreign policy has pointed out, there is as yet no effective European defence pillar of the kind envisaged by President Kennedy in his call for a greater European share in the Alliance a quarter of the century ago.[12] There is little justification for the unfavourable comparisons between West European and American defence costs and deployments, which show that Western European governments as a whole spend more t deploy fewer forces which are less well-equipped. Britain, which spends more *per capita* on defence than its European allies, has special interest in greater integration of national defence effort. More effective West European coordination on defence, particu larly between Britain, the Federal Republic and France, could not only strengthen European security but also act as a powerful force for detente and disarmament.

* * * * *

GOOD NEIGHBOUR AND PARTNER

Labour must promote foreign and defence policies without illusion, based on the notion of Britain as a good neighbour and partner. It should accept that, for the foreseeable future, Britain's fate lies with the European Community, and, in conjunction with sister parties, it must make a constructive contribution to the development of a Europe which will increasingly coordinate policies not only on economic but on industrial, environmental and social issues as well. The party must also develop a defence policy which assists both in the maintenance of collective security and the promotion of detente and disarmament. As a general principle, Labour is more likely to secure its objectives if it shifts its policies from unilateralism to a firm commitment to negotiated disarmament.

Conclusion: the Path to Power

The theme of this book has been that, if Labour is to win power in the 1990s, it will have to change radically. This concluding chapter summarizes the main changes which will be required, attempts to refute the arguments which will be deployed against the revisionist model, and considers the appropriate political strategy which the party has to adopt if it is to put itself in a position to replace the Tories as Britain's main governing party over the next decade.

* * * * *

THE NEW REVISIONISM

After three election defeats, Labour is in danger of becoming a permanent minority party. Its declining traditional base and its crippling political weakness in the South of England mean that, without substantial change, the Labour party could find it as difficult to win an election in the 1990s as it has done in the 1980s. Yet Labour must win in the 1990s. For without power, or its prospect, its *raison d'être* will gradually disappear. If it is serious about winning, it must decisively reject the following strategies. It cannot afford to be primarily a class party. This is partly a question of political arithmetic; by the 1990s, the manual working class will be in a substantial minority. It is also fundamentally alien to Democratic Socialist values. Labour stands not for the victory of one class or group over another but for a genuinely classless approach to politics and and society.

Nor can Labour find salvation as a purely trade union party. Although it will respect trade union views (and a large proportion of trade unionists will continue to vote Labour), it can never allow itself to be dominated by an interest group, however influential and powerful. Labour should be, and be seen to be, a broad based national party, concerned with national solutions for national problems. It must also reject the so-called 'rainbow coalition' idea of appealing to a ragbag of minority interests. Labour must be committed to equal rights and opportunities for all, irrespective of class, race and gender. But the problem with the 'coalition of minorities' strategy is that it turns off the majority and is, therefore, against the best interests of those it seeks to assist.

If Labour is to gain power in the 1990s, it must become a people's or citizens' party, capable of representing the whole nation. Its project should be to promote the general good by seeking to secure that common framework of rights and obligations which guarantee citizenship. It must also be a revisionist party, ready to reassess its values, strategies and policies in the light of economic and social change. What is urgently required is nothing less than a new 'model' Labour party, prepared to put forward an alternative political agenda for the 1990s.

The Labour party would be still the party of social justice, a fairer distribution of resources and a reduction in unjustified inequalities. But it will also underline its firm commitment to the expansion of freedom, opportunity and choice, including enthusiastic support for the higher standards of living. In contrast to Thatcherite Conservatives, it will also emphasize its backing for the idea of 'one nation', the notion that there are shared assumptions, common purposes and mutual obligations which need to be affirmed and, if possible, strengthened.

Above all, the new 'model' Labour party will be a party of citizen rights. It will champion the case for a comprehensive 'floor' of basic statutory rights – in the market, at work, in the provision of welfare services and benefits and, through a Bill of Rights, in political life as well. The concept of rights is potentially extremely powerful. First, it is expressed in terms of the individual, thus underlining that a major Socialist objective is to maximize individual empowerment. Secondly, it serves to humanize the process of change and helps ensure that everyone benefits from it. In that sense, it is egalitarian. Thirdly, if properly applied, it is an instrument for the improvement of efficiency as well as social advance. As such, it provides a key intellectual underpinning for the new political agenda.

As a party of change, Labour will accept the role of the market in large parts of the economy. Paradoxically, however, this will free Labour to develop a more credible theory of selective state intervention. Intervention will be necessary in cases where the market is ineffective or has to be supplemented or guided. Even where markets work effectively, rules, regulation and supervision will be required. All Western industrial economies are inevitably mixed economies which need the guiding hand of government if they are to operate effectively.

In policy terms, the new Labour party will strongly support competition, profitable investment and industrial innovation. But change cannot be left to market forces alone. Government will need to facilitate – and, where necessary, speed up – the process of adaptation, encouraging investment in research and development, promoting education and training, and revitalizing the idea of partnership between government and industry. Government will also be required to assist and cushion individuals, groups and regions who lose out. Hence the case for a floor of social rights and for regional and labour market policies. Increasingly, solutions will have to be found at a European level.

Learning the lessons of the 1970s and 1980s, Labour will be cautiously Keynesian, prepared to use all the available instruments – fiscal, monetary and exchange rate intervention – to sustain the level of demand at an appropriate level but aware of the need for a moderate, balanced approach. Acutely conscious of inflationary dangers, it will support the idea of a broad consensus between government, employers and unions on growth of incomes and back this up by pursuing firm monetary and exchange rate policies. It will work for sensible international coordination, including joining the exchange rate mechanism of the European Monetary System.

Labour will continue to give strong support to the state welfare services, which still receive such overwhelming popular backing. But it will demand value for money, higher standards and effective delivery of services. It will insist on efficient and accountable management, rigorous inspection and the establishment of a system of enforceable consumer rights, particularly in health and education. And it will require a more effective attack on poverty which, in the longer term, could well include the eventual integration of tax and benefits.

The revisionist Labour party will give high priority to democratic reform. It will support the idea of a Bill of Rights (based on the European Convention of Human Rights), argue for the introduction of a Freedom of Information Act, and back the reform of administrative law. It will want to strengthen the roles of the investigative committees of the House of Commons, revitalize local government, and establish elected assemblies, not only in Scotland and Wales, but in England as well. It will need to reconsider its position on electoral reform, as well as set up a Royal Commission on a Written Constitution.

Externally, Labour will promote foreign and defence policies without illusion, based on the notion of Britain as a good neighbour and partner. It will accept that, for the foreseeable future, Britain's fate lies with the European Community, and, in conjunction with sister parties, will make a constructive contribution to the development of a Europe which will increasingly coordinate policies not only on economic but on industrial, environmental and social issues as well. Labour must also develop a defence policy which assists both in the maintenance of collective security and in the promotion of detente and disarmament. As a general principle, Labour is more likely to secure its objectives if it shifts its policies away from unilateralism to a firm commitment to negotiated disarmament.

$$* \quad * \quad * \quad * \quad *$$

COUNTERING THE CRITICS

The fundamentalist left will claim that the revisionist model which has been advocated in this book is not 'Socialist'. There are, however, major flaws in their thinking. The first is that they believe that there is only one definition of Socialism – nationalization of the means of production. Yet the British Socialist tradition, like those of its continental sister parties, has always encompassed a number of strands. In the *Future of Socialism*, Crosland described as many as twelve different Socialist ideas, from which he extracted five main elements[1] – a concern for social welfare, a belief in the classless society and greater equality, support for fraternity and the cooperative ideal, rejection of the inefficiencies and unfairness of capitalism and a protest against poverty and physical squalour.

In this book I have firmly rejected the idea that there is a single definition of Socialism or one 'Big Idea'. Instead, I have argued that there are three main Socialist values – freedom, equality and community – which have to be balanced (and to some extent, traded off) against each other.[2] I have also advocated various instruments and policy initiatives, including selective state intervention, a 'floor' of basic rights, democratic reform and efficient welfare services by which a modern Labour government should seek to improve society in line with democratic Socialist values.

The second mistake made by the fundamentalists is to confuse ends and means. Nationalization or public ownership is not – and never can be – an aim or value like the expansion of freedom, the promotion of greater equality or the strengthening of community. It is merely one method (and often not the most appropriate) amongst a number of instruments and policies from which Socialists can select to further their aims and values.

The third error is to assume that Socialism is (or should be) something static. The reality is that, like all other political creeds, Socialism has to adapt if it is to survive. That is why I have argued so strongly that Labour needs continually to reassess its values and strategies and policies in the light of rapid economic, social and political change.

Another charge that will be levelled against the revisionist model both by the fundamentalist left and by right wing Conservatives is that, because it accepts the role of the market in large parts of the economy, it is therefore indistinguishable from Thatcherism. A moment's thought reveals that this accusation is baseless. There are clearly profound distinctions between the Thatcherite and the 'revisionist' Labour positions. These include different attitudes towards state intervention, welfare, taxation, citizen rights, democratic reforms and Britain's position in the world, as well as different starting points in terms of values and aspirations.

As to the criticism that the revisionist approach amounts to little more than the promise to 'manage capitalism better than the capitalists', this is more a reflection on the misconceptions of the critics than something of which the Labour party need feel ashamed. As the Soviet Union and Communist China have both recognized, the market is a highly effective device for coordinating and allocating economic activities. As such it should be supported by Socialists. But if the modern market economy is to function effectively, it needs 'managing'. Revisionist Socialists who understand the need for intervention and have worked out how and when to do it, are better equipped to do that 'managing' than doctrinaire market Conservatives who are against government intervention on principle.

A more plausible criticism of the 'new revisionism' is that it takes Labour too close to the political ground occupied by the Social and Liberal Democrats (SLD) and the 'rump' Social Democrats (SDP). Clearly there will still be crucial differences between a revisionist Labour party and the two smaller opposition parties. These include Labour's more robust approach to state intervention, its stronger commitment to the welfare state – and, on the level of values, its greater concern for social justice. But it would be foolish to deny that there will be substantial common ground.

A Labour party committed to a Bill of Rights and Freedom of Information Act, setting up a Royal Commission on the case for a written constitution and a reassessment of its approach to electoral reform and, more generally, an emphasis on citizen rights would obviously find itself close to the SLD and the SDP on democratic issues. A Labour party in favour of negotiated disarmament and of constructive developments in the European Community, would receive strong support on external policy from the two smaller opposition parties. In addition, the SLD and the SDP increasingly share Labour's determination to turn out the Conservatives and end Mrs Thatcher's reign.

In my view, the considerable area of agreement between a revisionist Labour party and the SDL and SDP should not be a matter for concern. On the contrary, it is likely to be a source of strength to Labour.

When Labour won the general election of 1945, it fought on a programme which, to a great extent, was based on ideas and policies which already had a wide measure of support across the political spectrum.[3] It drew its economic policies largely from Keynes and its welfare programme from Beveridge – both of whom were Liberals. In education, it was content to accept the framework established by the reforming Conservative, R. A. Butler, in the 1944 Education Act. The idea of a National Health Service, so skilfully brought into being by Aneurin Bevan in 1948, had already been extensively discussed during the war. Even Labour's nationalization proposals could, for the most part, be presented as practical responses to the recommendations of Royal Commissions or non-partisan investigatory committees.[4] Of course there were specifically Labour movement influences on the manifesto, including party conference, the trade unions and the Fabian Society. But Labour won in 1945 because it was closely identified with a widely endorsed alternative agenda which had emerged during the war.

Similarly in 1964 when Labour gained power under Harold Wilson, it projected themes which had already captured the progressive imagination. The importance of sustained economic growth was stressed by a considerable body of expert opinion; economic and industrial planning had become a fashionable idea by the beginning of the 1960s; while the need for increased social spending and institutional reform was a commonplace of media discussion and debate.

The Labour party's project for the 1990s must be to help forge a new consensus around an alternative agenda which, as in 1945 and 1964, is capable of uniting a majority behind it. It will be substantially assisted in that task if a number of its key ideas and policies are already supported by a broad swathe of progressive opinion.

*   *   *   *   *

A PROGRESSIVE CONSENSUS

The question remains: what kind of political strategy must Labour adopt if it is to put itself in a position to gain power in the 1990s?

I have already emphasized the size of the recovery that will be required for victory. Nationally, Labour needs a swing of over 8 per cent and an extra 97 seats. Moreover, its weakness in the South means that there is an additional geographical barrier which the party has to surmount. As the continuing electoral success of sister European Socialist and Social Democrat parties show, there is no inexorable iron law which prevents Labour from winning. But in British political conditions, it will not be easy.

Some Labour politicians have even argued that the combination of a 'first past the post' electoral system, a divided opposition and Labour's weakness in the South will make it impossible

for Labour to win the next election.[5] They therefore propose that
there should be an electoral pact between Labour and the two
smaller opposition parties by which the party in third place at
the 1987 election would agree to stand down in a number of
marginal seats. In this way, the handicap of the 'first past the
post' electoral system would be overcome by concentrating the
anti-Tory vote and extra Conservative seats would thus be
gained.

In theory, the case for an electoral pact is attractive. Voters,
particularly Labour voters in seats where Labour is third, are
already voting tactically in considerable numbers.[6] If it was
possible to formalize tactical voting through an electoral pact,
this could help turn out the Conservatives. Surely it would be
worth Labour forgoing putting up candidates in seats where it
was in a hopeless position if this sacrifice opened up the
possibility of power? The problem for the Labour party is that
making an electoral pact with the SLD and the SDP before the
next election would be an admission that it could not win on its
own. There is the additional difficulty that such a pact could
work more to the advantage of the centre party, at least in terms
of seats, than to the Labour party. This is because at present
Labour voters are more likely to vote for the centre party
candidates than centre voters are for Labour candidates.

In any case, only the 'rump' SDP, under David Owen, has
expressed any interest in electoral pacts. Paddy Ashdown, the
leader of the SLD, anxious to establish the identity of his new
party, has come out strongly against the idea, while the Labour
party has always been opposed. The obvious conclusion is that,
whatever the theoretical attractions, an electoral pact is unlikely
to be practical politics this side of the next general election.
There is, therefore, no immediate short cut to power. Over the
next few years, Labour will have to concentrate on the task of
changing itself. It has to make progress on a number of fronts at
once.

It is partly a question of how Labour manages its own affairs.
Under Neil Kinnock's courageous leadership, the National
Executive Committee has been increasingly prepared to act
against Trotskyite and other sectarian groupings. This resolute
line must be intensified. There is simply no place in a Labour
party, committed to parliamentary democracy, for those who
reject democratic values and procedures. For much of the 1980s,

these anti-democratic groups have fed off the party. Unhappily they are still entrenched in the Liverpool, London and other inner city areas. The NEC must not only expel individuals but close down and reconstitute local constituency parties in which these groups are strong.

Tough action against Trotskyites is not only right in principle. It will also pay electoral dividends. Neil Kinnock's attack on the behaviour of the Militant Tendency in Liverpool at the 1985 Bournemouth conference was rewarded by an immediate rise in Labour's poll ratings.[7] A Labour party which is seen to be effectively sorting out anti-democratic elements within its own ranks is more likely to be entrusted with running the country.

The case for transforming the Labour party into an individual membership party stands in its own right. Giving voting powers to individual party members in the election of the leader and deputy leader, in the selection and reselection of members of parliament and parliamentary candidates (and hopefully councillors as well), and in the choosing of conference delegates is preferable because it is the most democratic solution. But 'one member, one vote', especially if it can be backed up by an expansion of party membership, also has the merit of helping to ensure that the party and its representatives are more in touch with the mood of the voters. The spectacle on televison of conference delegates who speak in tones of hatred and abuse, the sectarian activities of too many London Labour councillors and the presence in parliament of Labour Members with close associations with Trotskyite groups – all these are highly damaging to Labour's cause. A broader based, more representative Labour party is likely to be more electable.

I have already argued above that it is crucial for Labour to convince voters that it is not 'in hock' to the unions. Moves towards a 'one member, one vote' party, combined with a scaling down of the 'block vote' at conference and support for the principle of state funding of political parties, would be a practical demonstration that Labour is responding to the electorate's concern. The 'new model' Labour party must be – and be seen to be – less dependent on the trade unions. Success in broadening the party base, in reducing the influence of the unions, and in throwing out anti-democratic elements will do much to increase the prestige and authority of the party leadership. This is very important. For it is essential for electoral victory that Labour projects itself as a credible alternative government.

At the 1945 election, Labour was able to play on the fact that Attlee, Bevin and Morrison had all been leading members of Churchill's War Cabinet.[8] In contrast, by the 1990s, few of Labour's prominent figures will have had any experience of government. This need not, however, be an insuperable handicap. After all, after thirteen years of Conservative rule, Harold Wilson's Labour party was in a similar position in 1964. Today's Labour party can, indeed, learn a great deal from Wilson's political strategy in the months leading up to the 1964 election. In a series of speeches stressing change, growth and modernization, he helped set the political agenda.[9] In this way, he overcame his party's lack of governmental experience and added to his own stature as a potential Prime Minister.

As in 1964, the overriding priority for the Labour party must now be to build up a progressive consensus of opinion around new issues and policies. It must set out an alternative agenda, based on citizen rights, democratic reform, selective government intervention, an efficient welfare state and a fresh and more realistic vision of Britain as a good partner and neighbour. A revisionist programme on these lines would give a firm foundation for a serious Labour challenge for power over the next decade. It would create a balanced and coherent framework of values and objectives. It would come to terms with economic and social change. And it would provide themes and policies which were in tune with the needs and aspirations of a majority of the voters, the essential prerequisite to political success.

The key to Labour's future thus lies in whether or not the party is prepared to revise its overall direction, strategies and policies in the light of changing circumstances. At the end of the 1980s, Labour is in danger of becoming a permanent minority party. Only the whole-hearted adoption of the new revisionism will give the Labour party the prospect of office in the 1990s.

A 'new model' Labour party, committed to citizen rights, accepting the market but upholding the case for selective state intervention, strongly supporting the welfare state but insisting on efficiency, attaching a high priority to democratic reforms and giving firm backing to the development of the European Community, the maintenance of collective security and progress on negotiated disarmament, could not only become a formidable challenger for power but will also be well equipped to tackle the challenges which are likely to face the United Kingdom over the next decade.

Notes and References

Introduction: the Case for Revisionism

1. Peter Kellner, *Independent*, 23 May 1988.
2. Eduard Bernstein, *Evolutionary Socialism* (New York: Schocken Books, 1961).
3. Bernstein, *Evolutionary Socialism*, pp. xxv–vi.
4. Bernstein, *Evolutionary Socialism*, p. 146.
5. Bernstein, *Evolutionary Socialism*, p. 210.
6. Bernstein, *Evolutionary Socialism*, p. 202.
7. Susan Crosland, *Tony Crosland* (London: Cape, 1982) p. 13.
8. Anthony Crosland, *The Future of Socialism* (London: Cape, 1956). pp. 75–6.
9. Crosland, *The Future of Socialism*, pp. 100–3.
10. Crosland, *The Future of Socialism*, p. 102.
11. Crosland, *The Future of Socialism*, p. 113.
12. Crosland, *The Future of Socialism*, p. 518.
13. Anthony Crosland, *Socialism Now* (London: Cape, 1979) p. 15.
14. Crosland, *The Future of Socialism*, p. 515.
15. Peter Gay, *The Dilemma of Democratic Socialism* (New York: Collier Books, 1962) pp. 276–89.
16. See David Lipsey, in David Lipsey and Dick Leonard (eds), *The Socialist Agenda* (London: Cape, 1981) p. 34.
17. The philosophical and analytical basis of the revisionist approach to politics is brilliantly described by Bryan Magee, in his *Popper* (London: Fontana, 1973) pp. 74–86.
18. All quotes are from the English text of the Bad Godesberg programme contained in Willi Eichler, *Fundamental Values and Basic Demands of Democratic Socialism*, Friedrich Ebert Foundation (1966).
19. Peter Kellner, *Independent*, 23 May 1988.
20. See edited speech by Oscar Lafontaine, *New Statesman and Society*, 9 September 1988.
21. See Giles and Lisanne Radice, *Socialists in the Recession* (London: Macmillan, 1986) p. 64.
22. Lisanne Radice, *Beatrice and Sidney Webb* (London: Macmillan, 1984).
23. See *Marxism Today* (October 1988) for a stimulating discussion of these changes.
24. Peter Jenkins, *The Thatcher Revolution* (London: Cape, 1988) p. 379.
25. For example, Giles Radice, *Independent*, 21 October 1987.
26. See Anthony Crosland, *The Conservative Enemy* (London: Cape, 1962) p. 7 on conservatism inside the Labour party.

27. Raymond Plant, *Citizenship, Rights and Socialism*, Fabian Society, 531 1988 p. 2; also Ross Terrill, *R. H. Tawney and His Times* (London: André Deutsch, 1973).

1 Labour's Decline

1. Ivor Crewe, in Dennis Kavanagh (ed.), *The Politics of the Labour Party* (London: Allen & Unwin, 1982) p. 12.
2. Martin Linton, *Labour Can Still Win*, Fabian Society, 532(1988) p. 3.
3. See Michael Stewart, in Wilfred Beckerman (ed.), *The Labour Government's Economic Record* (London: Duckworth, 1972).
4. See James Callaghan, *Time and Chance* (London: Collins, 1987) Chapter 19.
5. Joel Barnett, *Inside the Treasury* (London: André Deutsch, 1982) pp. 104–10; Susan Crosland, *Tony Crosland* (London: Cape, 1982) pp. 381–2.
6. Callaghan, *Time and Chance*, p. 462.
7. See Giles Radice, *The Significance of the British General Election*, *Government and Opposition* (Summer 1979) pp. 276–81.
8. Callaghan, *Time and Chance*, pp. 513–18 for Callaghan's reasons for delaying the election.
9. See Tony Benn, *Arguments for Socialism* (London: Cape, 1979) and *Arguments for Democracy* (London: Cape, 1981.)
10. See David and Maurice Kogan, *The Battle for the Labour Party* (London: Kogan Page, 1983).
11. David Butler and Dennis Kavanagh, *The British General Election of 1983* (London: Macmillan, 1984) pp. 296–7.
12. David Butler and Dennis Kavanagh, *The British General Election of 1987* (London: Macmillan, 1988) p. 271.
13. Butler and Kavanagh, *The British General Election of 1987*, p. 247.
14. Peter Kellner, *Independent*, 13 June 1987.
15. Ivor Crewe, *Guardian*, 16 June 1987.
16. *Sunday Times* 14 June 1987.
17. Butler and Kavanagh, *The British General Election of 1987*, p. 271.
18. *Independent*, 13 June 1987.
19. See Ivor Crewe, *Guardian*, 15 June 1987 and *Guardian*, 14 June 1983.
20. Anthony Heath, Roger Jowell and John Curtice, *How Britain Votes* (Oxford: Pergamon Press, 1985) p. 35.
21. Dennis Kavanagh, *The Times*, 25 September 1987.
22. *Guardian*, 15 June 1987.
23. John Curtice, *Must Labour Lose?*, *New Society*, 14 June 1987.

2 The Thatcherite Triumph

1. Hugo Young and Anne Sloman, *The Thatcher Phenomenon* (BBC 1986).
2. See Dennis Kavanagh, *Thatcherism and British Politics* (Oxford: Oxford University Press, 1987) pp. 292–7; also Social and Community Planning *British Social Attitudes*, (London: Gower, 1987).
3. Peter Jenkins, *Mrs Thatcher's Revolution* (London: Cape, 1987) p. 66.
4. Mrs Thatcher, *Let our children grow tall*, Centre for Policy Studies (1977); see also William Keegan, *Mrs Thatcher's Economic Experiment* (London: Allan Lane, 1984) Chapters 2 and 3.
5. Giles Radice, *The Significance of the British General Election, Government and Opposition* (Summer 1979) pp. 276–81.
6. See James Prior, *The Balance of Power* (London: Hamish Hamilton, 1986).
7. Jenkins, *Mrs Thatcher's Revolution*, p. 99.
8. Jenkins, *Mrs Thatcher's Revolution*, p. 164.
9. Jenkins, *Mrs Thatcher's Revolution*, p. 165.
10. Peter Riddell, *The Thatcher Government* (Oxford: Martin Robertson, 1983) pp. 239–40.
11. Jenkins, *Mrs Thatcher's Revolution*, p. 214.
12. Nigel Lawson, speech on monetary policy to Lombard Association (16 April 1986).
13. Interview, *Independent*, 4 September 1987.
14. Social and Community Planning, *British Social Attitudes*.
15. Ivor Crewe, *Guardian*, 16 June 1987.
16. *Sunday Express*, 24 July 1988.
17. *Sunday Times*, 4 December 1988.
18. *Sunday Times*, 12 June 1988.
19. Jenkins, *Mrs Thatcher's Revolution*, pp. 317–18.
20. *Financial Times*, 9 November 1987.
21. Jenkins, *Mrs Thatcher's Revolution*, p. 370.
22. Riddell, *The Thatcher Government*, p. 229.
23. Interview, *Independent*, 4 September 1987.
24. Hugo Young, *Guardian*, 12 July 1988.

3 Must Labour Lose?

1. *Must Labour Lose?* (Harmondsworth: Penguin, 1960) p. 119–20.
2. *Social Trends* (London: HMSO, 1988) p. 27.
3. *New Society*, 2 October 1987.
4. See Table 22, The Labour Party, *Labour and Britain in the 1990s* (May 1988).
5. *Sunday Times*, 14 June 1987.
6. *Labour and Britain in the 1990s*, p. 17.
7. Heath, Jowell and Curtice, *How Britain Votes*, p. 68.

8. *Labour and Britain in the 1990s*, p. 16.
9. Anthony Heath and Sarah K. McDonald, 'Social Change and the Future of the Left', *Political Quarterly* (December 1987) p. 372.
10. Robert Graham, *Financial Times Survey*, 18 January 1983.
11. Heath and McDonald, *Social Change and the Future of the Left*, p. 374.
12. Heath, Jowell and Curtice, *How Britain Votes*, Table 3.3
13. See pp. 139–42.
14. See Jenkins, *The Thatcher Revolution*, p. 240.
15. Hilary Wainwright, *Tale of Two Labour Parties* (London: Hogarth Press 1987) pp. 254–255.
16. Heath, Jowell and Curtice, *How Britain Votes*.
17. Attributed to Gerald Kaufman, MP.
18. Aneurin Bevan, *In Place of Fear* (London: MacGibbon and Kee 1961) p. 202.

4 A Balance of Values

1. Anthony Crosland, *The Future of Socialism* (London: Cape, 1956) p. 101.
2. 'Democratic Socialist Aims and Values', The Labour Party (1988).
3. J. M. Keynes, *The General Theory of Employment, Interest and Money*, (London: Macmillan, 1936) p. 383.
4. Roy Hattersley, *Choose Freedom* (London: Michael Joseph, 1987), p. 21.
5. Hattersley, *Choose Freedom*.
6. Crosland, *The Future of Socialism*, p. 104.
7. Bernard Crick, *Socialism* (Oxford: Oxford University Press 1987) p. 89.
8. John Rawls, *A Theory of Justice* (Oxford: Oxford University Press 1972) p. 203.
9. Hattersley, *Choose Freedom* and Bryan Gould, *Socialism and Freedom* (London: Macmillan, 1985).
10. Rawls, *A Theory of Justice*.
11. Crosland, *Socialism Now*, p. 15.
12. R. H. Tawney, *Equality* (London: Allen & Unwin, 1931).
13. Crick, *Socialism*, p. 88.
14. Plato, *Laws*, quoted in Karl Popper, *The Open Society and its Enemies*, vol.1 (London: Routledge & Kegan Paul, 1957) p. 96.
15. F. A. Hayek, *Law, Legislation and Liberty* (London: Routledge & Kegan Paul, 1982) vol. 2, p. 64.
16. J.-J. Rousseau, *Social Contract* (London: Dent, Everyman edn, 1966) p. 174.
17. Margaret Thatcher, *Let our children grow tall*, Centre for Policy Studies (1977).
18. Tawney, *Equality*, p. 113.

19. Hattersley, *Choose Freedom*, pp.39–40.
20. Douglas Jay made this point in his *Socialism in the new society* (London: Longman, 1962) p. 8.
21. Rawls, *A Theory of Justice* p. 82–3.
22. See Thomas Stark, *A new·A–Z of income and wealth*, Fabian Society (1987).
23. *Foreword to* 'Democratic Socialist Aims and Values'.
24. Hattersley, *Choose Freedom, p. xvi.*
25. 'Democratic Socialist Aims and Values', p. 3.
26. See the works of F. A. Hayek, Milton Friedman and Robert Nozick.
27. Isaiah Berlin, *Four Essays in Liberty* (Oxford: Oxford University Press, 1969) p. 148.
28. Gould, *Socialism and Freedom* pp. 28–9.
29. Rawls, *A Theory of Justice*, chapters II and III.
30. Tawney, *Equality*, p. 268.
31. Raymond Plant, 'Community: concept, conception and ideology', *Politics and Society*, vol. 8, no. 1 1978).
32. R. T. Wolf, *The Poverty of Liberalism* (Boston: Bevan Press, 1968) p. 184.
33. See F.A. Hayek, *Law, Legislation and Liberty, vol. 2 The Mirage of Social Justice*, (London: Routledge & Kegan Paul, 1976) and R. Nozick, *Anarchy, State and Utopia* (Oxford: Basil Blackwell, 1978).
34. *Woman's Own*, 31 October 1987.
35. See *Independent*, 11 August 1988.
36. David Marquand, *The Unprincipled Society* (London: Cape, 1988) p. 217.
37. Marquand, *The Unprincipled Society*, p. 217.
38. Giles Radice, *Community Socialism*, Fabian Society, pamphlet 464, (1979).

5 Rights and Obligations

1. See pp. 170–1.
2. Daniel Bell, *The Cultural Conditions of Capitalism* (London: Heinemann, 1979) p. 245.
   Gita Ionescu, *Politics and the Pursuit of Happiness* (London: Longman, 1984) p. 43.
   Alisdair Macintyre, *After Virtue: a Study in moral theory* (London: Duckworth, 1985) p. 263.
   Quoted in David Marquand, *The Unprincipled Society* (London: Cape, 1988) pp. 220–2.
3. See p. 55.

4. Margaret Macdonald, *Natural Rights* in Jeremy Waldron (ed.), *Theories of Rights* (Oxford: Oxford University Press, 1984) pp. 23–4.
5. John Locke, *Two Treatises of Government* ed Peter Laslett (Cambridge: Cambridge University Press 1960) pp. 301–2.
6. J. J. Rousseau, *The Social ·Contract* (London: Dent, Everyman edn 1966) p. 12.
7. Rousseau, *The Social Contract* p. 25.
8. Rousseau, *The Social Contract*, p. 13.
9. Bentham, *Anarchical Fallacies* (Edinburgh: Tait, 1843)
10. David Hume, *Of the Original Contract* in (*Social Contract*, Oxford: Oxford University Press 1946) p. 216.
11. Macdonald, *Theories of Rights*, pp. 32–3.
12. Thomas Paine, *Rights of Man* (Harmondsworth: Penguin, 1969) p. 136.
13. Rawls, *A Theory of Justice*, pp. 342–3.
14. Simone Weil, *The Need for Roots* (London and New York, Ark, 1987) p. 3.
15. Aristotle, *Politics*, Book I, II (Oxford: Clarendon Press, 1885) pp. 4–5.
16. Karl Popper, *The Open Society and its Enemies* (London: Routledge & Kegan Paul, 1957) vol. 1, p. 106.
17. Marquand, *The Unprincipled Society*, p. 226.
18. See pp. 168–73.
19. Raymond Plant, *Needs, Agency and Rights*, in C. J. C. Sampford and P. J. Galligan(eds), *Law, Rights and the Welfare State* (London: Croom Helm, 1986).
20. See pp. 137–9 and 154–7.
21. Michael Rustin, *For a Pluralist Socialism* (London: Verso Books, 1985).
22. See Lawrence Mead, *Beyond Entitlement: The Social Obligations of Citizenship* (New York: Free Press, 1986) and Raymond Plant, *Citizenship, Rights and Socialism*, Fabian Society, 531 (1988).
23. 'Economic Equality', in 'Social Justice and Economic Efficiency', The Labour Party (1988) p. 22.

6 State and Market

1. Samuel Brittan, *The Role and Limits of Government* (London: Temple Smith, 1983) p. 59.
2. Peter Kellner, in Ben Pimlott (ed.)*Fabian Essays in Socialist Thought* (London: Heinemann, 1984).
3. D. Green, *The New Right* (Brighton: Wheatsheaf, 1987) p. 150; R. Plant and K. Hooker, *The Rising Conservative Capitalism in Britain and the USA* (London: Methuen, 1988).
4. David Marquand, *The Unprincipled Society* (London, Cape, 1988) p. 102.

5. Marquand, *The Unprincipled Society*, p. 205.
6. Fred Hirsch, *The Social Limits to Growth* (London: Routledge & Kegan Paul, 1977).
7. See the occasional paper *Faith in the City*, prepared by the Theology and Social Values Group of the Diocese of Winchester's Working Group (1988) p. 27.
8. Gallup polls, etc.
9. Adam Smith, *The Wealth of Nations* (London: Methuen, 1961) p. 130.
10. J. K. Galbraith, *The Industrial State* (London: Hamish Hamilton, 1967).
11. See 'A Productive and a Competitive Economy', in 'Social Justice and Economic Efficiency, The Labour Party (1988) p. 5.
12. Speeches to May 1988 Congress of the European Trade Union Conference, and to September 1988 TUC Congress.
13. Chalmers Johnson, *MITI and the Japanese Miracle: Growth of Industrial Policy 1925–1975* (Stanford University Press, 1983) p. 318.
14. F. A. Hayek, *Law, Legislation and Liberty* (London: Routledge & Kegan Paul, 1979) vol. 3, p. 41.
15. D. Green, *The New Right* (Brighton: Wheatsheaf, 1987) Chapters 6 and 7.
16. J. K. Galbraith, *The Affluent Society* (Harmondsworth: Penguin Books 1987) 4th edn.
17. Speech to The Royal Society (1988).
18. See the speech of John Cunningham M.P, Shadow Environment Spokesman, in the debate on the Queen's Speech, *Hansard* (28 November 1988).
19. Hirsch, *Social Limits to Growth*, pp. 46–51.
20. Anthony Crosland, *Socialism Now* (London: Cape, 1974) p. 38.
21. Bryan Gould, *Financial Times*, 24th November 1987.

7 Economic and Industrial Policies for the 1990s

1. *United Kingdom*, OECD Economic Surveys 1987/88 (OECD, 1988) pp. 48–53.
2. United Kingdom, OECD Economic Surveys 1987/88. Table 9.
3. J. K. Galbraith, *Observer*, 31 August 1980.
4. *United Kingdom*, OECD Economic Surveys 1987/88, p. 65.
5. *United Kingdom*, p. 79.
6. *Towards Full Employment and Price Stability* (OECD, 1977) p. 103.
7. John Llewellyn, *Lessons from Two Oil Shocks*, OECD Working Paper, (1983) p. 5.
8. See Michael Stewart, *Controlling the Economic Future* (Brighton: Wheatsheaf Books, 1983).
9. Michael Stewart, *Keynes and After* (Harmondsworth: Penguin, 1986) 3rd edn.

10. See Giles and Lisanne Radice, *Socialists in the Recession* (London: Macmillan, 1986) Chapter 9.
11. *Japan*, OECD Economic Surveys 1987–8 (OECD, 1988).
12. William Keegan, *Britain Without Oil* (Harmondsworth: Penguin, 1985) p. 101.
13. Stewart, *Keynes and After*, p. 199.
14. See Giles Radice, *Independent*, 25 May 1988.
15. Paolo Cecchini, *The European Challenge 1992* (London: Wildwood House, 1988).
16. Martin Wolf, *Is there a British Miracle?*, *Financial Times*, 16 June 1988.
17. House of Lords Select Committee on Overseas Trade.
18. Michael Heseltine, *Where There's a Will* (London: Hutchinson, 1987).
19. *Times* 16 February 1987
20. *R & D 1988* (London: HMSO, 1988).
21. House of Lords Select Committee on Science and Technology Report, December 1984.
22. For example, *Competence and Competition* (NEDO/MSC, 1984); also various studies by the National Institute of Economic and Social Research.
23. Hilary Steedman, *Vocational Training in France and Britain*, National Institute Discussion Paper (January 1988).
24. Steedman, *Vocational Training*.
25. See Swedish Institute, *Swedish Labour Market Policy* (June 1987).
26. Department of Trade and Industry, *Regional Industrial Policy: some economic issues* (1983).

8 Trade Unions and the Labour market

1. MORI's *Sunday Times* study (August 1987).
2. See TUC, *Meeting the Challenge* (1988).
3. Giles Radice, *The Industrial Democrats* (London: Allen & Unwin, 1978) pp. 9–10.
4. Radice, *The Industrial Democrats*, p. 229.
5. NEDO, *Young People in the Labour Market* (July 1988).
6. Charles Leadbeater, *The Politics of Prosperity*, Fabian Society, 523 (1987) p. 2.
7. ACAS, 1987 Annual Report
8. Philip Bassett, *Fabian Society Discussion paper* 5 (November 1988).
9. Jim Conway Foundation Memorial Lecture (November 1987).
10. *Industrial Democracy* (TUC, 1974).
11. Report of the Committee of Inquiry on Industrial Democracy (London: HMSO, 1977).

12. William McCarthy, *The Future of Industrial Democracy*, Fabian Society, 526 (1988).
13. Anthony Crosland, *Socialism Now* (London: Cape, 1974) p. 83.

9 Reforming the Welfare State

 1. Social and Community Planning, *British Social Attitudes* (London: Gower, 1987).
 2. *Autumn Statement 1988* (London: HMSO, 1988), Table 1.10.
 3. *Autumn Statement 1988* (London: HMSO, 1988).
 4. *Guardian* 7 April 1988
 5. Social Services Select Committee, *Resourcing National Health Service: short term issues* (1 February 1988) para. 22.
 6. Speech to General Assembly of the Church of Scotland (22 May 1988).
 7. Gordon Best and Tony Culyer, King's Fund Institute paper.
 8. Social Services Select Committee, *The Future of the National Health Service* (July 1988) para 9.
 9. King's Fund Institute briefing paper 4, (1988) p. 10.
10. S. J. Prais and K. Wagner, *School Standards in England and Germany*, *NIESR Economic Review* (May 1985).
11. Joel Barnett, *Inside the Treasury* (London: André Deutsch, 1982) p. 32.
12. Treasury and Civil Service Select Committee (1988).
13. *The Nation's Health*, NAHA's evidence to the Prime Minister's review (1988).
14. Social Services Select Committee, *The Future of the National Health Service*, para. 183.
15. Giles Radice, *Equality and Quality*, Fabian Society, 514 (1986).
16. *Independent*, 19 February 1987.
17. *Parents in Partnership* (Labour Party, 1988).
18. *The Nation's Health*, para. 75.
19. Gordon Best, *The Future of NHS General Management*, King's Fund Project paper, 75 (1987).
20. Social Services Select Committee, *The Future of the National Health Service*.
21. A. W. Dilnot, J. A. Kay and C. N. Morris, *The Reform of Social Security* (Oxford: Clarendon Press, 1984) p. 29.
22. Dilnot, Kay and Morris, *The Reform of Social Security*, *passim*.
23. See A. B. Atkinson, *Rebuilding Social Security*, *New Society*, 26 July 1984.

10 The Democratic Agenda

 1. Answer to Written Question House of Commons, *Hansard* (7 July 1988).

2. See Peter Jenkins, *Mrs Thatcher's Revolution* (London: Cape, 1987) pp. 82–3 for Mrs Thatcher's anti-socialism.
3. Quoted in Peter Gay, *The Dilemma of Democratic Socialism* (New York: Collier Books, 1962) pp. 244–5.
4. Eduard Bernstein, *Evolutionary Socialism* (Schocken Books: New York, 1961) p. 144.
5. Bernstein, *Evolutionary Socialism*.
6. See pp. 141–2.
7. Quoted in Martin Linton, *The Swedish Road to Socialism*, Fabian Society, 503 (1985).
8. Jeremy Beecham, in *Labour's next move forward*, Fabian Society, 521 (1987) p. 22.
9. See Michael Zander, *A Bill of Rights?* (London: Sweet & Maxwell, 1985).
10. A. V. Dicey, *An Introduction to the Study of the Constitution* (London: Macmillan, 1959) 10th edn, p. 199 (Quoted in Anthony Lester, *Fundamental Rights: The United Kingdom Isolated?* (London: Sweet & Maxwell, 1984).)
11. Zander, *A Bill of Rights*, p. 45.
12. *Improving Management in Government: The Next Steps* (London: HMSO, 1988).
13. Lester, *Fundamental Rights*, p. 47.
14. Lester, *Fundamental Rights*, p. 65.
15. Harold Laski, *Liberty and the Modern State* (London: Allen & Unwin, 1948) p. 75.
16. *Report of the Select Committee on A Bill of Rights*.
17. Lester, *Fundamental Rights*, p. 71.
18. Jeffrey Jowell and Dawn Oliver (eds), *The Changing Constitution* (Oxford: Clarendon Press, 1985).
19. *Justice*, All Souls Report, *Administrative Justice and Some Necessary Reforms* (Oxford: Clarendon Press, 1988) and House of Commons *Civil Service Management Reform: the Next Steps* (1988) vol. 11, p. 35.
20. Peter Nielsen and Haydn Thomas, *Electoral Reform, A Priority for Labour* (Labour Campaign for Electoral Reform, 1987).
21. Peter Kellner, *Independent*, 13 June 1988.
22. Procedure Committee Report, Hansard July 1978.
23. *Hansard*, 25th June 1979.
24. Jowell and Oliver 25th June 1979, *The Changing Constitution*, p. 145.
25. John Stewart and Gerry Stoker, *From local administration to community government*, Fabian Research Series, 351 (1988).
26. David Blunkett and Keith Jackson, *Democracy in Crisis* (London: Hogarth Press, 1987).
27. See Labour party consultative paper, *Local government reform in England and Wales* (1987).
28. Press statement (17 November 1987).

11 Internationalism Without Illusions

1. Denis Healey, *Labour and a World Society*, Fabian Society, 501 (1985).
2. Guildhall Speech (16 November 1964).
3. David Reynolds, *A Special Relationship? America, Britain and the international order since the Second World War, International Affairs* (Winter 1985–6).
4. Preface to David Martin, *Bringing common sense to the Common Market*, Fabian Society, 525 (1988).
5. See pp. 118–19.
6. Michael Heseltine, *Where There's a Will* (London: Hutchinson, 1987) p. 260.
7. European Commission White Paper, *Completing the Internal Market* (June 1985) para. 8.
8. David Butler and Dennis Kavanagh, *The British General Election of 1987* (London: Macmillan, 1987) p. 247.
9. Mikhail Gorbachev, *Perestroika* (London: Collins, 1988).
10. Peter Jenkins, *Indewpendent*, 15 February 1988.
11. Peter Shore, 28 December 1987.
12. Christopher Tugendhat and William Wallace, *Options for British foreign policy in the 1990s* (RIIA, 1988) pp. 78–9.

Conclusion: the Path to Power

1. Anthony Crosland, *The Future of Socialism* (London: Cape, 1956) Chapters 43 and 5.
2. See pp. 63–5.
3. Paul Addison, *The Road to 1945* (London: Quartet Books, 1977) passim.
4. Harry Eckstein, *The English National Health Service* (New York: Harvard University Press, 1960) ix–x (quoted in Addison, *The Road to 1945*, p. 277).
5. For example, John Evans, MP and John Reid, MP.
6. David Butler and Dennis Kavanagh, *The British General Election of 1987* (London: Macmillan (1987) pp. 335–41, and Martin Linton, *Labour can still win*, Fabian Society, 532 (1988).
7. A point made by Martin Linton in *Labour's next moves forward*, Fabian Society, 521 (1987).
8. Kenneth Morgan, *Labour in Power* (Oxford: Clarendon Press, 1984) p. 24.
9. Harold Wilson, *The New Britain* (Harmondsworth: Penguin, 1964).

Index